Odyssey of an Eavesdropper

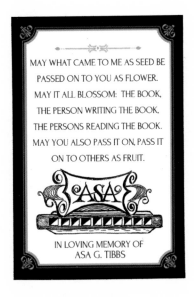

MAY WHAT CAME TO ME AS SEED BE
PASSED ON TO YOU AS FLOWER.
MAY IT ALL BLOSSOM: THE BOOK,
THE PERSON WRITING THE BOOK,
THE PERSONS READING THE BOOK.
MAY YOU ALSO PASS IT ON, PASS IT
ON TO OTHERS AS FRUIT.

IN LOVING MEMORY OF
ASA G. TIBBS

Odyssey of an Eavesdropper

My Life in Electronic Countermeasures and My Battle Against the FBI

Martin L. Kaiser III

with Robert S. Stokes

CARROLL & GRAF PUBLISHERS

NEW YORK

ODYSSEY OF AN EAVESDROPPER
My Life in Electronic Countermeasures and My Battle Against the FBI

Carroll & Graf Publishers
An Imprint of Avalon Publishing Group Inc.
245 West 17th Street
11th Floor
New York, NY 10011

AVALON
publishing group incorporated

First Carroll & Graf edition 2005

Library of Congress Cataloging-in-Publication Data is available.

ISBN-13: 978-0-78671-546-6
ISBN-10: 0-7867-1546-4

9 8 7 6 5 4 3 2 1

Interior design by Jamie McNeely
Printed in the United States of America
Distributed by Publishers Group West

To all "whistleblowers" and other seekers of the truth,
who continue to fight abusive systems everywhere

Contents

INTRODUCTION ix

PROLOGUE xv

PART 1: The Early Years

Chapter 1: Early Survival Lessons. 1

Chapter 2: Getting Serious About Electronics 14

PART 2: The New King of Electronic Countermeasures

Chapter 3: Stumbling into the Spy Racket 33

Chapter 4: The Michelangelo of Electronic Surveillance 56

Chapter 5: An Audience with J. Edgar Hoover 71

Chapter 6: A Fateful Meeting 83

Chapter 7: My Anwar Sadat Cadillac 91

Chapter 8: Road to Ruin 106

Chapter 9: Payback 128

PART 3: Trial by Fire

Chapter 10: A Gathering Storm. 141

Chapter 11: The Trial. 158

Chapter 12: More Trials and Survival Strategies 167

Chapter 13: Searching for Bugs in Corporate America 180

Chapter 14: Civil Suit and Countersuit 189

Chapter 15: The Aftermath 202

Chapter 16: "Enemy of the State" 211

Chapter 17: Looking Back 220

PART 4: The Road Ahead

Chapter 18: The Future of Privacy
in America—Or What's Left of It 233

APPENDIX: Audio Surveillance
and Countermeasures 249

GLOSSARY OF TERMS 288

ENDNOTES 294

ACKNOWLEDGMENTS 305

INDEX 307

ABOUT THE AUTHORS 312

Introduction

YOU PROBABLY DON'T recognize my name—unless you were in electronic surveillance. I once worked in the shadows of national security. If you ever passed me walking down a street in Washington or Baltimore, you would never have looked twice in my direction. I'm not the suave, debonair secret agent type. In fact, I have an Everyman face and physique that would never give you a clue about what I used to do—or the reputation I once had within the U.S. intelligence community.

Modesty aside, I was, to the FBI, the CIA, and the rest of the intel community, what "Q"—the British Secret Service technical genius—was to James Bond, Ian Fleming's dashing secret agent with a license to kill.

I had a license to design the deadliest eavesdropping devices you can imagine, and some that will forever remain classified. I built and supplied "bugs" to the FBI, the CIA, the DEA, Secret Service, the IRS, the U.S. Postal Service, and the intelligence commands of the army, navy, and air force.

With a hot-wired hearing aid the size of a thumbtack, I built eavesdropping devices that could bring down a government, prevent a terrorist attack, or provide blackmail to a government agency to smear a well-known American civil rights leader.

I built bugs that would fit inside picture frames, hotel room keyholes, fountain pens (an FBI favorite), office staplers, envelopes, wristwatches, cuff links, baseball caps, golf clubs, paperweights, the leg of a coffee table, reading glasses, the lining of a suit jacket or trousers, the hollow heel of a shoe, and telephones that captured room audio when hung up. I also built some of the first surveillance countermeasure gear ever used by the intel community, including an RF (radio frequency) detector with tonal readout (used to find bugs), a multiline telephone analyzer, and one of the first nonlinear junction detectors.*

I was considered by my colleagues to be the inspiration for Harry Caul, the paranoid eavesdropping expert played by Gene Hackman in Francis Ford Coppola's 1974 post-Watergate drama, *The Conversation.* I also provided technical expertise for the film. In the 1998 movie *Enemy of the State*, based loosely on my FBI story, I suggested and designed many of the eavesdropping dirty tricks used by Hackman in the role of Brill, a rogue ex-NSA surveillance expert.

I am essentially the Bill Gates of the U.S. eavesdropping biz, with far less fame and fortune. A columnist once referred to me as "the Michelangelo of electronic surveillance." I was as good as it got, and then some.

This book is about my journey through the dark side of U.S. intelligence operations, the high points, the low points, the colorful people with whom I worked and met, and the government agency that tried to destroy me when I inadvertently blew the whistle on a "cut out" operation.

My personal story is about growing up in a blue-collar family in the hard coal region of northeastern Pennsylvania, surviving years of physical and psychological abuse at the hands of my father, finally breaking free to demonstrate my talents and intellect in all things mechanical and electronic.

*See Glossary of Terms.

My story includes the intellectually challenging years of working as a research technician for RCA Laboratories in Princeton, New Jersey, and Barbados, West Indies, where I helped to develop the first link in the U.S. antimissile system, and how I accidentally happened upon a career in electronic surveillance and countermeasures.

It was in this field that I established a reputation for excellence within the U.S. intelligence community but then saw my reputation destroyed by abuse of power by a federal agency.

I make no apologies for the products I made or how they were used. Electronic surveillance, if used in a responsible manner, can provide the intelligence community with the information needed to save American lives—now more than ever! I took tremendous pride in what I designed and built.

There is a public misconception that those who make eavesdropping equipment for a living must be voyeurs who derive sadistic pleasure from violating an individual's right to privacy. That's not me. I hope the reader will understand that the technical side of countermeasure work always challenged me creatively and intellectually. In the end, it was the work itself that energized me—not the process of secretly invading people's lives.

I fervently believe in the individual's right to privacy and I am increasingly concerned about the government's encroachment on our constitutional rights and protections.

The cautionary tale in this book was the deliberate effort by the FBI and some of its agents to destroy me professionally. It is a story of how America's most powerful law enforcement agency carried out a vendetta against a law-abiding citizen whose only crime was telling the truth under oath before a Congressional committee.

As a result of my testimony before the National Wiretap Commission (composed of members of the House Select Committee on Intelligence) in 1975, I became a pariah within the intelligence community and was nearly driven into bankruptcy when my business dried up overnight and my clients stopped taking or returning my calls.

I was later indicted by the Justice Department and charged with illegal wiretapping, conspiracy, and transporting an illegal surveillance device across state lines. It took less than three hours for me to be found not guilty of all charges by a jury of my peers.

Frustrated by that verdict, the two FBI agents whose conversations were allegedly recorded by a device I installed for a client (with the clear admonition of "single-party consent"), sued me for civil damages, citing "professional embarrassment, humiliation and violation of their privacy."

[Of the fifty states, thirty-eight, as well as the District of Columbia, allow you to record a conversation to which you are a party without informing the other parties you are doing so—single-party consent.]

It cost me $300,000 in legal fees and millions in lost business, money I needed to protect my product inventions against piracy. The damage to my business, my professional reputation, and my health is inestimable and can never be recovered. I have no legal proof that the FBI intended to take revenge against me for my Congressional testimony, but it is the only reasonable and logical explanation for what transpired.

If you read my story with a fair and open mind, I believe you will agree.

This book also describes my experiences in conducting electronic countermeasures for corporate America and the relative ease with which eavesdropping takes place in the private sector. I discuss in detail the constant and growing use of electronic surveillance and invasion of privacy of all Americans in this post-9/11 era, and the war on terrorism and my concerns about where this trend is leading. In an appendix at the end of the book, I offer suggestions and recommendations for how you can protect yourself and your company from any type of eavesdropping.

Don't get me wrong. I am an American patriot, born and raised in a region of the country that believed in a bumper-sticker slogan popular in the 1960s and 1970s: "America—love it or leave it." I'm well aware of the threat of terrorism, what it means for all Americans, and the tough job our intelligence and law enforcement agencies have in defending us against this scourge. I'm also a law-abiding citizen who wholeheartedly believes in the rule of law. I also believe in the rights of the individual under the Constitution, particularly in the areas of privacy, free speech, and free enterprise.

Unfortunately, there were individuals in the employ of the country's most powerful law enforcement agency who let a personal agenda—to destroy me personally and professionally—take priority over their sworn allegiance to uphold the rule of law.

Why have I waited nearly twenty years to tell my story? Because in one respect the final chapter has not yet been written. My hope—perhaps a naïve one—is that I will finally receive an apology from someone in the Justice Department and an acknowledgment that I did nothing wrong.

Even after my testimony and the indictment on illegal wiretapping charges, I continued to believe that justice would be done. I remained silent because of concern and fear that I would only make things more difficult for my family and me by going public with what happened. But I've gradually come to realize that the clock will never be turned back. Restitution will not be part of my story.

However, this story is not simply about me. It's about the growing loss of privacy in the post-9/11 age of terror and the infringement of those freedoms by the intended reauthorization of the PATRIOT Act in 2005. It is about private-sector software downloadable from the Internet that can be used to secretly monitor business competition's e-mails, instant messages, programs, and keystrokes, all installed from a remote location for less than $200.

It's also about the twenty acres of mainframe underground computers at the supersecret National Security Agency (NSA—which some wags say stands for No Such Agency) at Fort Meade, Maryland, that has the ability to eavesdrop on all Americans' telephone, cell

phone, fax, and e-mail conversations with classified, prepro-
grammed, target-word recognition systems. Nowadays, the moment
they hear or read words like "bomb," "jihad," "Praise Allah,"
"Osama bin Laden," or thousands of other phrases with an identified
national security risk factor, those conversations are instantly
recorded and copied without individual or court approval, and an
investigation is launched.

Now is a perfect time to tell my story.

—MLK

May 1, 2005

Prologue

THE BAD THINGS in my life have somehow always been preceded by a telephone call. This time was no different.

It was a Monday morning, December 5, 1977. I was working in my electronics shop in Cockeysville, Maryland, putting the finishing touches on some bomb-detection and disposal equipment, electronic stethoscopes, and blasting machines. In order to survive the FBI-generated demise of my countermeasure and eavesdropping business since my testimony before the House Select Committee on Intelligence two years before, I had begun to focus my sales and marketing efforts in the improvised-bomb-detection market.

Outside my office window, a volatile mixture of rain and freezing temperatures had turned the roads into veritable skating rinks. The weather reflected my mood: dark, cold, and isolated. Despite being raised in this type of weather, winter was always a downer for me. I lived for moments of escape to the Caribbean. On this day, I had a serious case of the downs despite the antidepression medication I was taking.

I had been at work for about two hours when the phone rang. My secretary called from the other room that it was my attorney, Bernard "Bud" Fensterwald.

I liked Bud. I didn't always like what he had to say, but he was a straight shooter. I considered him a friend as well as my attorney. He had become a minor celebrity in defending James McCord, an ex-CIA agent and one of the Watergate burglary defendants who placed an eavesdropping device in the headquarters of the Democratic National Committee during President Nixon's reelection campaign in 1972. That's why I hired him. He had no illusions about the proclivity of the government or its agents to break the law as a means to an end. He also knew something about my business.

I had engaged Fensterwald to represent me when I was subpoenaed to testify before a grand jury in Winston-Salem, North Carolina, several months before. They questioned me about my role in the bugging of two FBI agents conducting interviews at the Northwestern Bank in Wilkesboro, North Carolina. Ever since the grand jury testimony, I had lived in constant dread, waiting for the proverbial other shoe to drop. I had come to hate the sound of a ringing telephone.

"Hi, Bud," I said. "What's up?"

"You won't believe this, Marty, but the bastards indicted you."

"No kidding," I said. My heart felt like it was in free fall. "For what? I've done nothing wrong."

"The FBI has a different view about that," said Fensterwald. "They've charged you with the intent to bug the FBI agents at Northwestern Bank, conspiracy with Ed Duncan and others to do the deed, and transporting the device across state lines for the purpose of using it to intercept oral communications."

"A lot of bullshit, Bud," I said, angrily. "You know what this is all about? This is retaliation for blowing the whistle on U.S. Recording. I was warned that the bureau would pull something like this."

Two years earlier, I had testified before the House Intelligence Committee about price markups I observed on invoices for eavesdropping equipment I had sold the FBI through U.S. Recording Company. Following my testimony, Luther Mook, a foreign intelligence agent, knocked on my door.

Mook warned me that the FBI intended to make me a "test case" under the criminal wiretap provision of the 1968 Omnibus Crime & Control Act. The act made it a crime to sell eavesdropping equipment to anyone but federal, state, or local law enforcement agencies. The "test case" scenario was a convenient cover for the FBI's real purpose in targeting me—payback for the embarrassment I'd created for the bureau, a cardinal sin in Hoover's FBI.

The indictment also confirmed a warning previously relayed to me by a retired intelligence officer for the Strategic Air Command. He said he had heard that if the FBI could not get me directly, they would get me through one of my customers. Northwestern Bank appeared to be that customer.

"Don't worry, Marty," said Fensterwald. "They'll never make it stick, but right now we've got more immediate things to deal with."

"Like what?"

"We have to prepare for your arraignment which is scheduled for December twelfth."

We left for North Carolina early that morning in what was mostly a hurry-up-and-wait exercise. I was the last of twenty-two other defendants, none of whom had lawyers to represent them. The process took all day until I could utter the words, "Not guilty," and fly back to Washington.

Fensterwald called the following day.

"The FBI wants to know when you intend to surrender," he asked.

When he said the word *surrender*, I flinched. I closed my eyes. I was a child again, gripped with shame about bringing home another poor report card and terrified of getting another beating from my father. I swallowed several times. I felt a sudden band of pain from one side of my head to the other. My mouth was so dry I could hardly speak.

"What . . . what do you mean, surrender, Bud?"

"Just what it sounds like, Marty," said Fensterwald. "They book you, fingerprint you, take your mug shot, and we go before a judge for a bond hearing."

"You mean they're going make me do a perp walk like some common criminal?"

"I don't think so, Marty, but they'll probably put the cuffs on you. Look, it'll take only a few minutes, so I suggest we get it over with."

"When?"

"How about tomorrow morning?"

"Do I have a choice?"

"Not really," said Fensterwald. "The FBI's already called."

The next morning my wife, Carmel, drove me to Fensterwald's office on K Street in downtown Washington. She and I hardly spoke. I told her I would meet her later, after it was over. She wanted to come to the court hearing but I absolutely refused. I was mortified. I still couldn't believe this was happening. To me. One of the good guys. A guy who had always played by the rules and who always told the truth no matter what the consequences were.

Fensterwald drove me over to the FBI office in the Old Post Office Building. I was dressed in a gray suit, starched white shirt, and dark tie as if I were going to a business meeting. When we arrived, Fensterwald started to introduce me but one of the agents interrupted him.

"Oh, yeah, Marty Kaiser," said one of the FBI agents. "We've been expecting you."

One agent gave me my Miranda warning against self-incrimination and then read the charges, basically the same as Fensterwald had described them over the phone. As I was being fingerprinted, another agent came over and smiled at me.

"Hey, Kaiser, didn't you go to Egypt a couple of years ago?" he asked.

"Yeah, that's right," I said.

"We've been trying to nail you for that too, but the fucking CIA got in our way."

I looked over at Fensterwald. He shook his head as if to say, "Ignore him."

After the fingerprinting was done and my mug shot taken, I used my two middle fingers to hold up the placard with my numbers on it. They turned to Fensterwald and told him he could meet me over in the courthouse. Bud nodded and tapped me on the shoulder.

"See you in a few minutes, Marty."

As soon as Fensterwald left the room, another agent came over to me and asked me to put my hands out. He was holding a set of shiny steel handcuffs.

"By the way," the agent asked. "Have you ever heard of a recorder that runs at fifteen thirty-seconds speed?"

"Are you sure it was fifteen thirty-seconds and not fifteen sixteenths?" I said.

"Well, I don't know."

In retrospect, that reference to the speed of tape recorders was a clue to the lies that would be told at my trial three months later by the FBI.

The agent put the cuffs on me, forcing the backs of my wrists together in front of me. Then they put leg irons on my ankles and a chain around my waist.

"Is this necessary?" I asked.

"Part of the arrest procedure," said the agent, grinning.

I took a deep breath, vowing not to let the bastards see me sweat.

A state police captain told me later it was part of the FBI's campaign of intimidation.

"They only do that with hardened criminals or if you pose a flight risk," he explained. "They were simply trying to get into your head."

Two agents took me downstairs and put me into a black, unmarked car for the ride over to the District of Columbia courthouse, three blocks away. I noticed they were driving on South Capitol Street, the same street U.S. Recording was located on, and I made a passing comment about it. They took me to a holding cell in the bowels of the D.C. jail and left with me a guy who was reading the sports pages. His feet rested on an old, scarred desk. He was the jailer in charge. He opened the cell door, motioned for me to walk in, and, with a loud clang, locked it behind me.

It was a space about thirty by twenty feet. It smelled of stale sweat and cleaning fluid. The sound of the key turning in the lock erased my short-lived sense of freedom. Oddly, I enjoyed the quiet of that cell. The steel seat was cold at first but I got used to it. Next to me on the seat was an apple, but I didn't eat it.

I was able to think clearly for the first time that day. The single thought that I repeated to myself was: *This is a war and I will survive this whatever it takes.* I waited there for what seemed like hours. Then the marshal came and led me upstairs into a practically empty courtroom. Fensterwald was waiting at the defense table. An assistant U.S. attorney was standing a few feet away behind the prosecution table.

U.S. Magistrate Jean Dwyer looked down at me from the bench.

"What's this man doing in handcuffs?" she asked the assistant U.S. attorney. He turned to one of the FBI agents and gestured to remove the handcuffs and leg irons.

I went over and stood next to Fensterwald. The U.S. Attorney read the charges and Fensterwald asked that I be released in my own recognizance. Judge Dwyer agreed. I relaxed for the first time that day. I thought I was free to go, but the system does not operate that way.

"The judge has to sign the release papers, Marty," said Fensterwald. "Hopefully, we'll be out of here shortly."

One of the bailiffs came over, took me by the arm, and escorted me downstairs and back to the holding cell.

After about five minutes, the jailer returned with a man also dressed in a suit and tie. He was put into the holding cell with me. He kept saying aloud, "Man, I've really done it this time. I've really done it this time . . ."

He looked at me as if he wanted to talk, but I ignored him. I figured he was an FBI plant who was placed in the cell with me to get me to say something negative about them or something that could be used against me. I was not about to play that game.

About two hours later, a bailiff delivered the release papers to the jailer. He looked at them, and looked in my direction, but went back to reading his *Washington Post*. Those papers sat on the edge of his desk for another hour. The jailer was probably waiting for me to beg him to release me, but I would not give him that satisfaction. Fuck him and fuck them!

Finally, three hours after the judge had ordered me released on my own recognizance, the jailer walked slowly over and unlocked the cell. He nodded at me as if to say, "You're free to go."

That was not true. My confinement by accusation was only beginning.

Part 1

The Early Years

Chapter 1

Early Survival
Lessons

WHEN I WAS growing up, my smile was my secret weapon. In the beginning, I had some memories to smile about. Roller skating, racing Radio Flyer wagons, hammering tin cans flat for the war effort, hanging in trees, flying kites, and watching the big steam locomotives as they passed over my street, smashing our pennies flat with their huge wheels.

One of my most exciting memories from that time was of sitting at the dinner table one evening and hearing the loud drone of an aircraft that sounded like it was just outside our window. We ran out the door and there above us was a huge Zeppelin dirigible. It seemed so close I could have reached out and touched it. People in the gondolas were waving handkerchiefs at us. I was so mesmerized by it that I fell off the porch backward and cut open my head. I remember the doctor sewing up my scalp and my father holding me still with his powerful hands.

But later on, from the age of eight or nine, my smile was a lie. It was the mask I presented to the outside world to camouflage my insecurity and the fear generated by the dysfunctional environment in which I was raised. It was the expression I would offer my father, hoping and praying—unsuccessfully—that it would help me avoid another beating.

I was the second of three sons born to Evelyn Sophronia Kaiser and Martin Luther Kaiser Jr. in the middle of the Great Depression in Wilkes-Barre, Pennsylvania, coal country. It was a time and place where fathers were expected to take a belt to their sons if they misbehaved. My father took this tradition to extremes. For reasons I only began to understand years later, I didn't have to misbehave to get hit. Simply failing to live up to my father's incredibly high standards was enough. Often, I was simply the most convenient target of his chronic dark moods.

On the other hand, he was an enormously generous man, often showering gifts on my mother, my brothers, Albert and Ronald, and me without explanation. He built a special chapel for his parents in the local Methodist church. He bought me my first U-control, spark-powered model airplane. He also gave me my first ham radio set, which opened an entire new world to me, providing an escape hatch from the world of fear and abuse that he also defined.

My gifts often seemed to follow a heavy dose of corporal punishment for some minor infraction. No doubt they were a peace offering to make amends for his inability to control his volcanic temper, a classic pattern practiced by fathers prone to abusing their children and spouses.

The gift I always wanted but never received was a simple word of praise.

My dad's unpredictable moods were tantamount to guerrilla warfare: days of placid normality punctuated by moments of sheer terror for my mother and me. My brothers were spared most of his wrath, another mystery that I would understand only when I grew older.

In retrospect, the emotional and physical abuse that filled my adolescent years was a crucible that toughened me for the battles—psychological and otherwise—that lay ahead.

As I grew up, my feelings toward my father were fear mixed with anger and resentment, but there was absolutely nothing I could do about it. By the time I left home at nineteen, I never wanted to see him again. My relationship with my mother was not so hot either, primarily because she had never tried to stop the abuse. I suppose she was too terrified, but at the time it was happening her inability to come to my defense mystified me. Perhaps that was one reason she drank.

The only positive result of those years was what psychologists have described as "cognitive giftedness in perceiving the intentions of others." In plain English, I developed an unerring perception of what was in the minds of total strangers by observing facial mannerisms, tone of voice, or body language. This talent has served me well during my business career when negotiating with a new customer, though I concede I have made some mistakes in judgment that have cost me dearly.

From adolescence until I was sent to college, I got whacked alongside the head or kicked in the butt about every other day by my father, who stood no taller than 5'7" but had the strongest, hardest hands I'd ever felt. He was a plumber who followed his father into the family business: "Martin L. Kaiser Co. Plumbing and Heating—The Better Kind!" He was used to handling heavy wrenches and pipes.

He also earned his master plumber's license by going to Pittsburgh's Carnegie Institute. I remember that because of his Carnegie belt, which he always wore and used to whack me with. He took the belt off so often it had a permanent crease in it where he would bend it double to give me a licking.

When my dad didn't have time to take off his belt, he would cuff me on the side of my head. He did it so often I had a perpetual ringing in my ears. I often got hit for thinking or saying literally nothing.

I would be sitting at the dinner table, quietly eating, when my father would ask, "What are you thinking?" I'd say, "Nothing." And WHACK, the sting of his calloused hand would send me sprawling.

"It's impossible to be thinking nothing," he would say, glaring at me.

Part of the frustration that fueled his temper, I believe, was the condition of my older brother, Al. He was born with a harelip and cleft palate. Of course, in those days there was no corrective surgery available for those deformities, and I am sure Al suffered psychologically from the comments of neighborhood kids. I think my father felt partially responsible for Al's condition, but he was powerless to correct it. That only made him more angry and frustrated, and I was his only available target.

That was part of his personality. He needed to be in control. He was a stubborn perfectionist as well as a visionary businessman. He had the wisdom to sell one of the first oil-fired furnaces when they were introduced in the late 1940s. And the temerity to offer it in the heart of Pennsylvania coal country. My dad's company storefront was dynamited or firebombed on four different occasions, most likely by thugs from John L. Lewis's United Mine Workers, who viewed him as a traitor for switching from coal to oil. The violence didn't scare him; it only made him more committed to doing things his way. I inherited those qualities of stubbornness and independence.

The other thing that drove my father to distraction was my failing grades in school. Years later I would realize that I had a learning disability that affected how I processed information. When I was tested as an adult, my IQ was 162. At the time, however, everyone, including my dad and me, simply thought I was the dumbest kid in class. It didn't help that my ears were still ringing from being whacked the day before. It only added to my low self-esteem and lack of confidence. I could not comprehend what I read. No matter how many times I read a sentence or paragraph, it was as if I had a concrete wall around my brain that refused to let the meaning penetrate.

And yet I had the knack for other kinds of mental gymnastics.

The *Wilkes-Barre Times Leader* had a daily maze. I eagerly looked forward to working on it. I would stare intently at the maze, mentally draw the solution, set the paper aside, draw the solution on a blank sheet of paper, and then hold it over the actual maze. I rarely was out of bounds.

What made my dad particularly angry was his belief that I was simply lazy and wouldn't apply myself. On the other hand, he saw that I got passing grades in math and science. That's because neither of those courses required much reading. Math for me was simply a bunch of numbers, drifting through my subconscious, that I instinctively understood. Science was learning how things worked, about which I had an innate understanding. But when it came time for report cards to go home, I would experience what I would later come to know as panic attacks—a weakness in my stomach and a pain that started in one temple and burned across my head to the other. I knew I was in for a beating.

The discipline from my father plus my feelings of insecurity driven by my reading problems led to my passion for ham radio. I built my first ham rig at age ten and I was hooked for life. It didn't occur to me at the time, but ham radio gave me the opportunity to be a star in my own personal galaxy. The power of one, literally and figuratively. I was no longer the dumbest kid on the block. I was call sign W3VCG, able to communicate with anyone on the planet, transformed by the magic of electronics. I loved the anonymity of it. I was never happier than when I was talking with a stranger hundreds or thousands of miles away. It fit my personality perfectly.

The other appeal of ham radio was the satisfaction of making something with my hands. I was always a tinkerer. After my first exposure to radio-controlled model airplanes at the age of eight, I made the leap straight to ham radio. But my fascination with electronics came even earlier. I remember sitting in the kitchen in our house on Horton Street and listening to an old General Electric tabletop radio next to the refrigerator. I would turn the radio around, exposing a forest of vacuum tubes and condensers, and imagine the Lone Ranger and Tonto, the Green Hornet, and The Shadow zipping through the tubes, wires, and filaments.

The first ham radio I built was a crude, crystal-controlled affair that I used to contact friends in and around Wilkes-Barre. The transmitter had a single 6L6 oscillator/amplifier and the receiver was a basic tunable National Radio NC53. Building that ham set gave me a feeling of satisfaction and independence that I would carry throughout my life.

At the same time, my friends and I were taking wire from old transformers and running it along cracks in the pavement from one house to another so we could send covert messages, i.e., four-letter words, back and forth between us by Morse code.

But then, building things was a tradition in my family. My great-grandfather on my father's side, William Kaiser, was a tin and copper smith. He was also a prolific inventor. During the Civil War, he rose to the rank of sergeant and saw action at the battles of Harpers Ferry and Falling Waters, West Virginia. My grandfather—Martin L. Kaiser Sr.— had a degree from the New York Technical School. In the early days of the Depression he invented a left- and right-hand valve seat for faucets, an external shaker for stoves, and numerous other plumbing and heating devices. My granddad was also the author of several books and articles on the subject of plumbing, including the 1905 classic "Repair Kinks for Plumbers." His brother Paul was the chief engineer at the DuPont Powder Company in the early part of the twentieth century. Another brother, Charles, was a world-renowned architect who designed the north face of the White House.

My father, Martin L. Kaiser Jr., was the first to introduce the new Motor Stoker furnace into northeastern Pennsylvania. When the temperature dropped, the stoker would automatically pull a new batch of coal from the coal bin, through a tube with an Archimedes screw inside, into the furnace, thus preventing the fire from ever going out. It saved someone the burden of going down into the cellar on a freezing winter night and shoveling more coal into the furnace to get the fire going again. It also removed the ashes from the firebox and dumped them into an ashcan. In the 1940s and 1950s in Wilkes-Barre and most of northeastern Pennsylvania, everyone had to have a Kaiser Motor Stoker furnace, and that included the hotels and office buildings. That was the case at least until the advent of the oil-fired furnace.

My father's brother, Albert, was the chief engineer of the West Virginia Pulp and Paper Company, where he invented the Marlboro cigarette flip-top box.

Following in the footsteps of my family, at age eleven I constructed a primitive diving helmet from scraps of tin and glass I found in my father's plumbing shop. I soldered it together, attached an air bottle from a World War II life raft to the front, and gave it a test run in Lake Nuangola, our summertime playground. It actually let me stay under water for several minutes, until the air ran out and I would get dizzy. I would refill the air bottle at a local gas station, not giving much thought to coating my lungs with oil! Not bad for a kid who had only read about hardhat diving in a men's magazine.

Looking back over the past forty years, it's amazing to realize that I have invented more than six hundred different devices for the electronic countermeasure, surveillance, and bomb-detection market. Unfortunately, many of these devices were later copied and their designs stolen by the very clients I was serving.

But ham radio was my refuge as a boy. As I mentioned, it was my only connection to the outside world and a source of bonding with the few friends I had. I joined a ham radio club at the YMCA when I was thirteen.

I met my best friend and ham radio partner when I entered Wyoming Seminary at fifteen. It was a college prep school in Kingston, located across the Susquehanna River from Wilkes-Barre. My friend was Tom Walsh. He had been born blind. I learned more from Tom about surviving bad times than from any seeing person.

We depended on each other. I was his eyesight and he was my moral support. I was closer to Tom than to my own brothers. When I got depressed about life at home, my painful shyness with girls, or my academic failures, he used to say, "You think you got problems, Marty?" Then he would laugh and I would laugh with him, all the while embarrassed that I was feeling sorry for myself.

Tom was an amazing person. He was always upbeat, full of life, and one of the wisest, most sensitive people I have ever known. He could listen to my tone of voice and know whether I was having a good day or not. He had a sixth sense about where everything was located within his immediate space. I always remember walking home from school with him. When we reached the beginning of his street, he would say, "Okay, let's race."

The first time he said that, I asked, "How're you going to do that? You might fall and hurt yourself or run into something." He would laugh and say, "Watch me." And then he would take off running like someone was chasing him. He often beat me to his house, somehow avoiding the trees and telephone poles that lined the four-foot-wide sidewalk.

We were inseparable in those days. I introduced Tom to ham radio and adapted his set so that he would know how to turn the dials to the precise settings by feeling the pointer on the meter from which the glass had been removed. When we got bored talking to each other late at night, we would communicate by Morse code. We were able to get our speed up to fifty words a minute.

One of our wildest adventures was letting Tom drive my mother's old hand-me-down '51 Caddy. We used to tool around in it at Kirby Park, a riverside park on the other side of the Susquehanna River from Wilkes-Barre, every day at noon lunch break. One day, he turned to me and said, "Could I drive?"

At first I thought he was joking, but he was absolutely serious.

"How're you going to do that?"

"You'll be my eyes," he said. "Just point me in the right direction and shout if we're about to smash into something."

"I don't know, Tom," I said.

"Stop worrying, Veece," he said. That was Tom's nickname for me. It was connected to the last three letters of my ham radio call sign: VCG. "It'll be a blast."

"Yeah, and I'll probably get a blast from my dad for letting you do it."

"Don't worry," said Tom. "He'll never find out."

"Okay," I said reluctantly, letting him slide into the driver's seat. He grasped the steering wheel as if he'd been driving all his life, and gunned the engine.

"Are we ready to roll?" he shouted. Before I could answer him, he floored the accelerator and the car leaped forward.

I'll never forget it. I was both scared and exhilarated. There was blind Tom driving around the field, yelling, hooting, and beating his left hand on the outside of the car door while I cracked up laughing. I was awed, and envious of my friend's self-confidence, his fearlessness, and his trust in me. In an odd sort of way, Tom was as much my mentor and role model as my best friend. I remember thinking later that if he could overcome his blindness with such fearlessness and confidence, I could certainly overcome my own problems.

One of my great regrets is that we didn't stay in touch. I heard that Tom went on to get his doctorate and became an influential member of the American Federation for the Blind.

My years at Wyoming Seminary were a constant struggle academically and socially. My only friends outside of Tom were a couple of guys I had introduced to ham radio. I didn't play sports for fear of being hit, and the trauma it would cause. I remained terribly shy with girls. I could never think of anything cool to say to them so I pretended not to hear them even when they whistled at me.

I joined the U.S. Army Reserve in my junior year and had my first opportunity to show off my Morse code capabilities. But essentially I couldn't wait for the last bell to ring so I could retreat to my home refuge of ham radio and hope for a reprieve from my father's bad moods.

Like most kids who hated school, I lived for the summers. We were not the wealthiest family in Wilkes-Barre, but my father and grandfather operated the most reliable plumbing business in town, which made it recession-proof. My father was fond of saying that no matter how little disposable income you had, you couldn't live without a working toilet, hot water for a bath, and heat to keep warm in the winter. Especially in Pennsylvania.

Eventually, with that kind of prosperity, my father was able to build a house in the Pocono Mountains on Lake Nuangola, where my mother, brothers, and I spent every summer. Not only did Lake Nuangola provide a respite from my father's unpredictable temper and judgmental attitude—he would join us at the lake on most evenings and head back to the shop in the early morning—it was there that I actually found something I was good at besides ham radio: sailing.

My dad bought me a "Moth" class sailboat and, with my younger brother Ron as crew, I consistently won races in that class every summer from the age of twelve until I left for college at nineteen. I also had a Barnegat Bay Sneakbox, which my brothers and I fooled around in. I can't remember how long it was but it definitely was big enough to make out with the girls in. It had a "gaff" sail that we dyed red in honor of "Red Sails in the Sunset," a popular song at the time.

The summer before my graduation from Wyoming Seminary was exciting for a different reason. I went on a church-sponsored fellowship for three months to Europe. It was 1953. The Korean War was just about to end in a truce at a place called Panmunjom, and Ike had been elected president the previous November. The trip was my first experience in another culture, and the first time away from home and the oppressive authority of my father. But only physically. He was always there in my head warning me to behave.

The most memorable part of the trip was crossing the Atlantic from New York to Le Havre, France, on the ocean liner *Stockholm*, which later rammed the *Andrea Doria* in the fog off the coast of Nantucket in July 1956.* Every morning I would get up to watch the sunrise, head straight for the bow, and look over the railing in hopes of seeing a dolphin.

*The *Andrea Doria* sank and fifty-six lives were lost, but the *Stockholm* was able to limp back into New York.

One morning I saw something that scared the pants off me. It was a round, gray object bobbing about ten feet off the side of the boat. I suddenly realized what it was: a World War II mine complete with detonators, metal spikes sticking out from various angles. I ran around desperately looking for someone in authority to tell. By the time I found a crewman, the mine was well behind us and I remained silent. I doubt that anyone would have believed me. I was just a sixteen-year-old kid. Nevertheless, I knew what it was.

We cycled through Scandinavia and most of the rest of Europe to Morocco, traveling from one youth hostel to the next. My calf muscles were three times their normal size by the end of the trip. Berlin was the most memorable city I visited, primarily because of the damage from World War II that was visible wherever you looked. The Marshall Plan was still in its infancy.

The most powerful impact of the trip was my first taste of independence. I was intoxicated by it. I could not wait to get out on my own, to college or elsewhere.

My one last barrier to freedom was summoning the courage to give my senior oration before the entire Wyoming Seminary student body of four hundred kids. This was the psychological equivalent of scaling the Great Wall of China, given my shyness and lack of confidence. However, it was a requirement for graduation, which was why it took me five years instead of the normal four to graduate. I finally got through it. The only thing I remember about giving the speech was the title: "The Dawn of the Space Age."

The most surprising thing was the applause I received when it was over. I couldn't believe it. Someone actually liked what I had to say. It certainly lacked the pizzazz of the speech given by another kid in my graduating class. His thesis was a hands-on demonstration about the dangers of gasoline. He used a one-foot-long piece of pipe with a flat base welded to one end. A spark plug was inserted through the side of the pipe. He put one drop of gasoline into the pipe and inserted a rubber cork into the top. When he fired the spark plug there was a huge BANG! and the cork punched a hole through the stained glass window above the lectern. The hole was so high up that no one had bothered to fix it by the time I graduated. He definitely got the biggest laugh of the day. The hole was still there when I attended my fiftieth class reunion.

I entered Lafayette College the following September, and my academic struggles continued to plague me. The only thing I accomplished that year was learning how to drink and making it through class the next day with a crashing hangover.

By the end of the first year, I was flunking out and totally demoralized. I enrolled in summer school but had little heart for it. On the weekends, I would retreat to our house on Lake Nuangola, where I had some of best memories of my youth. It was there one weekend that my life took a dramatic change of attitude and direction. I saw a beautiful, dark-haired girl walking down the steps of a cottage surrounded by several of her friends.

I thought, "She's the one. I want her."

Her name was Carmel Gabriele. She was seventeen and from Hazleton, about twenty miles from Wilkes-Barre. Pardon the cliché, but it really was love at first sight. Despite my shyness, I found the courage to ask her to go to a drive-in movie with me. To my surprise, she agreed, but with her three girlfriends in the back seat. I don't remember the name of the movie, but I know we didn't look at it much.

We saw each other almost every night for the rest of the summer. When she entered the University of Pennsylvania that fall, I switched to Rider College in Trenton, New Jersey. I wasn't going to let her get away. I took the train to Philadelphia every weekend to be with her.

My transfer to Rider didn't set any records academically, but I was in love and on my own. I saw light at the end of my tunnel. Within a year, Carmel and I were married. She dropped out of the university and moved to Trenton. Our first apartment was on the second floor of a walk-up in a low-rent part of town, and the landlord let me hook up my ham radio rig in the attic.

In June 1957, the end of that first year at Rider, three things happened that would propel my life and career in a new and fateful direction: I flunked out of college, still unable to overcome my reading comprehension deficits; I was about to become a father for the first time; and I found a job as a research technician for RCA Laboratories in Penns Neck, New Jersey, near Princeton.

The experience would prove to be the equivalent of getting a Ph.D. in electrical engineering. I had finally found something I loved and excelled at. Most important, it was something that would earn me the respect of my peers—and their praise—for the first time in my life.

Chapter 2

Getting Serious About Electronics

MY FIRST JOB at RCA was pretty low-tech: keep the lab glassware clean and ready for daily experiments. My salary was about $90 a week, but I quickly demonstrated that I was worth much more than that. I started working with scientists on image-conversion devices to increase the clarity and strength of the first-generation night vision devices.

Some of the men I worked for were giants in this field. They were led by Dr. George Morton, who did some of the groundbreaking work in television, as we know it today. I also worked with Dr. John Rudy, inventor of the infrared sniper scope used by American troops in World War II, and Dr. Alfred Sommers, who invented the Iconoscope, the image-conversion tube that made real-time video possible. My job was to be their "hands." I designed and built much of the circuitry that permitted these scientists to move ahead with their experiments.

I had unlimited use of vacuum chambers, glass-working equipment, and machine shops. One of my tasks was to blow the glass for experimental vacuum tubes and heat up the "getter"—the silver phosphorous at the top of the tube that removes the final bit of air.

For one project, Dr. Dave Kleitman handed me a flat cardboard box with a hundred or so small glass jars containing just about every chemical element known to mankind. His instructions were to evaporate a sample of each of the chemicals and see which one had the highest light output when struck by an electron beam. The electron beam is the portion of a TV picture tube that strikes the phosphor on the back side of the tube face to create the picture you see, or what scientists called image conversion.

A vacuum chamber is required to accomplish each step of this process. The vacuum machines in my lab consisted of a mechanical pump with a liquid nitrogen "trap," a stainless-steel base with feed-through conductors to allow various voltages to enter the chamber, and a thick glass dome measuring 18 inches in diameter and 24 inches high. A mechanical pump was then used to remove most of the air in the chamber. What little remained was frozen to the walls of the "trap" by the liquid nitrogen, thus assuring a near-perfect vacuum. Once a suitable vacuum was obtained, a voltage was applied to the two terminals connected to the crucible, and it turned white-hot. The material in the crucible was evaporated onto a glass slide.

After evaporating virtually every combination of chemicals, I settled on cesium iodide mixed with a bit of thallium as the most efficient evaporated phosphor in creating what would evolve into TV picture tubes.

Using that newfound knowledge, I noticed that some phosphors were not only excited by an electron beam, they were sensitive to light. Based on this knowledge, I came up with a totally new method for doing image conversion. I called it a flying spot scanner video pick-up device. It was the first such system that recognized the non-linear action of electrons in evaporated phosphors. I wrote up the summary and handed it to Dr. Morton, who passed it up the line. A few days later, my summary came back with a note that the concept had no commercial value, but to be on the safe side RCA would issue a public technical note to destroy its patent value. The reason RCA did that, I believe, was that they may have been embarrassed when they found out that the idea came from a lowly technician rather than from one of their highly paid, world-class engineers. I received a check in the amount of $75 for my effort.

When the Russians sent their first satellite around the back side of the moon in the late 1960s, I read in technical journals that they used my flying spot scanner system because of its basic simplicity. For free, of course.

The deeper I moved into the research of image-conversion devices, I realized that it was time to turn my amateur radio interests toward amateur television. I wrote extensively for technical journals, RCA in-house technical publications, and radio amateur magazines. I also had my own ham TV station on the air. At RCA, I met another amateur TV enthusiast, Bill Haldane, who would become a close friend and associate in Project CAMEBRIDGE, an "Over-the-Horizon Radar" system.

One of the great aspects of working at RCA back then was the freedom to do research and to follow our instincts wherever the research led. I had a well-stocked parts department and fully equipped machine shop at my disposal to produce virtually any piece of equipment I needed. There was another benefit of enormous value to me. Every so often, each lab would "clean house" and hold an auction for employees to bid on equipment that was no longer needed. Usually I bid five or ten cents on items and no more than a quarter. I kept dragging the stuff home and Carmel kept putting it out for the trash man. It didn't matter. By the time she did that, I was able to understand the thought process it took to make the device. It was like getting a Ph.D. in engineering for pennies. I bought one of the first CBS color wheel TV sets and one of the first CBS color wheel cameras in the mid 1950s, years before color became commercially available. I'm glad RCA won the FCC standards war. If CBS had won, every TV set would have been three times the size of the current sets.

One of the projects I worked on involved VVLF (Very Very Low Frequency) technology that included all frequencies below 100 Hertz

(Hz), or cycles per second, as they were then called. During the changeover from cycles to Hertz, I used to joke that it was a heck of a lot easier to ride a motorcycle than a motorhertz.

We spent most of our time working between 8 and 12 Hertz. The objective of the project was to develop a communication system for submarines. I spent an enormous amount of time in the library scouring Russian and German scientific papers regarding experiments with communication technology below 10 Hz. Despite the fact that I did not read or speak either language, I could look at a schematic and interpret the article describing it.

One interesting item that I uncovered during my research was the Germans' use of strobe lights to down our aircraft during World War II. They did that by pointing the strobe spotlight at our aircraft and adjusting the speed of the flash so that it momentarily stunned the pilot and made him think the aircraft's engines had stopped. The pilot would then jam the throttle forward, not realizing that he was already near full power, and put the plane into a flat spin, causing it to crash.

On the ground, the German strobe operators suffered a different but intense result. They either lost consciousness or vomited seemingly without stopping. The Germans soon realized that the frequency they had chosen for the strobe light intensity was close to 6.8 Hz, the resonant frequency of the human body. The infrared component of the strobe light was causing the problem. They solved it by wearing dark glasses that filtered out the infrared component.

In the lab, we stumbled across the same problem one day. We were generating tens of kilowatts of audio at 6.8 Hz frequency and were suddenly walking around like zombies, bumping into desks and walls, tripping over chairs, and losing our breakfast or lunch.

Life at the RCA labs was more fun than anyone should have been allowed to enjoy and still get paid for working there. A good example: One day Dr. Richard Klensch, one of the top scientists in the lab, took me outside to a small pond behind Lab 3, where the serious R&D was done. A narrow bridge crossed the pond, and in the middle of the bridge was a small hut that housed the test equipment.

We lowered a hydrophone (an underwater microphone) from the hut into the pond. Two hundred yards away at the edge of the pond was a rod ten feet long amd four inches in diameter driven flush into the ground. Next to the rod lay a small loudspeaker connected to a microphone in the pond house. The research was part of something called Project Pangloss—trying to figure out how to communicate with submarines in deep water (below 15,000 feet) at a frequency below 10 Hz.

My job was to drop a 10-pound cannon ball onto the iron rod when Klensch yelled "Go." He would in turn measure the shock wave that resulted from the impact. We had been at it for several hours when suddenly I saw an ambulance roaring across the field toward me. It stopped nearby and two men in white jackets jumped out. They slowly walked over to where I was holding a cannon ball above my head.

"Excuse me, sir," said one of the medics. "But what are you doing?"

Needless to say, my explanation caused my colleagues back in the main building to collapse in spasms of laughter. I assume someone from the lab had called the security office and advised them that some maniac was on the loose behind the building. After assuring them that I was sane and simply carrying out some basic research in shock wave vibration, the paramedics left, and Dr. Klensch and I continued with our experiment.

Another fascinating project I worked on was the TIROS 1 (Television InfraRed Observational Satellite), publicized as the world's first meteorological satellite. My assignment was to work on a portion of the imaging and ground control system. In fact, TIROS 1's primary mission had little to do with weather and everything to do with the U.S. cold war strategy vis-à-vis the Soviets.

It was common knowledge around the lab that when it was originally sent into earth orbit on April 1, 1960, TIROS 1 was an antisatellite satellite (ASAT), armed and ready to take out a Russian satellite in the same orbit in the event of Soviet ICBM missile attacks on the United States. Since the end of the Cold War in the early 1990s, TIROS 1 has been converted to its current low-earth orbit weather forecasting mission.

In late 1961, about four years after I joined RCA, Bill Haldane approached me one day at work and asked if I would like to go to Trinidad to work on an interesting project.

"What's it about, Bill?" I asked, excited about the possibility of living and working in another country.

"First I need to know whether you're willing to live outside the U.S. with your family for a year or more," he said.

"Let me talk to my wife and I'll let you know tomorrow."

When I got home, I grabbed an encyclopedia and found the location of Trinidad and Tobago on the map. It was a twin-island nation, the southernmost of the Caribbean's Leeward Islands and about seven miles off the coast of Venezuela. Carmel was a little reticent about picking up and moving our family, which now included our daughter, Carol, and our son, Marty, to a foreign country. But I was excited about it and she reluctantly agreed.

When I told Bill I was ready to go, he told me that the government of Trinidad and Tobago had turned thumbs down on our request. Our next choice was the island of Antigua, but they too said no. I later learned that both islands had rejected our request due to the growing strains in the relationship between the Kennedy administration and Cuba. The tensions that finally grew into the Cuban Missile Crisis that would take place later that year also played a large role in that rejection. What those governments must have known at the time, but I did not, was the purpose of the experiment—laying the groundwork for the development of the first early warning, antimissile defense system.

A few weeks later, Haldane advised me that RCA had decided to set up the project on the island of Barbados, where there was a small U.S. Navy base.

"How did we get permission from the government?" I asked.

"Simple," said Haldane. "We didn't tell the Barbadian government the nature of the project."

Weeks later, Bill informed me he was going to manage a similar project on the island of Jamaica to provide a second radar point for the project. He never did tell me how RCA convinced the Jamaican government to give permission for the experiment. Probably by not asking.

Bill asked if I was still game to go to Barbados and I assured him I was raring to go despite the fact that I had no idea what the project was all about. It didn't matter. I was ready to experience another culture, especially one with crystal-clear water for scuba diving, white sand beaches, and temperatures in the 80s and 90s year round.

That afternoon, I was finally briefed about a new high-frequency (1–30 MHz) Over-the-Horizon Radar (OHR) that an RCA technician had conceived. Essentially the project mission was to study the "flutter effect" caused by objects moving through the ionosphere. In those days, thanks to the early design of limiter stages in the receiver, one could readily hear the effect when an airplane flew between an FM transmitter and an FM receiver.

The Russians later tried to expand on the OHR concept by "chirping" the signal. Amateur radio operators were not very happy with the Russian system because it could be heard continuously from 3 to 30 MHz. It was affectionately dubbed "The Woodpecker" because that's exactly what it sounded like.

The project was funded by the air force at a price tag of $1 million. By today's standards, you couldn't buy and design the equipment needed to conduct the experiment for less than $30 million. That was my first task—to assemble the equipment needed for two forty-foot trailers loaded with the most sensitive receivers and transmitters available and put them on ships headed for Barbados and Jamaica.

I was transferred to the RCA Service Company and sent to Burlington, Massachusetts, to check out the hardware required for the project. When I arrived, much to my astonishment, I found nothing there. I was told I had three months to find (which meant beg, borrow, or steal from the RCA facility there) all of the equipment needed for those two forty-foot trailers.

By early April 1962, the two trailers had been assembled, tested, and ready to go. My wife and I closed our house in Pennington, New Jersey, and along with our two children, flew to Barbados on one of the first 707s to take to the air. When we left Idlewild airport the temperature was near zero. Two hours later we arrived in Barbados and the temperature was 88 degrees. Quite a difference, and a pleasant shock to the senses!

We checked in to a hotel that looked like something out of a Humphrey Bogart movie and was populated with plenty of indigenous insects. In its infinite wisdom, RCA would only allow us to stay at the cheapest lodging on the island on the east coast near the town of Bathsheba. The view was absolutely breathtaking, with the sea rolling in and the salt spray dripping from the trees and the eaves of the house.

A quaint English family ran the hotel, so for the continental breakfast we had toast presented in a toast rack, marmalade, tea, and mango juice. The morning after we arrived, Carmel, the children, and I walked down to the sea and waded into the water. I wasn't in the water five minutes when a Portuguese man-of-war draped itself over my right elbow, putting my arm out of action for the next few days.

I arranged to get a car from the only rental place on the island— Johnson's Stable and Garage. A 1958 VW beetle that had seen better days. But the engine turned over on the first try and we considered ourselves lucky to be mobile. We looked at a map to see how to get to the navy base. The owner of the hotel said the best route would be to head down the south coast to Bridgetown. From there, we would pick up Highway 1A and head up the west coast to the parish of Saint Lucy and the navy base on the northernmost point of the island.

Carmel looked at the map and asked, "Why should we go all the way to Bridgetown when we can cut across the island?"

We did just that. But with twelve-foot-high sugarcane at every corner, each intersection looks exactly like another, and it doesn't take long to get lost. Instead of taking half an hour to cross the island, it took us two and a half hours.

We had two priorities: to find more permanent, insect-free housing and to connect with the commander of the U.S. Navy base, where I had been assured I could set up shop for Project CAME-BRIDGE. When the car was delivered to our hotel we decided to take a ride around the island. With the kids in the back seat, we headed out. At one of the first roads leading to a beautiful, deserted beach, we passed man putting up a For Rent sign in front of a spacious stone house set back a few hundred feet from the road.

I stopped and asked him how much he was asking. He said, "One hundred fifty dollars a month." In U.S. dollars, that came to $75. Without even looking inside, I said, "We'll take it."

It turned out to be a dream house, with eighteen-foot ceilings, a living room the size of a small gymnasium, and three bedrooms tastefully furnished in teak and mahogany. The best part about it was that we lived one hundred feet from a private beach right next to the Sandy Lane Hotel, which is still the most exclusive hotel on the island today.

We spent the rest of the day transferring our suitcases and trunks from the hotel to the house. Most important, we fastened a Styrofoam float on Marty's back because we knew he would make a break for the beach whenever he could.

The following morning I was up early, knocking on the door of the navy base commander, Capt. Clyde McPherson. I had to find out where I could set up my trailer full of equipment when it finally arrived by tramp steamer. The moment I met him I knew by the blank expression in his eyes that no one from the RCA advance team had informed him of Project CAMEBRIDGE or of our intention to set up on his base.

It turned out that the four RCA advance men never left

Bridgetown, the island capital. Instead, they spent their time enjoying the warm Barbadian hospitality, fueled by the smooth Mount Gay rum and the strikingly beautiful island women.

I was basically on my own. After some protracted negotiations with Capt. McPherson, and helped considerably by my wife's kitchen politics—her cherry-cheesecake pies were always a deal-closer—he gave me a few hundred square feet of space on which to set up the project.

The eighteen-ton trailer full of equipment finally arrived from Massachusetts a month later by an inter-island cargo ship that resembled a slightly larger version of the *African Queen,* complete with a Bogart-like skipper at the helm.

"How're you gonna move this?" he asked, already knowing the answer.

"I'm still trying to find something strong enough," I said.

He laughed. "Good luck."

As they started to off-load the trailer, it began to swing from side to side and came perilously close to the water. Finally, on one long swing, the captain ordered the crane brakes released. With a loud and painful BANG, the trailer—packed with two one-million-watt peak-pulse-power transmitters and two 10,000-watt continuous wave transmitters, receivers, and synthesizers—was now solidly on Barbadian soil.

I thanked the skipper despite the less than gentle treatment, while hoping nothing had been damaged, and set about finding something powerful enough to tow the trailer to the north end of the island. I was successful after several trips to the local junkyard plus generous amounts of rum for my hastily assembled caravan crew.

The only problem with the tractor we found was that it had no brakes. However, with the help of a good mechanic we bypassed the brake system and got moving. I was overjoyed at my great luck, brakes or not.

We set out for the navy base the following day. My caravan consisted of me in my VW beetle leading the way, waving a large red flag out of the window, followed by the tractor towing the trailer, warning people to stay out of our way. As we passed through several small villages, many of its inhabitants ran out into the street, clapping their hands, waving, and jumping wildly with joy.

To this day, I'm still not sure what caused this reception. Perhaps the people thought the island had been taken over by Communists. More likely, our strange little caravan interrupted the tedium of another day in paradise.

After getting the trailer in place on the navy base, I began installing four huge log periodic antennas. They consisted of two 150-foot-long (1–30 MHz) vertical log periodic curtains and two (3–30 MHz) horizontal log periodic beams mounted on the hundred-foot towers that supported the curtain. These towers were supported by half-inch nylon rope, a rare luxury on the island.

In the beginning, Barbadian fisherman would "liberate" some of my nylon rope each night. I finally came up with a solution. I made several meaningless medallions of wood that I required the workers to wear around their necks while working on the antenna site. If they refused to wear them, I told the men, they would lose their virility. Since Barbadian men value their manhood above anything else, they didn't want to risk losing it for some rope. Within days, the after-hours nylon rope thefts stopped.

Before I could set up the antennas, however, I had another problem to solve. I hired a man with the only bulldozer on the island to clear the area of a grove of large manchineel trees. These trees bear a harmless-looking fruit similar to an apple, but in fact, the fruit and the tree sap are extremely poisonous.

According to the local legend, the reason the Spanish did not colonize the island was their initial landing at the edge of a forest of manchineel trees in the same location as my intended radar project. The conquistadors were poisoned by the tree's apples and leaves that rained down upon them as they waded ashore. Viewing the incident as a bad omen of their discovery, the Spanish pulled up anchor and left, leaving the island to the British explorers who came after them.

We learned firsthand how seriously the sap from the manchineel leaves could burn the skin. There were several of those trees in the backyard of the house we rented. My son, Marty, picked up the apples and started throwing them. Giving him a bath that night, my wife noticed his eye was swollen where he had rubbed it. It took months for the infection from the manchineel sap to heal.

Once the equipment was in place and the "illuminating points" were locked into the receivers, my family and I settled into the laid-back island life for which the Caribbean is known.

The only bit of excitement created by the project occurred several weeks after we had the antennas up and functioning. I heard the drone of a four-engine aircraft and looked up to see a red star and Soviet markings on the underside of a bomber cruising at about 1,000 feet with its bomb bay doors open and a large camera protruding from it. Others had seen the aircraft too. By the next morning, the American ambassador was banging on my door wanting to know exactly what the hell we were doing on the navy base that had made the Soviets so curious.

With the help of my wife's baking expertise plus my assurances to the ambassador that the project was merely some harmless research in expanding the reach of radar signals—I did not mention the system's antimissile tracking capability—we were allowed to stay. The next big flap was one of my own making, and my compulsion to tell the truth.

We had been in Barbados a little more than a year when I received a phone call one day from an air force procurement officer in Washington asking how the research was going. I told him everything was operating at high speed and going very well. Then he popped a more delicate question.

"How would you compare RCA's missile tracking system with a similar one Raytheon is working on?"

"What do you mean compare the two systems?" I asked, stalling for time. It was a loaded question, and we both knew it.

I was familiar with the Raytheon system from my research in the field. I also knew that Raytheon had invested far more in perfecting their system than RCA had—$68 million of Raytheon's own money compared to RCA's investment, which was basically limited to the $1 million air force contract.

"I mean which system would you choose if you were me?" said the officer.

"Off the record?" I asked.

"You bet."

"Based on the R&D investment alone, I'd go with Raytheon."

"Thanks."

Of course, my comment to the air force officer was not treated as confidential. It got back to my superiors at RCA Service Company campus in Cherry Hill, New Jersey. Within the month, I received a letter notifying me that I would be replaced on the Barbados project. I was directed to return to my original job as a technician, in Cherry Hill.

When I got back to work, I asked if there were any other overseas project opportunities. Yes, I was told. We have a job in Australia, but you would have to pay to take your family with you. That was tantamount to offering no job at all. I was also demoted from senior technician to technician. The explanation: I lacked an undergraduate degree.

The treatment was RCA's payback for my comments to the air force regarding the Barbados project. From then on until I left RCA six months later, I was treated as a virtual pariah and hidden in a basement workshop of one of the Project CAMEBRIDGE managers. It was the price for telling the truth. But truth-telling had been hard-wired into me from the time I was a kid, when my father would beat me for telling a lie. He also beat me if he didn't like the truth I was telling him, but not as badly as if I told a lie.

An ironic footnote to my management of Project CAMEBRIDGE

came the following year in a page one article in the *Trenton Evening Times*, September 18, 1964. It read:

> *Two new United States defense systems that can detect, intercept, and destroy enemy missiles far out in space have been revealed by President Lyndon Johnson. One of the systems, a radar-like beam, which bends around the earth's surface and upon which the new missile-destroying system depends, was developed under the direction of a 29-year-old Pennington (NJ) man, Martin Kaiser, of 418 Hale Street.*
>
> *The President said: "We now have developed and tested two systems with the ability to intercept and destroy armed satellites circling the earth in space. I can tell you today that these systems are in place, they are operationally ready and they are on the alert to protect this nation and the free world."*
>
> *Kaiser said he worked for the Radio Corporation of America Laboratories in Dutch Neck (Penns Neck), when, in 1962, an RCA engineer discovered the principle of the bending beam. Kaiser was appointed field manager and engineer for the project, known as CAMEBRIDGE, at an RCA Lab in Burlington, Mass. After three months, at the end of the 1962, all equipment was taken to Barbados, West Indies, and Kaiser managed the work there until June 1963. The young scientist hails from Wilkes-Barre, Pa. He is presently at Rider College, studying for a degree in management.*

A later incarnation of my OHR project became known by another name: Relocatable Over-The-Horizon Radar (ROTHR). The U.S. Navy developed the system to provide wide-area ocean surveillance for the nation's fleet defense from both sea and airborne threats. The first development system of ROTHR was tested on the east coast of the

United States and delivered to the navy's Fleet Surveillance Support command in Norfolk, Virginia, in 1988. The tactical military radar scanned the skies from Japan to the eastern U.S.S.R. looking for high-speed bombers. ROTHR performed its surveillance duties successfully and the navy intended to install twelve of these systems around the world during to provide the fleet with an early warning of Soviet attack.

However, with the collapse of Communism that began in 1989, and the decline in defense spending, it was decided to use ROTHR in a different role.

While testing the first production system, the radar operators noticed that ROTHR was not only tracking large commercial aircraft crossing the Caribbean, but also small twin- and single-engine planes. On May 1, 1989, ROTHR had provided the joint U.S. Coast Guard/U.S. Customs center in Miami with critical detection information that led to a pursuit and seizure of an aircraft carrying drugs to the Bahamas. This drug bust was the first one attributable to a long-range radar system. At the same time, Congress assigned to the Department of Defense the task of counter-drug detection and monitoring. As a result, the Pentagon decided to leave the ROTHR system at its test site in Virginia to search for drug smugglers in the Caribbean.

Since that time, the ROTHR system has been operating as part of the national counter-drug strategy in conjunction with the ship and airborne assets of the navy, customs, coast guard, and local law enforcement agencies. When the air route of a plane raises the suspicions of ROTHR operators, information on the target is passed to the Joint Interagency Task Force in Key West, Florida, via a secure communications link. Since 1992, information obtained by ROTHR has led to the seizure of over 50,000 kilograms of narcotics and tens of millions of dollars in cash and resources. I am proud to know that I contributed to the early development of the system.

I left RCA in Cherry Hill, New Jersey, within three months after returning from Barbados, and took a job with the Telerad

Manufacturing division of the Lionel Corporation (the model-train company), a defense electronics company in the Flemington/Pennington area, where I worked as a senior technician on the Atlas missile program.

My last project with Telerad was designing and building a dollar-bill changer for the Petrovend Corporation. They wanted to put them into all of their gas pumps. I built the prototype in a couple of weeks and it was field tested, but never used. That same year marked the introduction of something that would make cash transactions a whole lot scarcer—credit cards.

I also went back to Rider College to complete my undergraduate degree in business management. This time I was on the dean's list, thanks to a lot of help from my wife, but also as a result of my determination to overcome my comprehension problems.

My tenure with Telerad lasted about a year. I was bored, and tired of working for someone else. I completed my coursework at Rider, graduated in June 1965, and started looking around for a new challenge. I took a job with ENAC Triton Co., a small electronics firm located in Cockeysville, Maryland. They were building loran marine triangular location systems, something I'd never done before. These systems were the forerunner of the current GPS system. But within a few months, I knew it wasn't for me.

I came home one day and told my wife it was time for me to be my own boss. I knew as much as the guy running ENAC Triton and I told her that if he could do this so could I. She didn't like the idea. She was worried about health insurance coverage for her and the children, as well as a steady paycheck.

"Don't worry, Carmel," I told her. "It'll be fine. Trust me. You'll see."

Of course, she did worry and decided to get a substitute-teaching job in the Baltimore County schools to supplement my salary. Carmel taught for a year or so until my business started to take off. Then she stayed home to raise our two children, and helped out by keeping the books for the business. Later, after the children were grown and out of the house, she went back to college to complete her degree in nursing and eventually took a position with the American Cancer Society.

But in December 1965, it was the beginning of Martin L. Kaiser Inc., a small electronics company with a big future. It was risky, to be sure, but I was confident I would find companies with electricity-related problems that would hire me to solve them.

Part 2

The New King of Electronic Countermeasures

Chapter 3

Stumbling into the
Spy Racket

NOT KNOWING EXACTLY how to start a company, I picked up the Baltimore yellow pages and started down the list of companies. I called the maintenance department of the first company listed, Armco Steel.

I knew they must have something that operated on electricity, wasn't working, and that I could fix. Bingo! On my first call, the Armco maintenance manager, Fred Vogelgesang, answered the phone.

"Hi, my name is Marty Kaiser," I told him, "I'm starting my own electronics company. I can fix almost anything electronic and I was wondering if you had anything broken that you have not been able to get to work correctly."

"As a matter of fact, I do," said Vogelgesang. "Do you know what a Curtis Immerscope is?"

"Not really," I told him, "but if it runs on electric current, I can fix it."

"I like your honesty and your confidence, Marty," said Vogelgesang. "Come on over and let's talk."

I immediately jumped in my '57 Chevy and drove over to the Armco plant on the outskirts of Baltimore. Vogelgesang explained his problem with the broken Immerscope, a device that ultrasonically scans a glowing-hot steel ingot to detect any flaws or air bubbles that could result in a weakness in the steel.

"The Immerscope is a critical quality control device in the steel-making process," he said, "and it's constantly going down. If you can fix it, you've got a client right here."

I took it home in the trunk of my car, cleaned it up, and replaced all the high voltage wiring that had become degraded and brittle from the extreme heat encountered in a steel mill. I took the device back to Armco the next afternoon, connected it, and it worked as if it had just come off the assembly line.

Vogelgesang was ecstatic.

"Sit down, Marty, and let me make a few phone calls."

While I listened, he called about a dozen maintenance managers at manufacturing and steel plants in the Baltimore area. Within weeks, thanks to Fred's recommendation, I had over fifty industrial customers within easy driving distance. They included steel mills, copper refineries, bottling and canning companies, breweries, and some 100 other companies that desperately needed electronic devices repaired as fast as possible and for a reasonable price.

Not only was he generous in helping me find new customers, he taught me something about how to price my services.

I received a call from him at 2 A.M. one day. Armco's vacuum degassing furnace had been damaged by some molten steel that had struck it in the wrong place, causing it to shut down in the middle of the smelting process. The furnace was thirty feet in diameter and forty feet deep. I climbed down inside the furnace and found the burned wiring. After a few quick repairs, I had it up and running in a matter of minutes. I billed them $200. Fred called me a few days later and asked me to stop by his office. Before I could sit down, Vogelgesang handed me back my invoice.

"Put another zero on that invoice, Marty."

I looked at him to see if he was joking.

"You saved Armco Steel about two million bucks by repairing that furnace when you did," he told me. "You earned the money."

It was a valuable lesson. From then on, I began to charge my customers for the value of the service from their perspective instead of at an hourly rate.

Some of my favorite clients were local breweries. I serviced three of them on a regular basis, including American, National, and Schaefer. After working for them on various jobs, I learned that when the "new" beer came down the pipes very early in the morning, it was customary for all employees to drink as much beer as possible while the machinery cooled down. Soon that included me.

One day in the summer of 1966, I had just finished a job at American Brewery, including the usual liquid breakfast. After driving a few blocks in the warehouse and waterfront area of Baltimore, I realized I was totally lost. My momentary disorientation was no doubt influenced by the large quantity of beer I had drunk. I continued to drive around looking for a familiar landmark when I passed a gate with an unattended guard post in the middle of the driveway. A sign above the gate read:

U.S. ARMY INTELLIGENCE, FORT HOLABIRD

It was the first time I'd ever seen the gate or realized that a military facility was located in this area. Hey, I said to myself, maybe these guys have something that needs fixing. Following my instincts, I drove through the unguarded gate and meandered around the installation until I saw a door to a large warehouse. A sign above the door read:

U.S. ARMY INTELLIGENCE MATÉRIEL SUPPORT OFFICE (USAIMSO)

I parked the car, got out, and knocked on the door. There was no answer so I tried the door, which was open. I looked inside and saw a man in a suit and tie sitting behind a desk in a small, dimly lit, glass-enclosed office a few feet away.

I walked over to the office and opened the door. The sign on the man's desk read Captain Robert W. Doms, CIC [Counter Intelligence Corps]. There were shelves filled with electronic equipment all over the office.

"Can I help you?" he asked, standing up. He was a tall man with a bit of a paunch.

"Hi, I'm Marty Kaiser," I said. "The question is, can I help you?"

Doms gave me a strange look.

"What I mean is, do you have anything electronic that needs to be fixed because I'm the guy who can fix it. I can fix almost anything."

"How'd you get in here?" Doms asked.

"I drove."

"I mean how did you get past the guard?" said Doms.

"There was no guard," I said.

"Figures," he said. "So you say you can fix anything, eh?"

"That's right."

Doms smiled. He stood up, went over to one of the shelves at the rear of his office and brought back a box of about a dozen transmitters and microphones the size of a cigarette pack and smaller.

"Know what these are?" he asked

"Sure," I said. "They look like miniature microphones and transmitters. Who are you bugging with those?"

"It's none of your business," he said. "Can you fix them?"

He was wrong, as within a month, it would be my business in a big way. I later learned that USAIMSO was a centralized government depot for the purchase, distribution. and maintenance of intelligence property and apparatus worldwide. In Bob Doms's words, "Intelligence property can best be described as anything you need but which is not authorized."

Participating agencies included the FBI, CIA, the Bureau of Narcotics and Dangerous Drugs (later renamed the Drug Enforcement

Agency, or DEA), U.S. Secret Service, and the intelligence commands of the army, navy and air force. Without knowing it, I had just walked, literally and figuratively, into a potential bonanza of electronic repair work and a booming market for electronic surveillance equipment.

I picked up a couple of the transmitters and amplifiers and examined them more closely. Some of the items had tags attached showing financial values that were way overpriced.

"Sure, I can fix them," I told Doms, "but frankly, some of these are not worth the time or trouble. They're junk. I can build better transmitters and amplifiers than these and I'll do it for half the price you paid."

Doms raised his eyebrows.

"Why don't you repair the ones worth fixing," he said, skeptically, "and I'll think about your offer."

I worked late into the night and repaired the dozen or so miniature transmitters and amplifiers that were salvageable. I wrote out an invoice for $350 and went to bed. I was back in Doms's office by early the next morning to deliver the items. He was clearly impressed by my work and my fee.

"Nice job, Marty," said Doms. "We'll be in touch."

Throughout the remaining months of 1966, Doms would call me once or twice a week with repair jobs on a variety of surveillance equipment, including receivers, miniature microphones, and transmitters for room audio, recording systems, body transmitters, lie detectors, and spectrum analyzers (devices that troll the radio spectrum for clandestine transmitters and receivers). Each month my business was moving more substantially into the countermeasure and surveillance equipment market and away from heavy industry.

One day in January 1967, Doms took off the shelf a Fargo 435—the state of the art in eavesdropping in the 1950s and 1960s—by Leo Jones, one of the Technical Surveillance Countermeasures (TSCM) pioneers in the United States. Doms asked me if I could fix it. I opened the amplifier and found the circuitry was potted in epoxy. The epoxy concealed the simplicity of the circuit and had nothing to do with protecting it from dust, dirt, or moisture. It also helped to justify a higher price. Using epoxy also rendered the device unrepairable and hopefully generated new sales. I never epoxied any of my products, thus making them field-repairable and giving a better return on investment.

"I'll make you the same offer," I said. "I can make an amplifier better than this one with far more capacity at one-fifth the price you're paying for the Fargo 435."

"If you can deliver it," said Doms, "you'll have more work than you can handle from army intelligence as well as other agencies."

A week later, I was back in his shop with a test Model 1059 pre-amplifier. It had four inputs for microphones and two outputs for headsets and/or tape recorders compared to the Fargo 435 that had inputs for only one mike and one headset. Doms was impressed enough to give me an order on the spot for one hundred 1059s. I was able to build and deliver them four weeks later.

With that transaction, my career as a major manufacturer and supplier of eavesdropping equipment to the entire U.S. intelligence community was launched. Over the next ten years, I would sell more than 10,000 of these 1059 preamplifiers to a wide number of intelligence agencies, including the FBI, CIA, Secret Service, the Drug Enforcement Agency, and the counterintelligence commands of the army, navy and air force.

But the miniature transmitters that Doms had initially asked me to fix really intrigued me. The cost of making them was insignificant—less than ten dollars per transmitter—and they were easy to place and conceal. The bottom line in the bugging business was that the risk-reward ratio was heavily skewed in favor of the latter. Information obtained was often invaluable and the risk of being caught was extremely low. In the hands of a professional, one ten-dollar transmitter cleverly placed in an office, house, vehicle, or on the person of a surveillance target could yield intelligence in a day or a week that could take undercover agents months to collect.

I manufactured a wide variety of these bugs in a myriad of disguises. One of army intelligence's favorite eavesdropping attacks was concealing transmitters inside picture frames. USAIMSO, Doms's shop, at one time manufactured a half dozen different sizes of picture frames with prefitted slots for transmitters 3 inches by ¾ inch deep. That was also prior to the invention of transistors that then permitted the design of bugs the size of a sugar cube or smaller.

Another favorite transmitter the spooks at Fort Holabird in downtown Baltimore asked me to make during my early days there was the shoe-heel bug with a mercury battery. The device—the size of a tiny fingernail clipper—was hidden inside the false heel of a man's or woman's shoe. It transmitted audio for only a few hours, but if they were lucky that's all the time the surveillance techs needed to pick up valuable intelligence.

In those days before the passage of the Omnibus Crime Control and Safe Streets Act of 1968, which prohibited the sale or use of Title III devices (clandestine telephone and room eavesdropping devices primarily designed for the surreptitious interception of oral communication) to anyone except federal, state, or local law enforcement agencies, the types and uses of miniature transmitters were limited only by the imagination. The "primarily designed" part means that the device must change the operational utility of something. An example would be to make a transmitter that only fit into an ashtray.

They came in all sizes, shapes, and contexts. And I made many of them, hidden in wallets, wristwatches, voice pagers, wall outlets, eyeglass cases, office staplers and lamps, cigarette and match packs, ashtrays, fountain pens, briefcases, baseball caps (the hard metal button in the middle of the hat), and neckties.

I also built pencil-thin, flexible keyhole mikes similar to those used by the FBI in its room audio surveillance of Dr. Martin Luther King Jr. from the early 1960s to January 1966.

With the exception of the microphone concealed in the martini olive, one of the most surreptitious placements of an eavesdropping device ever conceived was designed by Winston Arrington. He called it a "bikini bug." It was hidden inside a sanitary napkin worn by an undercover agent. It's not known whether that bug was ever used operationally.

It didn't take long after I got into the bug-building business at Fort Holabird to see the potential danger of these little devices, so I decided I'd better get busy and start manufacturing countermeasure equipment to find them. In addition to the 1059 amplifier, I designed and built the 2050CA RF (radio frequency) detector, which became standard gear for TSCM professionals.

RF transmitters are the toughest type of eavesdropping devices to find because they exist in a space generally filled with tremendous amounts of radio frequency energy. This energy includes all FM and AM radio stations, cell phones, TV stations, etc. The challenge is to try to distinguish the RF transmitter from all other signals in the room. An RF bug is usually designed to operate on frequencies not occupied by commercial users. The operative word is "usually." The ideal bug has low harmonic (multiples of the base frequency) output that makes the signal more difficult to detect. It can also be turned off remotely, in order to hide its existence from standard countermeasure efforts.

The RF bug, a miniature FM transmitter, was at the heart of the Watergate scandal that forced President Richard Nixon to resign in disgrace in August 1974. It was the kind of listening device James McCord hid in the ceiling of the Watergate office of the Democratic Party chief, Larry O'Brien, during the 1972 presidential election. The White House plumbers also tapped O'Brien's telephone.

The LP (listening post) was set up across the street in a Howard Johnson's motel room, where the FM receiver was located. As often happens in the "positive side" of audio surveillance, McCord and his colleagues were caught returning to the scene of the crime, in this case to replace a faulty transmitter with a new one.

Depending on the transmitter's frequency, O'Brien might have discovered the bug if he had happened to have an FM radio in his office and knew the telltale sounds of a secret microphone on the premises. By surfing the FM band on the radio, the bug would have caused a dead spot on the dial resulting in no reception or just a soft hiss below the level of ordinary static. Turning to that dead spot and raising the volume would have caused the same kind of squeal heard in public address systems when the amplifier is set too high. TSCM people call it the feedback effect, a sure sign that the room is bugged.

I'm intimately familiar with these details of the Watergate bugging in June 1972 because it was my model 2050 RF detector that found the bug during a countermeasure operation led by Capt. Larry Linville of the Metropolitan Washington Police Bomb Squad.

The first RF detectors I made were the 2050 models. The RF detector I showed the bureau and J. Edgar Hoover was the improved version called 2050C. When I added the suggested tone generator, it became the 2050CA.

The Capitol Police first saw the device in a flowerpot in the foyer of the entrance to the Democratic Party headquarters in the Watergate complex, and thought it was a bomb. But when Linville showed up, he realized it was a listening device and suggested they bring in the countermeasure equipment—mine. They eventually found the other bug in the removable tile ceiling of O'Brien's office.

The U.S. intelligence community, as well as the American public, came late to the electronic surveillance party both in detecting bugs and on the positive side: planting them.

The Soviet Union, thanks to the brilliance of an electrical engineer named Leon Theremin, was already experimenting with electronic surveillance in the 1920s. Theremin, the father of electronic music (his so-called "ether music" was the basis for the design of the Moog synthesizer popularized by, among others, the Beach Boys), initially devised an electronic night watchman that would open doors at a hand signal. He also worked for decades in the Soviet KGB's "mailboxes," top-secret research centers, designing various electronic espionage systems.

Theremin's story reads like something out of a John Le Carré novel. Ostensibly, the engineer was given permission by Stalin to take up residence in New York City in 1928 to promote his eponymous musical instrument. During that time there he married an African-American ballet dancer, Iavana Williams. In 1938, Theremin was kidnapped from his apartment by agents of the NKVD (forerunners of the KGB, the Soviet security apparatus), taken back to Russia, and accused by Stalin of spreading anti-Soviet propaganda.

Despite rumors of his execution in the West, Theremin was actually interned in Magadan, a notoriously brutal Siberian labor camp, where he was put to work on sophisticated electronic eavesdropping devices. He supervised the bugging of both the American embassy and Stalin's private apartment. For this work, he was awarded the Stalin Prize first class, Russia's highest honor, while still in prison. After Stalin's death, Theremin was released from prison and became a teacher at the Moscow Conservatory of Music.

The most famous listening device Theremin invented was found in the U.S. embassy in Moscow, hidden inside a wooden carving of the Great Seal of the United States. It was presented by a group of Russian schoolchildren to the U.S. Ambassador to Moscow, Averill Harriman, in 1946, shortly after the end of World War II in Europe, at a time when Stalin was consolidating his conquests within the Iron Curtain bloc. The Great Seal bugging coincided with start of the Cold War in earnest. The device, known as "The Thing" in intelligence circles, hung on a wall in the ambassador's private study. It was far ahead of its time because it carried no wires, electrical circuits, or batteries to wear out. Its inherent genius was its simplicity.

It worked by beaming an ultra-high-frequency radio signal at the Great Seal from a van parked near the building. The room conversation entered the carving in holes drilled below the bald eagle's beak. The radio frequency signal from the van was picked up by a short antenna that entered the device, which looked like a small tunafish can. On one side of the can, a resonant cavity held a thin metallic membrane that vibrated at a rate determined by the voices striking it. The signal carrying the room conversation then returned to the van at three times the frequency of the original input signal, was detected, monitored, and recorded. Soviet intelligence was able to record conversations for nearly six years until the device was discovered during a routine physical, not electronic, security check.

The American public's naïveté about electronic snooping was challenged for the first time in May 1960. That's when Henry Cabot Lodge, the U.S. Ambassador to the United Nations under Eisenhower, displayed to the UN general assembly the hand-carved wooden replica of the Great Seal with the resonant RF cavity and copper antenna hidden inside it. Lodge charged that more than 100 similar eavesdropping devices had been recovered in U.S. missions and residences throughout the U.S.S.R. and Eastern Europe. This revelation made the word "bugging" a universal term and created widespread public fascination with electronic surveillance that has not abated since.

The Great Seal incident was the first time U.S. intelligence had seen a passive eavesdropping device illuminated by radio signals from a remote directional antenna. Our intelligence community spent millions of dollars trying to imitate the technology but was never able to come up with a viable product. Peter Wright, an agent with Britain's MI5, claims the agency later produced a copy of the Great Seal device (code-named SATYR) that was supposedly used by British and U.S. intelligence. Due to the classified nature of the work, it has never been revealed how successful the British or the CIA were in copying the device.

By the time I entered the picture in early 1966, army intelligence was anxious to develop a countermeasure device that could locate these RF-powered transmitters that could be turned on and off remotely. The Model 2050CA RF detector filled that requirement.

A good portion of my early work at Fort Holabird also involved repairing polygraph machines (lie detector systems), which seemed to always be breaking down. Whether the machines were being used for training purposes or in actual interrogations was not clear, but they were obviously getting a lot of use. When I asked the question once, I got the intelligence community mantra from Doms: "You don't have a need to know." In intelligence circles, the phrase was an early variation on "Don't ask, don't tell."

What I learned about the functions of lie detectors convinced me that I would never take a lie detector test if I were trying to prove my innocence, because it was too susceptible to manipulation. The machine proved easy to defeat. One strategy I devised was to disrupt the voltage that is naturally created on your skin (the galvanic skin response) when you're hooked up to the machine's sensors. I did this by placing a common watch battery between my toes. When I wanted the needles to go haywire, I simply squeezed my toes. So, when they asked a test question to measure my truthful response, I squeezed my toes. Without a baseline truthful response indicator, the polygraph operator could not determine the validity of any response. Therefore, the test could not be validated.

I never tested this strategy during actual interrogation. Years later, when the FBI questioned me regarding the Northwestern Bank episode, I refused to answer any of their questions. It was my constitutional right, and the charges were false in the first place.

Within six months of that initial meeting with Doms, the majority of my business had moved from heavy industry repairs for civilian companies to repairing and producing various electronic transmitters and receivers for various branches of the U.S. government. Doms and the other intelligence officers at Fort Holabird liked my work so much that I was invited to teach the DASE (Defense Against Sound Entry) course.

My part of the DASE training focused on identifying telephone tap techniques (both offensive and defensive surveillance) and detecting radio-frequency transmitters. The primary way to identify phone taps back then was by measuring the amount of line voltage on the target phone line. This was before the development of the time-domain reflectometer that measured the line voltage and how it changed when there was a "parasite" (a bug) on the line.

The standard amount of voltage on a phone line is forty-eight volts when the handset is in the "on hook" (hung up) position. The voltage comes from batteries at the telephone company's central office. If a parallel bug (*across* the two wires) is on the line, the voltage may drop from forty-eight to forty-two volts. Detecting this type of eavesdropping attack meant tracing the wires back through a building or climbing a lot of telephone poles until the original forty-eight volts was found, and that was generally where the devices was located.

A series tap (using only one wire) affected what is known as the loop current. Normal loop current is twenty milliamperes, and if that drops it is an indication of a tap. Again, the wires must be traced back to the location where the loop current returns to normal.

My specialty was teaching the detection of RF transmitters. When I first started doing business with army intelligence at Fort Holabird, the state-of-the-art device for identifying RF listening devices was the Mason A-2 receiver, which had a spectrum analyzer attached to it. A spectrum analyzer allows you to see what you are listening to. But within six months of my involvement there, I had designed and built a much better mousetrap, due to its portability, for RF devices—my 2050CA RF detector.

Most clandestine audio intelligence is gathered at between 200 and 5000 megahertz (MHz). Despite the best countermeasure equipment available, a professional eavesdropper who knows his business can hide an RF transmitter right next to a high-wattage FM or AM station, or TV station, and never have the signal discovered. Back in the 1970s, I taught classes about two basic RF transmitters: self-excited and crystal controlled. A self-excited transmitter is one where the frequency is determined by the components used. These devices would change frequency as the battery weakened, the temperature changed, or the surroundings changed. They needed a tunable receiver to follow these changes.

Those little transmitters were devastatingly effective. The ones I built were the size of a button, and provided three to four weeks operation with standard nine-volt battery. Transmitting range was one mile and often clear as a bell. You could put them anywhere. They worked in a flowerpot, under a chair, down the side of a sofa cushion, behind a book on a shelf. Some bugs were so small and thin you could slip them into the spine of a book, and even if the target picked up the book to read, the bug still captured and transmitted clear audio.

The other type of transmitter was a crystal-controlled device that captured audio and transmitted it on a specific frequency. These devices did not change frequency based on their surroundings. After explaining the most common types of transmitters and how they worked, I would let my students—army intelligence agents, FBI agents, and CIA operatives—put on the earphones plugged into the 2050CA RF detector and try to find some of the transmitters I had hidden at various locations in the room. The 2050CA sounds much like the well-known Geiger counter. The closer you get to the transmitter, the higher the pitch of the tone. They found all of the transmitters.

But often the training and instruction I provided was as basic as how to operate a reel-to-reel Uher 4000 tape recorder, the eavesdropping recorder of choice back in the 1970s, and how not to compromise the operation. I sold hundreds of Uher recorders to the army, FBI, and numerous other intelligence agencies over the years. Not every agent had the technical know-how or dexterity to operate one correctly. Most important, they had to remember that the audio input jack on the Uher also became the audio output jack during replay.

One night an FBI agent was tapping a telephone conversation and decided to listen to what he was recording to make sure the reel-to-reel recorder was working. Suddenly, the conversation he was secretly recording was broadcast back into the telephone line and both the agent and the target heard it, blowing the tap. An urgent memo went out from Director Hoover's desk the next morning, informing everyone about the problem. The solution, I advised, was to unplug the tap when listening to the tape. Not exactly rocket science, but then I had to remind myself that this was the FBI, not RCA.

The army offered two other eight-week tech classes at the facility, photo interpretation and lock-picking/surreptitious entry techniques. The latter course was originally titled "Methods of Entry," but after the news media got wind of the name the course was euphemistically renamed Defense Against Methods of Entry (DAME). Regardless of the titles, both the DAME and DASE courses were taught with a focus on offensive operations that made operational sense. The attitude among the intelligence professionals back then was that the best defense was an aggressive offense.

The reader should note that from the late 1960s to the mid-1970s in the United States it was like the Wild West as far as the methods of illegal surveillance and entry employed by a variety of domestic intelligence agencies led by the FBI were concerned. Targets of these warrantless surveillances included the antiwar movement, New Left and black liberation groups, the Socialist Workers Party, and right-wing organizations like the Ku Klux Klan, as well as targeted members of the media.

According to *The Lawless State: The Crimes of the U.S. Intelligence Agencies,* by Morton H. Halperin et al., published in 1976, following the Watergate scandal and congressional investigations into various intelligence agencies, the FBI, "acting without legal authority, placed 'wildcat' or 'suicide' taps and bugs on antiwar groups despite the fact that the United States Supreme Court held in 1972 that a warrant was required in any domestic security case."

According to the same source, "the FBI's illegal burglary program was also extensive through this period. It is known that the FBI conducted at least 239 'black-bag jobs' aimed at fifteen domestic groups and over ninety burglaries against the Socialist Workers Party during this time. In 1973 and 1974, FBI agents conducted numerous burglaries against the families and friends of members of the Weather Underground (a Left Wing extremist group linked to various bombings of government buildings and other crimes during the 1970s) to look for evidence of their possible whereabouts." These illegal "sneak and peeks" were orchestrated by none other than W. Mark Felt, the ranking deputy director of the bureau at the time, who recently admitted to being Woodward and Bernstein's "Deep Throat" Watergate source. Felt was convicted in 1980 of authorizing the illegal break-ins, but was later pardoned by President Reagan.

The FBI had its own lock picking and illegal entry program at its training center in Quantico, Virginia, but by mid-1966, word had reached the bureau that there was a new guy teaching TSCM (Technical Security Countermeasures) at Fort Holabird who knew his stuff—me. They started signing up their technical people for my courses. This was the start of my relationship with the FBI, one that looked very promising at that point in my life.

The first students in my DASE course were army intelligence officers. Despite their military title, the theory of electronics always seemed beyond their ability to comprehend. Granted, there was only so much you could learn in a six-hour course, but rarely did my students seem to understand the basics by the end of the day. I worked with some capable people at Fort Holabird, but for the most part, the term army intelligence, as applied to the people I taught there, was an oxymoron.

While the students' comprehension of electronic countermeasures and how to plant bugs was never that impressive, they were obviously extremely busy in another aspect of intelligence work during my time at Fort Holabird. Between 1967 and 1970, following the riots in Detroit and Newark, New Jersey, army counterintelligence agents conducted a "sweeping campaign of civilian surveillance which ultimately affected more than 100,000 citizens" connected to various domestic organizations. It was never clear to me if the army agents employed electronic eavesdropping on their domestic targets. The tech work was probably left to the soundmen at the FBI.

The files compiled by army intelligence units in the surveillance of various domestic organizations during the late 1960s and early 1970s were massive, and Fort Holabird was the operational hub. According to Halperin et al.,

> *a computerized Spot Report Index, started in 1968 at Ft Holabird, received as many as 1,200 reports a month (of domestic groups referred to as "subversive files") during 1969. According to the Senate Subcommittee on Constitutional Rights, the dossiers may have been "one of the most extraordinary chronicles of domestic political activity ever compiled."*
>
> *Army [intelligence] agents infiltrated Resurrection City during the 1968 Poor People's March on Washington. Agents also posed as students to monitor classes in Black Studies at New York University. . . . Army Intelligence agents also infiltrated the October and November 1969 [antiwar] Moratorium marches around the country. Military personnel even posed as newspaper reporters and television newsmen during the 1968 Democratic National Convention in Chicago to tape interviews with demonstration leaders.*

As my tenure progressed at Fort Holabird, the intelligence agencies sending staff to attend my countermeasure class expanded to the FBI, the CIA, and the Secret Service, as well as those from state and local law enforcement organizations. As my class rolls expanded so did my contacts and sales of eavesdropping and detection devices. Often my manufacture and sales were in response to individual threats. A prime example of that was the SCAN 23 that I made for the U.S. Capitol Police.

In the late 1960s and early 1970s, the nation's capital was constantly awash in marches, street demonstrations, and occasionally, protests that developed into riots provoked by the antiwar movement.

The Capitol Police were on constant crowd control and riot duty, and the protestors came with their own hand-held, CB communication devices. There were often so many CB radios on the air at one time that all twenty-three of the CB frequencies were occupied. The Capitol Police came to me and asked if I could build a device that would indicate transmitter operation on all CB frequencies at once. Thus the SCAN 23 was born.

The SCAN 23 simultaneously indicated all frequency usage instantly. The unit contained a broadband receiver covering all CB channels and individual filters, which, when activated, would turn on a light for that channel. The police could then watch the light panel and zero in on a specific protestor to see which light came on when he or she lifted their transceiver to talk. That channel could then be monitored and/or "neutralized" (the communication broken or misdirected). A portable CB transceiver was included in the package if the police chose to use that.

On the strength of my initial preamplifier sales to the folks at Fort Holabird, I developed a transmitter locator and tracking system that I believed superior to any comparable device then available on the market. Through my contacts with the FBI in my DASE countermeasure-training course, I was able to expand my network of friends within the bureau.

In April 1967, I arranged an appointment with Mr. William Baker, chief of the FBI Communications Section, and Dr. Briggs White, an assistant to Director J. Edgar Hoover, to discuss my services and some ideas for countermeasure equipment that I was developing.

At their offices in the Old Post Office Building in downtown Washington, I demonstrated for them the prototypes of my transmitter locator and tracking system. In addition, I asked them to consider my services in performing repairs on countermeasure equipment similar to those I did for army intelligence at Fort Holabird. During that meeting, we were joined by John M. Matter, Chief of the FBI's Technical Section. Matter was so impressed with the prototype that he immediately placed an order for the transmitter locator. Later, the FBI would order dozens of the transmitter location detectors.

More than a decade earlier, in November 1964, Matter had supervised a project that, when revealed in 1976 during the Church investigations, would give a black eye to the squeaky-clean image of the FBI for years to come. (The 1975–76 review of U.S. intelligence agency operations by the Senate Select Committee on Intelligence Activities, commonly known as the Church Committee, was chaired by Sen. Frank Church, D-Idaho.)

Matter had prepared, at the request of William Sullivan, assistant director of the FBI's Domestic Intelligence Division, a composite tape recording of the most salacious episodes captured by FBI-planted microphones hidden in the hotel rooms occupied by Dr. Martin Luther King Jr. as the civil rights leader moved from city to city leading the civil rights movement. (In October 1964, it had been announced that King was being awarded the Nobel Peace Prize.)

That audiotape contained sexual conversations and the sounds of sexual intercourse between King and several different female partners with whom he carried on extramarital affairs, including several nights in January 1964 when King was staying at The Willard Hotel in Washington, across the street from the U.S. Treasury Department.

The tape was accompanied by an anonymous letter written by Sullivan himself (as reported in David J. Garrow's 1981 book, *The FBI and Martin Luther King, Jr.*). In the letter, Sullivan, the fourth-ranking official in the FBI, urged King, in so many words, to commit suicide or face the humiliation of having the tape released to the media.

The letter read in part: *King, there is only one thing left for you to do. You know what it is. You have just 34 days in which to do it . . . You are done. There is but one way out for you. You better take it before your filthy, abnormal fraudulent self is bared to the nation . . .*

The tape and the letter were flown by an FBI agent to Miami, where it was mailed to King at the Southern Christian Leadership Conference headquarters in Atlanta. The action epitomized the decade-long attempt by Hoover and others in the FBI to destroy Dr. King and his leadership of the civil rights movement.

Deke DeLoach, one of the assistant FBI directors, even offered a copy of a King surveillance transcript to *Newsweek*'s Washington bureau chief (later executive editor of the *Washington Post*) Benjamin Bradlee. Bradlee reportedly refused to accept it and mentioned the approach to a *Newsweek* colleague, Jay Iselin. A few days later, Attorney General Nicholas Katzenbach learned that the FBI was trying to leak these transcripts to the media and spoke to Assistant Attorney General Burke Marshall about it. Both men were angered about the intentional FBI leaks, but when they brought it to Lyndon Johnson's attention, Johnson said only that he would "look into the matter." In fact, LBJ tried to protect the FBI by discrediting Bradlee as an unreliable source. He also instructed his press secretary, Bill Moyers, to warn the FBI that Bradlee was telling everyone about the bureau's attempted leaks of the eavesdropping transcripts to smear King.

During my initial meeting with John Matter in 1967, I became acquainted with a company called U.S. Recording Company (USRC). It was a name that would become synonymous with some of the most embarrassing moments from the FBI's past, and the codeword that indirectly led to the destruction of my business with the intelligence community. This book will chronicle the details of that experience in chapter 8, *Road to Ruin*.

Matter explained that negotiations for orders would be conducted directly with the FBI. However, I should expect to receive the purchase orders from the U.S. Recording Company. I, in turn, should bill U.S. Recording for the items that were delivered to the bureau. Although the procedure seemed odd, I was anxious for the business and didn't raise any objections. I figured the FBI knew the law better than I did regarding this equipment. How naïve and trusting I was! After all, this was the FBI, at that time the paradigm of what I believed to be honesty and integrity in law enforcement.

Matter then drove me to the offices of U.S. Recording Company on South Capitol Street and introduced me to Joseph Tait, president of the company.

Tait had been the owner and operator of the company since 1938. He'd been doing business with the government since 1943, when army intelligence asked for the FBI's help in purchasing two microphones for an eavesdropping operation. The FBI turned to USRC to serve as the intermediary in the purchase. From 1963 until 1975, when I testified before the National Wiretap Commission, USRC was virtually the sole supplier of electronic equipment to the FBI.

The FBI encouraged this role with USRC because it allowed them to circumvent government procurement statutes and regulations, which required all purchases over $2,500 to be put out for public bid. During the investigations of USRC and their inflated prices on equipment that I testified about, FBI officials initially justified this sole-source relationship with USRC under a specific exemption for purchases that required confidentiality for national security reasons. Later, following my testimony before the National Wiretap Commission in 1975, and investigations by the House Select Committee on Intelligence, the Justice Department, and the General Accounting Office, evidence emerged that did not support this explanation. The Justice Department eventually found that the bureau and some of its agents had abused that special relationship with USRC.

Several days after meeting with John Matter, I received a purchase order from USRC for the Model 2050CA RF locator, with instructions to deliver the equipment to their facility on South Capitol Street. Although this transaction occurred before the passage of the Omnibus Crime Control and Safe Streets Act, which expressly prohibited selling eavesdropping equipment to anyone except federal, state, or local law enforcement agencies, my instincts for self-preservation took over. Because the FBI was the actual customer, I felt it was important to follow Matter's instructions and deliver it directly to his shop. I also wanted to develop closer relationships with the technicians and the people at the bureau who would be using my equipment. I made it a point to hand-deliver the equipment to John Matter's office in the Old Post Office Building in downtown Washington, D.C.

By the end of 1968, I had developed a complete product line of countermeasure equipment for the U.S. intelligence community. With the encouragement of the army's Intelligence (and Security) Command (INSCOM) at Fort Holabird, I went on to develop a telephone analyzer that could check multiple lines simultaneously. Its primary function was to determine if a telephone had been modified for eavesdropping while the handset was hung up.

In early 1969, I put all the products together into a portable countermeasure kit that was instantly popular with army intelligence personnel. After consultation with John Matter, I developed a more compact version of the countermeasure kit for use by the bureau's field agents. In April, the FBI ordered sixty-seven of the countermeasure kits at $1,000 apiece.

In June 1969, I received my first order for equipment from the FBI, via U.S. Recording Company. The order was for pure surveillance equipment that was clearly prohibited under Title III of the Omnibus Crime Control and Safe Streets Act of 1968 from being sold to non–law enforcement entities.

The law also made it a crime punishable by a $10,000 fine and up to five years in prison even to advertise electronic bugging devices. Despite my insistence on delivering the gear directly to the FBI, I was worried about the fact that a commercial entity like U.S. Recording Company was showing up on my sales invoices. I expressed that concern to Matter and others at the bureau.

"Don't worry about it, Marty," Matter told me. "It's all legal, but I'll make sure that Joe Tait puts a disclaimer on U.S. Recording invoices from now on."

"Thanks, John," I said. "I appreciate it. I'm just trying to obey the law." It seem ironic that I needed to say this to an FBI special agent.

Soon thereafter, a U.S. Recording Company purchase order arrived in the mail bearing the notation at the top of the page: "THIS

ORDER COMPLIES WITH THE PROVISIONS OF THE OMNIBUS CRIME CONTROL AND SAFE STREETS ACT OF 1968."

On March 12, 1969, the Justice Department issued Memorandum Nr. 613 to all U.S. attorneys, providing guidance, interpretations and procedure for enforcement of Title III of the act. To alleviate my continued concerns about the U.S. Recording arrangement, Matter sent me a copy of the memorandum, which I tacked up on the bulletin board above my desk. I studied this memorandum very carefully and concluded that my practice of negotiating and delivering surveillance equipment directly to the FBI placed my conduct fully within the scope of legal and permissible activity as detailed by the Omnibus Crime Act. In retrospect, I should have consulted an attorney.

Regardless of the assurances of Matter and the other FBI technical people, something just didn't sound right regarding their invoice arrangement with U.S. Recording. And there was no one that I felt I could confide in regarding my concerns. My instincts would eventually prove correct.

The original order for surveillance equipment was rapidly followed by larger and more comprehensive orders for additional wiretaps, quick-drop bugs, and body transmitters. I even built a miniature transmitter to be hidden inside a toothpaste tube. By the end of 1969, the FBI had made dozens of purchases from me totaling more than $100,000 in gross sales.

By early 1970, my customers for surveillance products had expanded beyond the FBI to include the Secret Service, the Internal Revenue Service, the Department of Transportation, and the intelligence commands of all of the armed forces. The FBI was still my major customer, accounting for more than half of all sales, averaging about $200,000 a year. Yet, they were the only government agency using a commercial entity as a middleman. I worried about that, but I assured myself that if anyone respected and operated within the law, it would have to be the FBI.

How naïve I was!

Chapter 4

The Michelangelo of Electronic Surveillance

AS MY BUSINESS in electronic surveillance grew during the early 1970s, so did my reputation both within the intelligence community and outside it. I was making a full line of countermeasure products while continuing to teach telephone tap detection and RF countermeasure strategies at U.S. Army Intelligence, Fort Holabird, Maryland. I also began to teach a basic course in electronic surveillance at the Pennsylvania State Police Academy in Hershey. In addition, I started getting requests from state and local agencies to conduct countermeasure "sweeps" of telephone systems and conference rooms for line taps and quick-drop transmitters.

I was even featured in local newspaper columns. Lou Panos, a columnist for the *Baltimore Sun,* referred to me as "the Michelangelo of electronic surveillance." Modesty aside, I was an artist when it came to designing and building surveillance equipment, and a perfectionist driven by the challenge of every new problem. And I was never happier than when I was at my workbench coming up with a new solution to a problem. I couldn't wait to get up in the morning and go to work.

Despite my increasing professional success and prosperity, my lifestyle, and that of my family, did not change. We continued to live in the same modest, four-bedroom house that we bought when we moved to Cockeysville from New Jersey in 1964. We were able to take a few more vacations in the Caribbean and I was able to indulge my favorite recreation of scuba diving more often. I was also able to move my workshop from the cellar of my house into a plant facility, where I employed from six to eight technicians. But for the most part, I would take the profits from the business and plow them back into the company.

My relationship with my father continued to be chilly. I would see him during a few holiday visits when my brothers and their families were in attendance. But I never saw him or spoke to him alone. The memories of my childhood and the abuse he inflicted on me were still as fresh and vivid as on the days when it happened.

I often worked weekends and pulled all-nighters to deliver special orders needed on a particular project. It wasn't really work to me but something I loved doing, and I took tremendous pride in what I produced. In a way, I felt guilty that I was having so much fun. I had been raised to believe that work was serious business and not something that made you happy. My equipment was as good as it got in the countermeasure business and was certainly the most reasonable in terms of price.

In many ways, I was developing technology applications back in the 1970s that became available only in the 1990s. For example, I invented something I named the call diverter. The local phone companies now offer the same technology, known as call forwarding. I also designed a device attached to the fuel pump of a car that could kill the engine when activated by a special remote transmitter. In 2003, several Web-based devices that could immobilize with a computer keystroke the cars of customers who missed their monthly car payments were being marketed to auto finance companies.

But my first love was countermeasure devices. The only problem was that as quickly as I built the products, someone would steal my idea, stick a couple of bells and whistles on it, and christen it with a sexy new name. In the beginning, I tried to patent a couple of the devices, but it proved to be enormously expensive and ultimately offered no protection against theft. My best strategy was to build new products and add improvements to them faster than those making the knockoffs.

As much as I loved making eavesdropping and countermeasure devices, finding them sometimes gave me an even greater thrill, particularly when the guy doing the planting was at the top of his game. It was sort of an electronic *mano a mano,* and I never lost.

One of the most significant eavesdropping finds I made came in October 1970 after getting a call from Trooper Norval Cooper of the Maryland State Police, who provided security for Governor Marvin Mandel. Cooper had bought some countermeasure equipment from me and he wanted me to come over and walk him through the use of it.

We started with Mandel's main phone system, and it was clean. Then we checked all of the other phones in his outer office. They also checked out okay. I was about to leave when I saw the red civil defense phone on the governor's desk.

"What about checking that one?" I asked.

Cooper shrugged.

"Who would want to bug a phone that's never used?" he asked. "But if you want to, go ahead."

When I took the cover off the red phone I immediately saw two wires—I can't remember the colors, but they were most certainly not white, which they should have been. Those wires were connected to the two white wires that went to the earpiece in the handset. I could see that the hook-switch contacts that short out the earpiece when the handset is hung up had been compromised. And one of the two wires that came from the hook-switch had been removed. That made the handset earpiece a hot microphone. What we had was a telephone compromise, or more specifically, a hook-switch bypass. It essentially made the phone in the hung-up position a room eavesdropping device capable of picking up conversations and transmitting them to a recorder somewhere inside or outside the building. It was the genius of "hiding in plain sight."

I placed the 1059 preamplifier across the wires that led to the earpiece, held down the hook-switch, and clearly heard room conversation. Cooper and I traced the cable from the "hot wire" back to the frame room. (A frame room is a closet or small room where all telephone lines terminate.) Inside the frame room are six- to eight-foot-high racks with rows and rows of terminals. Each telephone line is connected to punch terminals, usually fifty terminals per telephone.

We found the terminal block for the hot line. Then we identified the two suspect wires of the same color that we saw in the red phone and connected the 1059 to those wires. Bingo! We heard conversation from the governor's office loud and clear. Those wires exited the building in a large cable bundle, but I never found out where they led. It was Cooper's job to trace where those wires ended up. That was confidential information to which I never became privy.

But the story didn't end there. Trooper Cooper immediately notified Governor Mandel of the phone bug. The governor called Governor Russell Peterson of Delaware about the discovery and then offered to send Trooper Cooper down to Dover to check Peterson's red civil defense phone. Governor Peterson said he appreciated the offer. A few days later, Cooper found that Peterson's civil defense phone had a similar hook-switch bypass compromise.

According to George O'Toole, who interviewed me for a story about eavesdropping in *Harper's Magazine*, both of these civil defense phones were part of the National Warning System, a special telephone network designed to provide communication between state and federal governments in the event of a national crisis. The system makes use of the Pentagon's classified telephone system and is reported to have three main terminals: the subterranean headquarters of the North American Aerospace Defense Command (NORAD) at Cheyenne Mountain, near Colorado Springs; an emergency command post near Washington, D.C.; and a two-story underground building in Denton, Texas.

When the bugging of the Maryland and Delaware civil defense phones became public, other governors had their civil defense hotlines checked. According to O'Toole, at least four more hotlines—in Arkansas, Illinois, Pennsylvania, and Utah—were found to be bugged. Governor Lester Maddox of Georgia—renowned for favoring axe handles—didn't go to the trouble to check his telephone hotline for a compromise. He reportedly ripped it right out of the office wall.

No one ever found out who had engaged in this widespread campaign to bug state governors through their civil defense hotlines. American Telephone & Telegraph (AT&T), which had installed the phones, offered the improbable explanation that the phones had been hot-wired by mistake. Attorney General John Mitchell, in an ironic pre-Watergate statement, told the media he had personally investigated the matter of the bugged civil defense hotlines and found it "to be merely a case of defective equipment."

One of the most fascinating aspects of the discovery of the Maryland governor's office being bugged was ruminating on the conversations that the red phone may have transmitted to unknown persons during the governorship of Spiro Agnew, who became Richard Nixon's vice presidential running mate in the 1968 election.

The phone was installed in 1966 during the Johnson administration, shortly before Agnew was elected governor. If the red civil defense phone was already wired for sound, it would have been operating throughout his governorship and capturing potentially damaging conversations between Agnew and others. Agnew, of course, resigned from the Nixon administration in 1973, amid charges that he had accepted payoffs while sitting in the Governor's Mansion in Annapolis.

The question remains: Who would have had reason and motive or opportunity to bug a national civil defense hotline? The suspects ranged from Hoover's FBI (Hoover was notorious for collecting all sorts of salacious personal information on national political figures at state or local levels who might one day end up in Washington in the federal government) to Lyndon Johnson, who was known to play hardball in order to get his legislation through the Congress, and other partisan Democrats at the state or national level. Due to the number of retired spooks from the various intelligence agencies in the Baltimore-Washington area, the bugger could have been some freelance eavesdropper who saw an opportunity to bug a controversial politician and sell the results of compromising conversations to the highest bidder.

About a year later, Trooper Norval Cooper was also instrumental in bringing me in to check the phone system in the Baltimore office of Maryland Attorney General Milton Allen. This job was far more challenging than finding the compromised telephone in Governor Mandel's office. It became clear early on in my sweep of the office that I was going up against a professional wire tapper.

Milton Allen was leading a campaign to crack down on the city's major drug dealers, and they suspected that the dealers were being tipped off just before authorities raided various drug houses. By the time investigators and SWAT teams showed up at these locations, the dealers and their drugs would be long gone.

I started by sweeping the office with my RF detector and found nothing. Then I started on the phone lines. I had been told by Allen to specifically check his phone lines as well as those of his deputies, Stephen Montanarelli and Benjamin Brown, plus their secretaries. But since those lines were part of a cable bundle involving dozens of other lines in the attorney general's office, I had to check each line myself, one at a time. I spent the entire first day checking phone lines and found nothing hot. On the morning of my second day, however, a strange thing happened.

As I was checking the wire pairs in the frame room that led into Allen's direct phone line, someone in Allen's office picked up the phone and I heard his voice. Then I went to the next set of terminals and heard the man's voice again. Why is this happening? I wondered. Why do I hear his voice on two different line pairs?

Then it hit me. The wiretapper had used spare wires in the cable bundle adjacent to the five wire pairs of lines going to and coming from Allen's office. What that did was to build an induction transformer that could pick up all conversation going through the cable bundle for all phone lines. Any conversation that went on in the wire bundle leading to Allen's phones or his deputies would be picked up by the wiretap.

We traced the cable from the frame room outside Allen's office to the basement of the courthouse building. There, in the civil defense emergency shelter, we found the cable and evidence of where a tape recorder had sat on an empty water drum. The two wires leading from the phone line cable to the recorder were gone. There was even an ashtray filled with cigarette butts where the guy operating the tape recorder had killed time while waiting to illegally eavesdrop and record the conversations.

The scariest part of the whole deal was that the wiretapper had obviously been tipped off in advance that someone was coming to sweep the lines. Milton Allen never found out who did the job, but I must say whoever it was, he was one of the best I'd ever been up against.

When Allen left his position as State Attorney General a few years later, he told a reporter about the countermeasure sweep that found the telephone tap in the courthouse basement. It was the first time it had been made public. When the reporter asked him who did the sweep, he blocked on my name for a moment.

"You know him," Allen told the reporter. "Everyone knows him. He's that world-famous guy. Marty . . . Marty Kaiser."

I meant to write Milton Allen a thank-you note for those kind words, including the hyperbole, but never got around to it. My reputation as well as my business was definitely growing. I wasn't world-famous, but I was moving in that direction.

I had been teaching countermeasures at Fort Holabird for several years when I made my first contact with the CIA in the early 1970s.

His name was Bob Jones, chief of the CIA's Interagency Training Center. As I recall, Jones was not taking the class but he had heard about me, and he introduced himself during a break in the class. He told me he had seen some of the quick-drop bugs and transmitters I had made for the FBI and army intelligence and he was impressed enough to place an order for some items. The orders were strictly for equipment on the positive side—including wiretapping gear and fountain pen bugs.

The CIA had a particular yen for my fountain pen transmitters. Like army intelligence, the agency was into using subminiature microphones hidden in picture frames. There must have been a factory operation somewhere in the Baltimore-Washington area that turned out thousands of picture frames of various sizes with the slots already hollowed out for transmitters to support the intelligence community in its room eavesdropping operations.

One of the most memorable devices I built for the CIA was a transmitter inside a field telephone line used along the Demilitarized Zone (DMZ) in Korea. One of Bob Jones's technical people at the agency said they intended to enclose my bug in mercury fulminate, a highly volatile chemical that would cause the device to explode if it got into the wrong hands. If someone started bending it or happened to drop it in their curiosity to identify it, ka-BOOM. I always wondered how the army or the CIA could make sure the device wouldn't fall into friendly hands by mistake, and get dropped by someone with no clue to its menace.

Another interesting countermeasure device I worked on for the intelligence community in the early 1970s was what was known in the trade as the TEMPEST attack. TEMPEST stands for Telecommunications Electronics Material Protected from Emanating Spurious Transmissions, a system of measuring the electromagnetic radiation "signals" that are generated by an electric typewriter. The Russians first used the attack in the late 1960s, using a scanning receiver to capture the radiation signals produced by an IBM electronic typewriter.

The receiver decoded the signals and fed them into a second IBM type-writer that created an exact copy of the text generated by the original machine.

Dr. Wim van Eck, a member of the bioengineering group of the electronics department of the University of Twente in The Nether-lands, was the first scientist to identify this eavesdropping risk. In the landmark 1985 paper "Electromagnetic Radiation from Video Display Units: An Eavesdropping Risk?" published in *Computers & Security*, a trade periodical, van Eck demonstrated that you could capture radiation field signals (or interference) by a normal TV mon-itor and transmit it to a receiver to reconstruct the images or letters on an electronic typewriter located in a van across the street from the building from which the signals emanated. That's where the eaves-dropping attack got its most common name: the van Eck attack.

My countermeasure to the van Eck attack was to build what I called a "spark gap jammer" device. Essentially it would produce a spark signal that would jam or obliterate the broadband signals being produced by the IBM electronic typewriters. I sold a ton of those in the early 1970s to army intelligence until other companies started ripping off my design.

I later developed the "pipe banger" to counter the use of clan-destine contact microphones attached to pipes, walls, and air condi-tioning or heating ducts. When it is operating, tiny hammers bang away on the surface to which it is attached, totally drowning out any ability to capture human voices.

Another defense against the van Eck attack that has been used effectively by the intelligence community is a finely woven steel mesh screen enclosure that can be set up in a motel or hotel room encasing the computer and operator. The only problem is that the screens are so tightly woven you need a portable air conditioning unit inside the enclosure to allow the operator to breathe comfortably.

Every so often my countermeasure equipment would even pick up eavesdropping devices by accident. One day during the winter of

1971, I was testing a new RF receiver in my workshop in Timonium about a half mile away from the Timonium Racetrack. I was surfing up and down the FM frequency dial when I heard some background noise, but I couldn't figure out what or where it was. I monitored the same frequency with the RF receiver every week or so for months and I would always pick up the same background noise.

Finally, one day after the racing season began, I tuned the receiver to the same point on the dial and I heard the sound of an announcer calling a horse race. Then I heard the voices of the judges talking about the photo-finish results of the race. It was quickly apparent that someone—most likely a bookie—had placed a hidden transmitter in the judge's booth. During a close race that resulted in a photo finish there was always a delay in announcing the winner while the judges conferred. Someone was down in the paddock with a receiver getting the decision of the judges before it was posted. He probably held up a handful of hundred-dollar bills, claiming his horse to be the winner, and there was always somebody ready to take the bet. Easy money. I recorded the conversations and turned them over to the Baltimore County Police. They caught a guy in the paddock wearing the receiver, but I don't know if they ever pressed charges against him.

That was a typical response in the corporate sector or in private industry. The main thing they wanted was to stop the bugging. Despite the Omnibus Crime Act and its penalty, lawyers always told me that proving intent and getting a conviction for eavesdropping was always more difficult than it would seem to be.

I had another involvement with the Timonium Racetrack a couple of years later. Some guy showed up at my office with something that looked like a dog collar training receiver. He wanted me to rig up the receiver with a hair-fine wire antenna. His crackpot idea was that he would shove the receiver up the horse's rear end and comb the fine wire into the tail. Then he would send a signal to shock the horse as he was entering the homestretch of a race. His name was

Fred Bennett of Fred Bennett, Incorporated . . . FBI. Get it? I promptly showed him the door and told him not to come back. An FBI friend later told me Fred was not an agent, but you couldn't get me to buy it.

That was the price to be paid for getting a reputation as the guy to call about eavesdropping devices. I often received phone calls and visits from countless people who were mentally unstable and clearly paranoid.

One sad little fellow showed up at my door convinced that Martians were tracking him. At the confidential request of his spouse, I cobbled together what I called a Martian Ray Detector from some scraps of material in my shop and gave it to him, hoping it might ease his pain and paranoia. But he returned to my shop several times during the month, each time in a more depressed state. On one occasion, he told me, he had even parked in the Baltimore Harbor Tunnel to try to escape them, backing up traffic until the police came and made him move.

Finally, in desperation, he used a pair of ordinary gas pliers to yank out one of his molars. He fervently believed that the tooth concealed a homing device that Martians were using to track him. He wrapped the tooth in aluminum foil so the Martians couldn't track it and brought it to my shop for my examination. Out of curiosity, I had my dentist X-ray the tooth, but it revealed only a silver filling. A Martian antenna? Not wanting to fuel his deteriorating mental state, I told him the tooth was clear of anything suspicious.

The man's wife came with him on his next visit. I quietly advised her to take him to a local hospital for psychiatric observation. I never heard what happened to him, but I felt great empathy for the guy, never suspecting that I would have a mental breakdown of my own years later. But mine, however, was not paranoia-induced.

During the 1970s and 1980s, with Cold War paranoia in high gear, the Russians were probably more effective in bugging us than we them, because they were more creative and relentless in their pursuit of intelligence data than we were and more willing to take risks.

Following the Great Seal caper in Moscow, a transmitter was found in the heel of the U.S. ambassador's shoe in Vienna and another device was found hidden in the leg of a coffee table in an Eastern Bloc U.S. embassy. Such Soviet monitoring techniques have been regularly discovered and occasionally publicized during the post–World War II period. Soviet eavesdropping incidents revealed during the 1980s alone were alarming in their scope and brazenness.

In 1984, we found that an unsecured shipment of typewriters for the U.S. embassy in Moscow had been bugged and transmitting intelligence data for years. In 1985, there were media reports that the Soviets were using invisible "spydust" to facilitate tracking and electronic monitoring of U.S. diplomats.

In 1987, we found indications that even the new embassy we built in Moscow had been wired for sound. Almost every office space had been infected, requiring us to tear down the entire building and rebuild the place from scratch with U.S. contractors brought in to do the work.

At the time, U.S. Representative Dick Armey of Texas called the building "Nothing but an eight-story microphone plugged into the Politburo."

In the 1990s, the United States found that clandestine microphones had been operating in the Leningrad consulate for many years. I remember one strategy the Russian agents used in Washington for passing espionage data that took the FBI and CIA years to figure out.

Most Americans know that the FBI conducted a constant, 24/7 surveillance of the Soviet embassy on Wisconsin Avenue in northwest Washington, photographing every person who went in or out of there. Sometime in the early 1970s, the surveillance team would see the same Soviet agents loitering outside the embassy's front gate, though the Soviet agents would never enter. The agents would stand and smoke a cigarette, as if waiting to meet someone, but no meeting would ever take place.

Through various sources, the FBI would get reports that the Soviet agents were continuing to pass intelligence or information regarding attempts to recruit U.S. government employees to spy for them to their KGB handlers inside the embassy. Unfortunately, the FBI was unable to prove it. Without physical proof that the Soviets were spying and passing data to their government, the FBI could neither arrest them nor deport them. The agents would not dare enter the Soviet embassy for fear of blowing their undercover status.

This pas de deux went on, according to my sources, for more than a year, until one FBI agent on the surveillance detail noticed that the Soviet agents always appeared to stand in the same spot on the sidewalk outside the embassy.

Later that night, the FBI brought out a construction crew and tore up the sidewalk to see if there was some reason for standing in the same spot on the sidewalk. Sure enough, they found an induction coil buried in the concrete that served as a receiver of intelligence data.

The FBI finally figured out that the Soviet agents had a miniature induction coil in their heel of their shoe. They would come to the spot on the sidewalk in front of the embassy, push the "play" button on the mini tape recorder in their pocket and download that intelligence through the induction coil in their heel to the induction coil pickup buried in the concrete. That data would be relayed to a recorder inside the embassy.

Only the Soviets could have come up with something that brazen and devious.

Throughout the early 1970s, my business with the FBI and other intelligence agencies continued to grow, as well as my reputation for being the go-to guy for both countermeasure and bugging devices. In fact, there were instances when I was given credit or blame for incidents in which I wasn't even involved.

One example involved the CIA spying on the columnist Jack Anderson and his associate, Les Whitten, in 1972, called Operation Mudhen. According to a memorandum obtained by Whitten through a Freedom of Information request, CIA director Richard Helms was scheduled to have lunch on March 14, 1972, with Anderson, code-named BRANDY. The memorandum indicated that the purpose of the meeting was to "dissuade BRANDY from publishing certain classified material in his forthcoming book." The memo referred to *The Anderson Papers*, a book that was published by Random House a year after the lunch with Helms.

The CIA memorandum in question went on to state:

"It was pointed out to the Director of Security that the Director (Helms) should be apprised of the possibility that BRANDY may seek audio coverage of the meeting. This conclusion can be based on the following factors:

a. Recent [CIA] coverage at the Empress Restaurant, Washington, D.C. revealed BRANDY in possession of portable recording equipment;

b. There is a distinct possibility that BRANDY may utilize the services of one (DELETED) . . ."

That's where I came in. A footnote in the book *Secret Agenda: Watergate, Deep Throat, and the CIA,* by Jim Hougan, read, "The deleted section appears to refer to one of two men: private investigator Richard Bast, who sometimes worked with Anderson, or Martin Kaiser, a former supplier of sophisticated audio equipment to the FBI."

To the best of my knowledge, I never met or talked to Jack Anderson.

However, I do remember speaking to Dick Bast during that period. As I recall, he inquired about some recording equipment, though he didn't say what it was for or for whom—and I never asked. My policy has always been that the less I know about the bugging operations of my customers, the better for me. But by that date, it would have been against the law to sell Bast bugging equipment anyway.

The most memorable aspect of my conversation with Bast was the enormous contempt he exhibited for the FBI. I believe his attitude was linked to the bureau's penchant under Hoover to collect personal information on various politicians and celebrities that could later be used against them. He also seemed angry about the FBI's arrest and treatment of Anderson's reporter, Whitten. The FBI had grilled Whitten for eight hours regarding the source of the documents he was given, involving a six-day takeover of the Bureau of Indian Affairs by 800 militant Native Americans. The FBI threatened to charge Whitten with a felony for receiving the documents.

At the time I was shocked by Bast's tone of voice when he referred to the FBI. Of course, that was when they were still one of my best customers.

Chapter 5

An Audience with J. Edgar Hoover

BUSINESS CONTINUED TO boom throughout the early 1970s. A drumbeat of requests came from the FBI and the investigative branches of other agencies, including the Internal Revenue Service, the Secret Service, the U.S. Postal Service, and even the Atomic Energy Commission (AEC) for countermeasure and eavesdropping equipment. I even developed a heat-based detection system for the Treasury Department's Alcohol, Tobacco and Firearms division that could identify illegal whiskey stills in the woods.

I continued teaching my countermeasure classes at Fort Holabird and the Pennsylvania State Police Academy, as well as demonstrating my equipment for various state and local law enforcement agencies in the Baltimore-Washington area.

Requests from private industry to conduct sweeps and audio/video surveillance of corporate facilities continued to multiply, but for the most part I refused to do them unless it was for a client who had purchased equipment. Offering to do a sweep for a customer was essentially my way of marketing my products. The truth was that I did not enjoy doing sweeps. I personally felt that there was too much hype among practitioners about the threat, and I didn't play that game. The countermeasure industry at this point was starting to fill up with retired spooks, many of them without principles, scruples, or the expertise to conduct a competent sweep.

With Watergate in the news every day, paranoia concerning electronic surveillance seemed to be reaching epidemic proportions. This fear of being bugged was driving up the demand from the private and public sector for countermeasure services, and the very people hired to protect companies from the threat were in effect nurturing the paranoia. What compounded the problem of bogus countermeasure services was the lack of any licensing or professional standards.

Anyone could hang out a shingle advertising himself as an electronic security expert. With federal intelligence agency experience on someone's résumé, regardless of what he actually did for the agency, he had the seal of approval of a TSCM expert. With a marginal investment in some black boxes with colored lights, switches, and a monitor, a neophyte countermeasure technician could hire himself out at exorbitant day rates to search offices and boardrooms for bugs.

At the end of the day, the client would be given a thumbs up and peace of mind that he was not bugged. Whether the threat was actually real was never clear. In a few cases, the unscrupulous TSCM technician would "discover" a transmitter he had allegedly found under the desk or stuck in the chair cushion. He would then present it to the client as proof that his paranoia was well founded, thus ensuring a return visit for his expensive services.

Even among honest countermeasure technicians, the level of competence was shockingly inconsistent. I once sold a private investigator one of my RF bug detectors. A year later, he brought it back and said he thought it needed servicing because of overuse. When I took it apart to clean it, I immediately noticed that it wasn't working at all. There was no battery inside! When the guy returned to pick up the equipment the next day, I asked him how he much he really used the device.

"To be honest, it hasn't worked right for quite a while," he said.

"That's because it runs on a battery," I told him.

He shook his head in embarrassment and asked what I owed him. "No charge, but let me know how it works with a battery in it."

One of the most unusual countermeasure assignments I did accept was for a bank near my hometown of Wilkes-Barre, Pennsylvania. It wasn't a normal countermeasure job, but rather setting a trap to catch a thief.

The bank's auditors had found short counts at the end of several weeks, and it was clear that one of their employees was stealing hundreds of dollars a week the hard way—in quarters. I set up a miniature video camera inside an emergency light panel located in the underground coin-drop area. The light panel was intended to provide light in the event of a power outage. It also shed light on the identity of the thief—the bank president. The hidden camera caught him filling up his cowboy boots with quarters each night, walking coolly past the guard on duty, his boots packed so tight with silver they didn't even jingle.

By early 1971, I was making weekly visits to the FBI technical branch located in the Old Post Office Building in downtown Washington. I was on a first-name basis with most of the sound people. I was still doing equipment repair and selling various eavesdropping equipment to the bureau, including pen mikes and quick-drop bugs. I continued to follow the policy of sending invoices to U.S. Recording Company but delivering the equipment directly to the FBI.

John Matter, the FBI laboratories chief, had asked if I could add a tone generator to my 2050C RF detector. He said some of his technical people had trouble looking at the meter while waving the antenna around when they got something hot.

"Put some sort of alert tone in it, Marty," he said, "and we'd be interested in buying a bunch of them."

"You got it, John," I told him. "I'll have a sample for you to look at in a week."

I went back to my shop and worked all night to produce the prototype of the 2050CA RF detector with a tone generator. I considered calling Matter and making an appointment with him that next day, but I didn't want him to get the idea that producing these RF detectors was that simple. If Matter thought I could bang out this equipment in less than a day, he might devalue it and beat me down on the price. So I waited and thoroughly tested it. It worked like a charm.

By Thursday, I was ready to take my new product over to the FBI lab, but suddenly I was struck by what anyone would have considered a crazy idea: I was going to call J. Edgar Hoover himself and show him what I had produced for his beloved FBI.

By now, I had been doing business with the bureau for nearly four years. Despite Hoover's reputation for knowing everything that went on within the bureau and everyone who worked there, I doubted that the guys in the tech branch had ever mentioned my name to him or to his assistant directors. I wanted some recognition for my work, I suppose, and who better to be recognized by but the man at the top? Besides, I had always been fascinated with Hoover, the legend, and the environment of fear he had created within the FBI. When he spoke, agents told me, people under him literally jumped, often misinterpreting mere observations for command decisions.

One of my favorite Hoover stories was supposedly triggered by the comment he had written on the cover page of a report he had reviewed. After reading the report, Hoover handed it to one of his assistant directors. At the top of the page, Hoover had scrawled in bold letters: WATCH THE BORDERS!

Without reading the report or asking Hoover what he meant by the note, one of the assistant directors dispatched two teams of agents to the Mexican and Canadian borders to confer with the border patrol about any suspicious incidents. Only later did one of the assistant directors realize that Hoover was making a cautionary note about the uneven left and right margins of the report's pages.

Another story that reflected Hoover's tyrannical nature and the impact of his commands on rank-and-file agents had to do with the tradition of shaking the director's hand at the end of their training. If Hoover didn't like the way a new agent looked or something a new agent said, he would have him fired.

The story goes that as one new agents' class left the Director's office, Hoover called one of the trainers aside and said, "Get rid of the pinhead." When the class got back to the FBI academy, the instructors measured the head of each man in the class. To be safe, they fired the two men with the smallest heads.

Despite Hoover's intimidating reputation, I was feeling cocky as I dialed the main number of the FBI and asked to be connected to the Director. Suddenly, I was speaking with Helen Gandy, Hoover's personal secretary.

"My name is Martin Kaiser and I would like to speak to Mr. Hoover," I said.

"What is the nature of your call?" Miss Gandy asked.

"I have just developed a new countermeasure device and I wanted to come over to show the prototype to the Director."

There was a pause and then Hoover came on the line abruptly. His voice was low and raspy.

"Who's calling?" he growled.

"Good morning, Mr. Hoover," I said, taking a deep breath. "My name is Martin Kaiser. I'm a countermeasures expert. You probably don't know my name, but I've sold a lot of electronic equipment to the bureau in the past several years. I've developed a new device that the bureau might be interested in using. It helps to find hidden transmitters with a tone-generated signal."

"Sounds interesting, Mr. Kaiser," he said in flat, detached tone. "Bring it over and I'll take a look at it."

I was stunned. I had just received a personal invitation from J. Edgar Hoover to come over and demonstrate a piece of countermeasure equipment.

"Mr. Kaiser. Are you still there?"

"Ah, yes, sir, I'm here," I said, trying not to burst out laughing at my good fortune. "Ah, Mr. Hoover, when would it be convenient for me, I mean convenient for you, to look at the equipment."

"Miss Gandy will arrange an appointment," he said, hanging up.

Miss Gandy came on the line and we agreed on a time two days hence. The meeting was scheduled for 10 A.M. I wore my best dark suit and a white shirt and made sure my black shoes were polished to a high gloss. Hoover's reputation for sartorial standards was legendary. I didn't want to disappoint him.

I got off the elevator a few minutes before ten and entered Hoover's anteroom where Helen Gandy sat at a desk guarding the entry to her boss's office. The one thing I remember was seeing the white plaster death mask of John Dillinger, the original Public Enemy Number One, its lifeless eyes looking down at me from its position on a side wall.

I walked over to Miss Gandy's desk and started to introduce myself. But she nodded and gestured toward the door to Hoover's office.

"The Director is expecting you," she said, opening the door.

Holding the door open for me to enter the room, she said, "Mr. Hoover, Mr. Martin Kaiser is here to see you."

Hoover looked up from his desk, nodded, and stood up.

"Come in, Mr. Kaiser," he said. "Come in and have a seat."

He pointed to the couch to my right that faced his desk, but he made no attempt to shake my hand. That was another part of the legend. Hoover never shook hands unless protocol required it. He reportedly had a phobia about germs and was known to wash his hands as many as a dozen times a day.

As I looked around the room, I realized something was out of sync. Then it hit me. Hoover's desk was built on a four-inch platform, and the legs of the chairs and the couch had been cut down so visitors would be looking up at the legendary G-man. I wasn't going to play his game. I took a seat on the arm of the couch so that I could look directly into Hoover's eyes.

He stood silently, watching my reaction. And then there was a hint of a smile from his bulldog face. I think he admired my spunk.

"Well, Mr. Kaiser, tell me about this device," said Hoover.

I don't remember the rest of the conversation. It didn't last more than a few minutes. I explained the operation of the RF bug detector. Despite his age—he was seventy-six at the time—he seemed quite alert and knowledgeable about electronic surveillance. He asked the right questions, short and to the point. As suddenly as the meeting began, it was over. Hoover walked back to his desk and picked up the phone.

"I'm going to call my people in the technical branch to take a look at your equipment," he said. Turning away, he spoke into the phone.

"Mr. Walters. This is the Director. I'm sending Mr. Martin Kaiser over to see you. He has a new piece of countermeasure equipment he has made that he thinks might be of use to the bureau." There was a pause. "Yes, that's right, Martin Kaiser."

Hoover hung up the phone and pushed an intercom on his telephone, asking that Miss Gandy send in an FBI agent to escort me across the street to the technical branch.

"Thank you for coming in Mr. Kaiser," he said.

"Thank you for the opportunity to meet you, sir," I said.

And that was the end of my ten-minute audience with J. Edgar Hoover.

The agent walked me across Constitution Avenue to the technical branch located in the Old Post Office Building. There I met with Jack Walters, one of the engineers. One of the first things I noticed when I entered the office were the pinball machines lined up against one wall. I doubted that they were there for the agents' recreation. Walters later explained that the bureau was checking the machines to see if they had been fixed to favor the house. These machines were part of the gambling action in the state of Nevada, the only state in the country where gambling was legal in 1971.

I demonstrated the 2050CA RF detector to Walters and he called several other sound people in the office to look at it. The consensus among the group was extremely positive, as John Matter had predicted. The bureau ended up purchasing a large number of those RF detectors with a tone generator, and my business with the FBI continued to increase.

It was during this period in 1971 that I met Special Agent Marion Wright of the FBI's Baltimore field office. Wright was the Baltimore office's top technical person in charge of countermeasure and eavesdropping operations. Wright and I became close friends— or so I thought until I read his reports obtained during the discovery phase of my 1978 trial, describing in detail our conversations, including what kinds of sandwiches we had for lunch.

Although I realize that Wright's first loyalty was to the FBI, I ended up feeling betrayed considering the favors that I did for him. One day he showed up at my shop in Timonium, and after some small talk he actually said, "Hey, Marty. I need a favor."

"Sure, Marion," I said, "What is it?"

"I need to buy some transmitters."

"No problem."

"But I need to buy them off the books," he said. "No invoices. Just cash and carry."

"Why can't you just purchase them through normal channels?" I asked, not wanting to say no to him, but nervous about the implications of what he was suggesting.

He laughed as if the answer to that question was obvious. This was the era of "black bag jobs" by the bureau, and deniability. A lot of warrantless burglaries took place during that period to plant hidden room and phone bugs on individuals involved with various antiwar and civil rights organizations.

It was estimated that Hoover's clandestine surveillance operations were probably in excess of a thousand bugs in working operation at any one time, and special measures had to be taken to keep the purchase of eavesdropping under the radar. This meant the funding had been disguised so as not to tip off the Congress to what was going on.

If even one of the FBI's fifty-nine field offices requested miniature transmitters, it meant creating a paper trail for the devices. It was much simpler for everyone concerned to do things off the books.

Wright told me he would buy the transmitters out of his discretionary fund account, which amounted to $25 a week. The FBI under Hoover was traditionally stingy when it came to paying for lunch or dinner or even coffee for information sources or informants.

Despite my misgivings about the arrangement, I rationalized that I was doing a favor for a friend and protecting my business relationship with the bureau. At $90 per transmitter, I sold Wright about fifteen bugs over a period of eighteen months, and he paid me a portion of the balance on a monthly basis. The entire process provided complete deniability. I should also add that it took Marion a long time to pay me back the cost of the transmitters. And when he didn't have enough petty cash, I loaned him bugs that he eventually returned weeks or months later.

The other favor I did for Wright made me a lot more nervous, and I vowed I would never do it again. One morning during the fall of 1971, he called me and asked, "Marty, what are doing right now?"

"I'm working, Marion. What's up?"

"I need a big favor."

"What's that?"

"I'm doing some business over here in your neighborhood," he said, "and I'm getting hungry. Could you come over and watch things while I go get lunch?"

"Doing some business" was code for conducting some sort of clandestine electronic surveillance.

"Well, what exactly do you want me to do, Marion?" I asked nervously.

"Piece of cake, Marty. Just come over as soon as you can." He gave me the address of an apartment house in Cockeysville and hung up.

I've always had a problem saying no to requests for favors, no matter how big or small. My shrink has told me for years that it's related to my need to be liked and my not wanting to disappoint people. This behavior no doubt stems from my dysfunctional relationship with my father, whom I spent what seemed like a lifetime trying to satisfy but always coming up short.

So I jumped into my car and drove over to the address that Wright had given me. I found the apartment and knocked on the door. Marion opened it and pulled me inside quickly. The apartment was vacant except for a couple of chairs and a reel-to-reel tape recorder sitting on a table. There was another agent sitting at the recorder with headphones on, listening to a conversation.

"All you have to do is turn on the recorder when the person picks up the phone," he said, "and turn it off when the conversation ends."

"How long will you be gone?" I asked.

"Couple of hours."

Wright and the other agent did not come back for five hours. I don't remember the conversations that were bugged or who was being bugged. The entire time, I had visions that someone would realize their phone was being tapped and come busting through the door with their guns blazing away. That was the first and last time I ever participated in an FBI eavesdropping operation. But the Baltimore field office was clearly engaged in a lot of phone and room electronic surveillance.

I know this because of a visit I once made to see Wright at the Baltimore field office, located near the Inner Harbor area. We met in the parking lot behind the building, and as we approached the guard at the back door Marion suddenly grabbed my left arm firmly and held his handcuffs so the guard could see them. I wasn't pleased about the impression he gave the guard, but I guess that was the only way to get me into the building without any record of my having been there.

Once inside, I sat drinking coffee for a while and had to use the men's room. Wright told me to go down the hallway and look for the third door on the left. I went down the hallway, stopped at what I thought was the third door, and opened it. I was amazed by what I saw:

There was an entire room filled with women sitting at desks with headphones or transcribing from reel-to-reel recorders captured conversations from telephone and room bugs. I closed the door as quickly as I opened it and never mentioned it to Wright. That was the last time I visited his office.

One day in late summer 1972, I had an appointment with William Harward, chief of the FBI's Research and Development Division. I had made some improvements in some miniature transmitters and wanted to show them to him. He was on the phone when I arrived and he gestured for me to take a seat. I said I preferred to stand and he told me he would be just another moment.

As I stood beside his desk, I glanced down and saw an invoice from U.S. Recording Company to the FBI for two of my body transmitters. They were the very same transmitters I had delivered to John Matter not more than two weeks earlier. When I glanced at the price on the invoice, I couldn't believe it. My cost to U.S. Recording had been $150 for the body transmitters, but on this invoice to the FBI, the cost was $195, a 30% markup.

I didn't understand it at first, but instinctively I knew it meant trouble. Perhaps not now but eventually.

Harward finally hung up the phone and we talked about some new telephone number decoder I was developing, as well as body transmitters with a greater transmitting distance. But I was listening with only half my brain. The other half was trying to decide what to do about what I had seen on his desk.

Should I say something? If so, to whom? And what would be the cost of opening my mouth? I was afraid to even think about it. It meant walking away from my best customer who was spending nearly $100,000 a year on my equipment. My business employees as well as my own family were depending on me for support. I decided to ignore it. Perhaps it was simply an accounting error, though I doubted it.

Three years later, when I testified before the National Wiretap Commission regarding that price markup, it would mean the end of my business relationship with the FBI and the entire intelligence community.

But in late 1972, before my testimony to the Commission, I received a letter from Joe Tait of U.S. Recording Company insisting that I deliver the FBI equipment orders directly to USRC rather than to the bureau, as had been my practice for several years. With the memory of that price markup on those two body transmitters still fresh, I was not about to change my policy. Regardless of FBI assurances that the arrangement with U.S. Recording was legal, my instincts told me otherwise. I continued to deliver the equipment to the bureau. My refusal to go along with the demand from U.S. Recording began to lead to deterioration in my business relationship with the bureau.

In 1973, the total amount of my sales to the bureau was about $30,000, compared to the previous year when sales had totaled over $100,000. My company still had an overall gross sales level of $250,000, but that was because I was now selling surveillance equipment to the entire intelligence community.

The reason for the precipitous drop in sales to the FBI? I was clearly not playing by the rules, rules being set by people at the top levels of the bureau. Joe Tait, the president of U.S. Recording, and John Mohr, the fourth-highest-ranking agent in the FBI and chief of purchasing, were buddies and poker partners.

Their relationship would cause more than a few raised eyebrows in 1975 when House Intelligence Committee investigators began scrutinizing the price markup scheme, as well as Tait's role as the host of poker weekends at the Blue Ridge Rod and Gun Club in the Shenandoah Valley of Virginia for more than a dozen FBI and CIA agents.

Chapter 6

A Fateful Meeting

BY 1972, IT was clear that I had to find new customers and new markets for my products, or new products altogether. As I had done in my early days in the countermeasure business, I evaluated the newest threats to law enforcement and responded to a need: detection equipment for bombs. Starting in 1970, state and local law enforcement agencies were faced with a dramatic increase in bomb-related incidents from various organizations.

The Weather Underground, a splinter faction of Students for a Democratic Society (SDS), was responsible for more than twenty bombings between 1970 and 1975. Those bombings included the New York City Police Department headquarters and the barbershop in the U.S. Capitol Building. In 1972, the FALN (Spanish initials for the Armed Forces of National Liberation), a Puerto Rican radical group, set off a bomb in Fraunces Tavern in lower Manhattan, killing four people and wounding two dozen others.

A Croatian nationalist set off a bomb at LaGuardia Airport in New York in April 1975, killing eleven persons and wounding more than fifty. And in 1978, Ted Kaczynski, the Unabomber, would begin his eighteen-year-long campaign of sending mail bombs to people, killing three and wounding twenty-nine. The 1970s would be what one bomb disposal technician called the "Decade of the Bomb."

In response to the early indications of this threat, I developed an electronic stethoscope for detection of mechanical timing devices, commonly employed to detonate bombs. This device was received with great enthusiasm by federal, state, and local law enforcement agencies. Picatinny Arsenal in Dover, New Jersey, placed an initial order for eighty-four of my new stethoscopes.

During my countermeasure work and teaching assignment at Fort Holabird, I met a Washington, D.C., police officer named Larry Linville. (He would earn his fifteen minutes of fame as the man who actually found the Watergate bugs with my equipment.) We had coffee one day during a break in the countermeasure class and he asked me if he could use my 1059 amplifier and contact microphone for bomb detection work. I listened to his stories about working on suspicious packages and realized that in order to help in bomb detection I would have to makes some changes to my 1059 amplifier and add an automatic gain [volume] control (AGC). I went back to my shop that day and immediately began to build the 2049M stethoscope that would be the same basic amplifier used for transmitter detection, but with an increased volume control that would help bomb squad people find explosive devices.

I built two switches on the 2049 stethoscope for bomb detection work. The tone switch controlled a low-pass and high-pass filter much like the bass and treble controls on your stereo. The low-pass position is used when listening to soft-sided packages, such as attaché cases and suitcases, while the high-pass position is used for listening to "crisp" sounds, such as those made by metal striking metal, for example, clocks in pipe bombs. The second switch on the stethoscope selects either the AGC or the manual volume control. The AGC position is used by the technicians to avoid hearing loss from loud sounds. If the probe is placed solidly on one surface, the AGC is turned off and the manual volume [gain] control is used for maximum sensitivity.

Larry introduced me to other police officers in the local area who were doing "double duty" as bomb detection personnel. Sergeant Gil Karner, with the Baltimore City Police Department, told me about a loosely knit association of bomb technicians that was forming nationally.

In early 1972, I became a charter member of the IABTI, the International Association of Bomb Technicians & Investigators. It was one of the best career decisions I have ever made. Even during the period of my indictment and criminal trial on allegedly bugging the FBI, the organization never stopped supporting me or my position that I had done nothing wrong.

From that point on, I developed and marketed a full range of anti-bomb equipment with particular emphasis on firing-system detection and bomb dismantling. During this period, the National Bomb Data Center conducted a survey of bomb stethoscopes and found my product to be the most effective of all stethoscopes on the market. By 1974, my business was equally divided between the sale of counter-measure and surveillance equipment to the intelligence community and bomb detection equipment to military, state, and local law enforcement agencies.

May 2, 1972, as I remember, started out to be a normal day. I was working on some body transmitters for the FBI and I had a call from my contact at the CIA regarding their interest in my portable coun-termeasure kit.

I was also expecting a visit of Marion Wright from the FBI's Bal-timore office, but he never showed up. Later I realized why. I turned on the local newsradio station and heard that J. Edgar Hoover had died of a heart attack. Despite his age, seventy-seven, he had seemed in good health the time I had met him the year before. I wondered if his death had anything to do with the "Washington Merry-Go-Round" column by Jack Anderson that had appeared the day before in the *Washington Post*.

The column revealed documents describing the FBI's electronic surveillance of Dr. Martin Luther King Jr.'s sex life, as well as personal information on the private lives of famous athletes, entertainers, and actors, such as Marlon Brando. The fact that the FBI had bugged King was not news, but the details in the column were obviously based on FBI documents that someone had leaked.

Hoover had been betrayed by his own people, something that never would have happened years earlier. I wondered if the bureau had ever used any of my transmitters to bug King's hotel rooms. I put the thought out of my mind. My attitude, at least back then, was that if they didn't get the surveillance equipment from me they would get it from someone else.

Later that year, there was a knock at my office door. I looked through the peephole and saw a man who looked like he had just come from a homeless shelter. He wore a faded plaid sport coat, striped pants, and tennis shoes. And he looked like he hadn't shaved in a couple of days. My first thought was that he was another refugee from a mental institution who was convinced that Martians were communicating with him through mysterious transmitters embedded in his scalp. Perhaps he wanted me to do a countermeasure body sweep to find it.

Opening the door a crack, I asked him what he wanted.

"My name is Ed Duncan," he said. "I'm president and chairman of Northwestern Bank in North Wilkesboro, North Carolina."

Sure you are, I thought, and I'm the pope.

"Look, Mr. Duncan, I'm working on a highly classified project right now and I can't permit anyone to come into my shop," I told him. "Why don't you come back in an hour or so and we can talk."

"Back in an hour," he said, nodding.

I thought the hour-long wait would give me some time to figure out what to do with him, or better yet, that he might decide not to come back. I wasn't that lucky. Little did I know that this meeting with Ed Duncan was the seed of the controversy that would ultimately come close to ruining my life.

True to his word, Duncan was back at my door an hour later. I invited him in and asked what he wanted.

"I have some security problems at my bank," he said, "and I want you to come down and train my security officer."

"What kind of problems?" I asked.

"The goddamned IRS is investigating me and I think they're bugging the phones and the offices."

"Where did you get my name?"

"You come highly recommended," said Duncan.

"From whom?"

"Never mind," he said. "I have a lot of contacts in the intelligence community."

Later, through my own contacts, his story checked out and then some. It turns out that Duncan was a superpatriot who was always ready to fund off-the-books black ops jobs (highly classified spy operations that were denied if the operators were caught) for the alphabet government agencies. These spook connections of Duncan's were also confirmed by a story I later heard from a scuba diver in the Cayman Islands when I started vacationing there in the mid 1970s.

The dive master, Clint Ebanks, told me that as a teenager in the mid 1960s he and his friends once discovered a cache of dozens of machine guns at the bottom of a swimming hole near the center of Georgetown, the capital of the Cayman Islands. As teenagers will do, Ebanks and his friends put a machine gun on each shoulder and marched into town like mercenaries on a Hollywood film set.

Ebanks and other sources told me the weapons came from a CIA Strike Team waiting to go ashore at Cuba's Bay of Pigs in the early hours of the April 1961 invasion. When it became clear the invasion was collapsing, the Strike Team aborted its mission and headed their boat for the nearest friendly island—Grand Cayman. The team beached the boat and dumped their weapons in the swimming hole near the island's capital, hoping one day to reclaim the weapons for another operation. Word had it that the team split up, pretended to be tourists, and eventually made their way back to their own country weeks later. The Strike Team boat remained beached on Grand Cayman for months until it was appropriated by Bob Soto who ran a local scuba diving operation.

Within days after the local police, tipped off by the gun-toting teens, took control of the weapons, word of the incident reached Jim Bodden, the recognized father of Cayman tourism and scion of one of the oldest families on the island. Bodden knew whom to call to resolve the problem and permanently bury any evidence of that aborted operation—Ed Duncan.

The swimming hole was quickly filled in with crushed limestone, and the Cayman Islands branch of Northwestern Bank was built literally overnight on the spot. The bank was built in such a hurry there was no time to fiddle with such things as design. It wound up with the drive-in window on the wrong side (they drive on the left in Cayman).

That day in 1972 in my office, Duncan was angry. He believed the IRS was tapping the bank's phones, and he felt he had a legal right to prevent this invasion of privacy.

"What do you think?" he asked.

"Well, there's no law against checking to see if your conversations are being monitored."

"Good," said Duncan. "I'll send my security guy, Jerry Starr, up here in a couple of days. You can show him how to use the equipment and he can bring it back with him to do the sweep."

I showed Duncan the types of countermeasure gear that would be needed for the sweep and he wrote me out a check for them on the spot. We shook hands and he left. That would be the last time I would actually see Duncan until April 1978.

Jerry Starr came to Baltimore the following week and spent a day with me learning how to use the equipment. But as so often happens, Starr was still not up to speed on how the equipment worked. About two weeks after his visit, he called and asked if I would come down to the bank and walk him through a sweep with the equipment.

Normally, I refused to do on-site instruction of the equipment, but the bank had purchased a lot of expensive gear from me and I liked Ed Duncan and Starr. I told Starr I would come, and the bank sent one of its company aircraft to pick me up at Baltimore-Washington International Airport the following afternoon.

On landing at the airport in North Wilkesboro, North Carolina, the pilot pushed a button on the instrument panel of the Fairchild Turboprop and the doors of a very large hangar slid open. Inside the hangar were at least six beautiful white aircraft with the Northwestern Bank logo on the tail. They ranged in size from a four-engine turboprop down to the classic Twin Beech. I was very impressed but also curious. What was a small North Carolina country bank doing with all these airplanes, I wondered at the time. Starr later told me that one of the planes was reserved for the exclusive use of North Carolina Senator Sam Ervin, chairman of the Senate committee that investigated Watergate. That still didn't explain the other five aircraft and their use.

We decided to sweep all of the buildings—about five—in the bank complex. The minute I turned on my receiver, I heard the sound of a time clock clicking off the seconds. It was obviously somewhere in one of the buildings, but where? After several hours, I located the exact clock. By holding the receiver speaker near the bottom of a nearby locked door, I got the loud feedback squeal of a listening device. It was somewhere behind the door of the comptroller's office.

I left the rest of the job to Jerry Starr. According to FBI directives, any clandestine listening device found in a residence or on commercial property was supposed to be reported to them. That meant getting involved with local law enforcement. I left that decision to Ed Duncan and his people and returned to Baltimore that same day. Before I left, my equipment was picking up a signal of another transmitter somewhere in the main bank building. Eventually I found that one too. It was a device that only the federal government would have had access to. Known in the trade as a "key logger," it was a transmitter attached to the bank's computer designed to capture all of the bank's data financial data and confidential documents on the hard drive.

Starr called me the next day and said he had found the listening device hidden inside a hollowed-out Bible in a bookcase in the comptroller's office. The IRS, to put it mildly, was not amused that their bugs were found. Case closed, client served—or so I thought.

Chapter 7

My Anwar Sadat
Cadillac

THE SUMMER AND fall of 1973 were an interesting time in political and black ops circles. From the testimony of John Dean before the Senate Watergate committee to the indictments of H. R. Haldeman and John Ehrlichman and the Saturday Night Massacre, there seemed to be no end to the daily revelations on the television news or in the *Washington Post* about the Watergate scandal. And the constant refrain of the now-familiar mantra: What did the president know and when did he know it?

But the disclosure by White House aide Alexander Butterfield before the Senate committee that Nixon had a secret, voice-activated taping system in the Oval Office made that question irrelevant. His own words would lead to his downfall.

From a strictly technical perspective, the taping story was the only one that really fascinated me. After all, that was my business. As I remember, the system had been installed sometime in 1969 by the Secret Service and had been maintained by the agency. According to Butterfield, the system taped all conversations in the Oval Office, Nixon's Executive Office Building retreat, the Cabinet room, several private White House rooms, and the president's cabin at Camp David. It sounded like there were more bugs in the White House than in a CIA safe house.

That meant a lot of microphones and reel-to-reel tape recorders. The Secret Service had been a steady customer of mine since the late 1960s when I made contact with several of the agents at Fort Holabird. But most of the equipment I sold them had been body transmitters or countermeasure sweep gear.

The entrepreneur in me wondered which of my competitors had supplied them with the transmitters and recorders for the taping system and what had they charged. A lot more than I did, I bet. In addition to making the highest-quality surveillance equipment, I always set the most reasonable prices. But the technician in me always wondered about the quality of the captured audio. Were they using Shure or Knowles miniature microphones? I made a mental note to ask one of my Secret Service or FBI contacts about the equipment used at the White House, but the opportunity never presented itself.

Was I surprised by Butterfield's disclosure of the taping system in the White House? When someone asked me that question— a few of my friends did—I laughed and shook my head. When it came to eavesdropping, presidents indulged in it for the same reasons that spooks did: power, information, and gaining an edge on the opposition.

At that point in my experience working in the "community," I automatically assumed that there were no protected conversations anytime, anywhere, and I acted accordingly.

For example: Curiosity got the best of me one day and I decided to test the ten-terminal telephone block on the wall of my rented building. The first two lines were mine but the other ones still had the standard forty-eight volts on them. Suddenly someone picked up a telephone on one of those lines and I heard their conversation. It turned out it was from one of the companies that had previously occupied my building. That partial relocation is typical of how the telephone matrix works. The telephone company moves the telephone number from one location to the next following the company as it moves, but leaves behind the line. I thought, hey, this is a great way to bug a company. Just go to its previous location and look for the telephone lines that have been left behind.

The CIA continued to be a regular customer for my countermeasure gear, body transmitters, and quick-drop bugs. As I previously indicated, my primary contact was Bob Jones, chief of the Interagency Training Center. But in the late summer of 1973, I met a supposedly ex-CIA agent who would have a prominent place in my personal rogues gallery of spies that I knew and worked with during my forty years of association with the intelligence community. His name was Frank Terpil.

The true story of Frank Terpil will probably never be known. In the world of spies, truth is a fungible commodity, a subjective analysis of facts whose only value is as a means to an end, a target acquisition strategy. It's a world encased in an infinity of mirrors where what you see is often not what you get or want. Frank's story was a lot like that for me.

The Frank Terpil I knew was a street-smart, funny guy with an iconoclastic sense of humor and a compulsion to tell the most amazing stories. Whether the stories were true or simply embroideries on the truth were beside the point. He was a born storyteller.

The public record on Terpil was that of a kid from Brooklyn, New York, who was busted at fifteen for selling a machine gun to a high school classmate, an experience he would duplicate as an adult—selling guns and getting busted. With only a high school education, he was hired in 1965 by the CIA, where he served as a courier and communications specialist until he allegedly resigned from the agency in 1972. His last station was India, where he was suspected of smuggling gems in a diplomatic pouch and running a black market money-changing scheme between Afghanistan and New Delhi.

Terpil would later establish a reputation as an international supplier of weapons, explosives, surveillance equipment, and assassination devices to some of the world's most infamous dictators, including Idi Amin of Uganda, Jean-Claude Duvalier of Haiti, the Shah of Iran, and Mu'ammar Gadhafi of Libya.

In late 1979, he was arrested, indicted, and convicted in absentia of selling 10,000 machine guns, plastic explosives, and poison dart fountain pens to undercover New York cops posing as Latin American terrorists. The U.S. government sent out a team of agents to kidnap him in Jamaica, and he was returned to the United States and put in jail. Someone accidentally left his cell door open and he worked his way back to his home in Alexandria, Virginia, got his passport, and left for Syria.

Several months later, he was indicted again along with another ex-CIA agent, Edwin Wilson, for training terrorists in Libya and selling twenty tons of C-4 plastic explosive to Libya's Gadhafi. This time U.S. authorities were not successful in getting him back to the States. Obviously, he had a gold-plated get-out-of-jail card from his former employer. From the Middle East, he showed up on the island of Grenada just prior to the U.S. invasion there in 1982, and after that he appeared in Nicaragua.

In 1984, there were rumors of his death and burial in Damascus, but it turned out to be more tradecraft than truth. In 1987 and 1988, the word among the spooks was that Terpil was traveling regularly through Central and Eastern Europe on diplomatic passports provided by the communist governments of Czechoslovakia and Romania.

He was last heard of in Cuba in 1995, reportedly under house arrest by Castro's government. But knowing Frank, he has probably schmoozed his way into Castro's inner circle by now to serve as his adviser on countermeasures and dirty tricks.

I met Terpil that summer of 1973 when he showed up one day at my shop unannounced. At the time, he handed me a business card that indicated he was a salesman with a company called American Overseas Agencies (AOA). The company acted as a middleman to purchase electronic surveillance detection equipment for foreign clients. He was interested in buying two telephone analyzers, which I eventually sold to him.

Months later, Frank would give me another business card for a company called NAPCO (National Auto Parts Company). NAPCO, he told me, bought used transmissions for tanks and other military vehicles, as well as an outdated weapons system that it sold to third world armed forces.

I later learned that both companies were CIA proprietaries— shell companies, facades behind which agents could ply their trade. Despite his contention that he was no longer with the agency, I didn't buy it for a minute. My experience with agency types was that they never completely severed their ties with their former boss. They were always on call, like cops or emergency room physicians.

During that first visit, Terpil said he had heard good things about me and my equipment from his contacts in the agency and he wanted to represent me to foreign governments who were actively interested in buying the best surveillance and countermeasure equipment. I told him I was always interested in expanding my customer base.

The one thing I remember from that first meeting with Terpil was when he pulled out a small automatic pistol and boasted that he could "take this baby through any airport security system in the world."

"How so?" I asked.

"It's made of ceramic and fires ceramic bullets," Terpil explained, laughing. "The magic of technology."

That was Frank, a born salesman, always pushing products.

And then there were the photos that he showed me of him and Jean-Claude Duvalier, the Haitian dictator, in the early 1970s before Duvalier was overthrown in a coup. The first photo showed Terpil and Duvalier with their arms around each other, smiling into the camera. A matching photo was taken of the two men from the rear, with both men holding .45 caliber pistols behind each other's back.

"What's the message here?" I asked.

"There's always a flip side to every story," said Terpil.

Throughout the next year, we saw each other frequently at my shop and became very good friends. We often had lunch together. He bought a lot of my equipment, but more often than not, he would simply drop by to shoot the breeze. Sometimes we talked shop about new surveillance equipment or bomb detection gear on the market. But we had an unspoken agreement: He never asked me who my clients were or what I was selling them, and I reciprocated.

I even had him and his wife and children over for dinner one night. His wife, Marilyn, said very little. As usual, Frank kept us in stitches with stories of his early years with the CIA. The one thing I remember about Frank's wife that night was a silver spray can that she kept beside her at all times. She never touched it and I wondered whether there was a tape recorder inside it or if it was simply a fancy can of mace. I heard later that she also worked for the agency. Terpil left his wife a few years later for a young Filipino woman he met at a Bloomingdale's cosmetics counter in suburban Washington.

I was always impressed by Frank's knowledge of explosives. Despite his contention that he was self-taught, he had obviously picked up a lot of knowledge from his former employer about bomb making, as well as the most effective uses of different types of bomb materials.

One story he told me regarding his clients was about building radios with bombs in them in Libya. The detonators were wired to the dial tuner, and he warned the people he was working with not to turn on the radios for any reason. Terpil left to confer with one of the Libyan intelligence people.

"I hadn't walked more than a hundred yards," he told me, "when BOOM—there was this tremendous explosion. There wasn't enough left of the guy to fill a paper bag. I guess he just couldn't resist playing that radio."

Years later, I read that Terpil was suspected of helping Libyan intelligence agents "not known for their great technical expertise" build the bomb that blew up Pan Am Flight 103 over Lockerbie, Scotland. And when British intelligence asked the CIA about him, the agency refused to open his file.

When I read the story, some questions came to mind: Was Frank Terpil still working for the CIA when I met him? And, how could a man whom I had briefly come to know as a funny, gregarious, regular guy also be a psychopath? While he sold his murderous skills as well as explosives and weapons to terrorists throughout the world at a tidy profit, was he impervious to the violence for which he was indirectly responsible?

I believe the answer to the first question is yes, based on my experience when I went to Cairo to train Anwar Sadat's intelligence services. As for the psychopath question, I have no answer. I guess that's the mark of an effective spy: an amoral individual who flies under his own flag.

In late summer 1974, shortly after Nixon resigned rather than face impeachment over the Watergate cover-up, I got a call from my CIA contact. He asked if I would be interested in selling a large quantity of countermeasure and eavesdropping equipment to a foreign government and then going abroad to train its intelligence service in the use of it.

"Absolutely," I asked. "Who is it?"

"Egypt," he said.

"What do they want?"

"Everything in your countermeasure inventory, but no bugging stuff."

"No problem," I told him.

I later learned that my countermeasure equipment and training services were part of a wish list by Egypt's Anwar Sadat and granted by Secretary of State Henry Kissinger to achieve a disengagement agreement between Israel, Egypt, and Syria following the Yom Kippur War in October 1973. Thanks to Frank, I got the contract. He still had solid connections with the Agency and he must have put in a good word with the folks in the purchasing section.

The CIA had two requirements when I went to their office in Crystal City, Virginia, to sign the contract: Remove the "Made in Japan" label on any equipment of mine that were made from parts produced in Japan, and do not mention anything about products made by Audio Intelligence Devices (AID). AID, based in Ft. Lauderdale, Florida, was then a major supplier of positive surveillance devices to federal and state government agencies and one of my competitors.

The implication was that the United States did not want to be accused of selling bugging devices to the Egyptians, should the devices be discovered. The Israelis wanted to keep an edge in that category of surveillance and they did, thanks to Uncle Sam. According to my intelligence contacts, the Israelis had world-class techs in phone taps and room bugs.

Of course, the day I arrived in Cairo, the first thing that Egyptian intelligence did was to take me to a closet and show off all of their transmitters and miniature microphones with the AID logo on the boxes. I was dying to ask them who the middleman was on the deal. I assumed it was Terpil.

A week before I left for Egypt, Frank made one of his unannounced visits to my shop. It was a typical Frank visit. A lot of small talk, a couple of funny stories, and then, as if to let me know he was still well connected in the Agency, he congratulated me on getting the contract to train Sadat's palace security. He even knew the exact dollar amount of the contract—$55,000.

That convinced me that he was still working for the agency if only in a contract mode. The last thing my agency contact, Al Montefusco, told me after I signed the contract was, "Mum's the word, Marty. This is a sensitive deal." Terpil also asked me if I could do some modifications to some of the equipment I was bringing to Cairo. I told him I had to follow the specifications in the contract.

I left for Cairo in early November 1974, with a short stopover in London to brief the tech people with British intelligence—MI5 and MI6—at the agency's request. I conducted the briefing in an office somewhere in the center of London. I have two memories of that London meeting: Everyone in the room wore a military uniform with lots of ribbons, and they were interested in radio-controlled car bombs.

I was supposed to brief them about countermeasures as well as bomb detection. But this was the height of IRA bombings in Northern Ireland, and they wanted to know the most unlikely spots to place a bomb in a car. I didn't know about the most unlikely place, but the most logical one, I suggested, was under the dashboard, connected to the car antenna for maximum range.

Eyebrows shot up all over the room with my explanations and some of the people scribbled notes hurriedly on their legal pads. After a few more questions about car bombs, the two-hour briefing was over. They thanked me and I was whisked back to the airport for the flight to Cairo.

Later, from agency contacts, I learned that the notes British intelligence took at my briefing were stamped Top Secret, put in a safe, and forgotten. A typical British intelligence reaction to their American cousins in the spy trade—there's nothing you can tell us about this spy business. We've been at it longer and done it better.

I boarded a Lufthansa flight for Cairo with a stop in Athens en route. I awoke when I felt the plane descending, assuming that we were about to land in Athens. Then the captain came on the intercom telling us the aircraft was being diverted to a Greek airbase at Tsaloniki. I didn't know if we were being hijacked or what, but I was more curious than nervous. A stewardess stopped at my seat, probably responding to my confused expression.

"Why is the flight being diverted?" I asked.

"No need to worry," she said. "Can I get you something?"

"Yeah, bring me a Cuban cigar and a tin of caviar."

The stewardess smiled and walked away. Either she was an accomplished actress or the diversion was not that serious. Suddenly the plane landed, turned around, but remained on the tarmac. Within minutes, about a dozen men in black Special Operations uniforms and balaclavas covering their faces appeared at the front of the plane carrying submachine guns. They walked slowly down the aisle staring at each passenger, obviously looking for someone.

I smiled at them as they walked by, relieved that I was not on their most wanted list. Within minutes, the captain came on the intercom again to apologize for the unscheduled diversion. We skipped Athens and headed straight for Egypt.

It was morning by the time I arrived in Cairo and I felt edgy from lack of sleep. I was also overdressed for the climate, although November was considered pleasant compared to the blast-furnace summers. To make matters worse, my suitcase was missing. The surveillance gear had been shipped weeks before so I wasn't concerned about that. But as I went through customs, a man in a uniform came over and told me to follow him. He took me to a room with a desk and a chair. My bag stood in the middle of the room.

"Is that your luggage?" the customs official asked.

"Yes," I told him.

"You can take it with you now."

An escort drove me from the airport to the Nile Hilton. When I got to my room, I checked to see if any of the baggage tricks Terpil had taught me had worked. He had told me to put a small thread under the collars of my shirts and at various other locations, and make a note of their placement. Sure enough, they were all displaced. Obviously someone had gone through my bag. Terpil confirmed my suspicion some months later when he asked me why I had packed a can of tunafish and a chain and lock. I told him I always took tunafish with me to a foreign country so I would have something to eat if I couldn't take the local cuisine. I brought the chain to lock my suitcase to the bed. I had never been to the Middle East before and my expectations were colored by the negative stereotypes of people from this part of the world.

"You really had them scratching their heads, Marty," he said, laughing.

My first impression during the drive to the hotel was surprise at how modern the city was with its high-rise buildings. I was fascinated with the broad, European style boulevards bursting with trucks, luxury cars and ox-drawn carts of merchants hawking their wares and pedestrians walking casually in front of traffic as if they owned the street.

I had never been in the middle of such a mass of people. The unwelcoming aspects of the city were the black smoke and auto exhaust fumes that hung in the air like a shroud, and the incessant blaring of horns, something one of my hosts called a "Cairo symphony." Some symphony!

When we arrived at the hotel and before I retired to my room, one of the people hanging around the front entrance was asked by my escort to take my bag out of the trunk and put in on the hotel trolley. He did it and then put out his hand asking for a tip. My escort slapped him hard across the face. I was stunned. This was my first experience of the Middle East. I was not prepared for this type of behavior.

"Why did you do that?" I asked him.

The escort shook his head as if to say, "You don't understand," and went inside the hotel to take care of my room reservation. When I looked around to give the man a tip, he had disappeared. My introduction to Egypt was not terrific so far. As I entered the hotel, I saw Frank Terpil walking across the lobby with a big smile on his face. I must admit it was nice to see a friendly face from home.

"Marty," he said, vigorously shaking my hand. "How are you doing?"

"Hi, Frank," I said. "What are you doing here?"

"I'm providing customer service, just like you."

Then he introduced me to a guy standing beside him who looked like a NFL linebacker. He was about six foot five and looked like he could lift the front end of a two-ton truck with one hand. Obviously, he was Frank's muscle.

"This is Omar. He'll be your contact while you're here," said Frank. "If you need me for anything, ask Omar to call me."

Omar nodded but said nothing. We rode in the elevator to the seventh floor. When we reached the floor and opened the door to my room, Frank turned to Omar and said, "All right, give him back his stuff."

Omar smiled and silently handed me my wristwatch, keys, wallet, and even my belt. I felt like I was the audience member guinea pig in a magic act, except the magician never asked me to volunteer. What he had done was more amazing because he'd picked my pocket with the biggest hands I'd ever seen. Frank laughed.

"You take care, Marty," he said, walking back to the elevator with Omar the pickpocket. "I'll see you around."

I never understood the point of that exercise except perhaps the unspoken message from Terpil that things were never what they appeared to be in his line of work, especially in Cairo. And I never saw Omar again, although I knew he was always somewhere in the background.

My assignment was to train the three top people in President Sadat's palace security operation. We worked in a large, ornate room in the palace. The primary aspect of the job was instructing them in the use of the countermeasure equipment they had purchased, specifically the telephone analyzer. Essentially, they asked me how to help them defeat Israeli phone taps. Somehow I had a feeling that this was not the reason Kissinger included my services on Anwar Sadat's negotiation wish list.

During one of my first days in Cairo, I was introduced to President Sadat by his security detail. He nodded but we didn't shake hands and then I was escorted out of his office. I guess that was part of his security policy—not to let anyone get too close. Seven years later, on the eighth anniversary of the Yom Kippur War, Sadat's security proved to be fatally ineffective and he was gunned down by his own troops.

Egyptian intelligence had seized a lot of Israeli bugging equipment during the war, including the infamous Israeli telephone poles—poles with cross arms that were loaded with batteries and enough memory circuit units to store a day's conversations inside. The Egyptians even took me out into the desert on a couple of occasions to show me some examples of Israel's phone tap tradecraft.

One day my hosts said they wanted to show me something I might find interesting. We drove to a different part of the city to an enormous warehouse the size of two aircraft hangars. Inside the warehouse was the greatest collection of captured Israeli weapons and electronics I've ever seen or heard of, including bugging and countermeasure equipment.

Egyptian intelligence apparently had no clue how much of it worked or its threat capacity to capture conversations. Of course, all of the eavesdropping gear was made in the United States. The tip-off to the Egyptians' lack of expertise regarding electronic surveillance threats emerged as we were discussing light beam transmitters. It absolutely fascinated them that a light beam could carry room conversations. We spent an entire day in an alley behind their headquarters setting up a crude light beam transmitter made from parts in the countermeasure kit I supplied to them. Israel and other countries had used that type of attack for more than a decade at that point, and Egyptian intelligence had been completely unaware of it.

Perhaps the best part of my assignment in Egypt was the mixture of work and play. My hosts were warm and generous and loved to party. No alcohol, of course, but we ate at a different restaurant every night during my three weeks in Cairo. We were entertained by the most exotic belly dancers in town and would finally end up at a tobacco café where a hookah would be brought to our table. Cuban cigar leaves would follow that on a gold tray, and your preference of a variety of drugs from cocaine to hashish. I abstained except for a few puffs on a good cigar with a Cuban leaf.

During my stay in Cairo, I ran into Frank Terpil several times in the lobby or the bar of the Nile Hilton, but those meetings were random and brief.

"Hi, how's it going? See you later."

About a week before I left, he invited me for dinner. We went to a traditional Egyptian restaurant and the maître d' asked if I liked lamb chops. I answered in the affirmative. A couple of minutes later, he pointed to the corner of the restaurant near the kitchen.

"How's that?" he asked.

I looked in the direction of his hand and there was a man with a smile on his face holding a baby lamb on a leash.

Oh, no, I thought, suddenly losing my appetite for lamb. I glanced at Frank and he nodded.

"Well, Marty, at least you know it's fresh," he said, following that with his usual unforgettable laughter.

Neither of us said much during dinner. There was nothing new to tell him about the folks I was instructing, and Frank seemed preoccupied, subdued. We went back to the hotel after dinner and I shook his hand and thanked him. I had a feeling I would not see him again. And I was right. From the grapevine, I heard he was doing deals in Lebanon and Libya after Cairo, and I never heard from him again.

I was happy to get home to my family, to my workshop, and to the good old U.S.A. Three weeks had seemed like three months. I decided to do something I had never done before: reward myself for a job well done. When I received the check for the Cairo assignment, I went to the local Cadillac dealer and paid cash for a brand-new, fire-engine-red, four-door sedan. My father and grandfather had always driven Cadillacs because the cars were distinctive, well made, and reflected a certain status of the owner. For me, it was simply a matter of giving myself a long-overdue pat on the back.

A year later, following my testimony before the National Wiretap Commission, the FBI would open an investigation into my sale of equipment and training for the Egyptian government. They already had me in their crosshairs.

It was about that time in 1974 that I also began to expand my business into the bomb detection market. I was no longer affiliated with the countermeasure course at Fort Holabird, and many of the officers I had made initial contact with had retired. I helped to establish and implement the navy's Improvised Explosive Device Detection (IEDD) school at Indian Head on the southeast side of Washington. I taught at the school for over a decade.

The FBI, always in my thoughts, would very soon become like a proverbial bad penny, continually coming back into my life with no objective except to disrupt and destroy.

Chapter 8

Road to Ruin

DESPITE MY LIFELONG habit of looking at the dark side, life was sweet in the mid 1970s. I was king of the hill in the electronic surveillance business, both positive and countermeasure. My client list was a Who's Who in the intelligence community, including the various alphabet agencies—FBI, CIA, DOD, DIA, NIS, NSA, DMA, and DEA—as well as the Secret Service, the intelligence commands of the army, navy, air force, customs, and state and local law enforcement agencies.

I enjoyed driving my shiny new red Cadillac (often thinking of Tom Walsh, my blind childhood friend driving my mother's old Caddy), compliments of Egypt's Anwar Sadat for training his palace security guard. A local columnist referred to me as the "Michelangelo of electronic surveillance." An FBI memorandum even referred to me as a "well-known electronics genius." Honestly, I was as good as it got in the world of electronic eavesdropping.

My business of designing and manufacturing the finest quality spookware in the United States—devices that included amplifiers, receivers, RF detectors, telephone analyzers, clandestine transmitters, and body mikes—was booming, as was my bomb detection business. I employed seven technicians in my cramped office next to

Brooks Robinson's sporting goods shop in Cockeysville, and the phone rang seven days a week with orders. I once thought it would be neat to go into business with Brooks. We could call the company "Bats, Balls, and Bugs."

I was finally earning real money. More important, I was recognized for my talent and expertise. That was my real bottom line. And I was having lots of fun.

Unwittingly, my life was about to change with a phone call. A phone call that would almost result in my destruction, professionally and personally. Shakespeare had it right: The past is prologue. You never know when the Law of Unintended Consequences will come back to bite you in the ass.

The phone call came in early 1975. The caller was Michael Hirschman, chief investigative counsel for the National Wiretap Commission. The commission was charged with reviewing Title III of the Omnibus Crime Control and Safe Streets Act of 1968 to determine the effectiveness of wiretapping as a crime-fighting tool. Title III also prohibited companies from advertising or selling eavesdropping devices to anyone except federal, state, or local law enforcement agencies. Hirschman wanted to see copies of all of my invoices relating to sales of electronic surveillance devices. I voluntarily complied with his requests, knowing that a refusal would probably trigger a subpoena.

A couple of months later, I received another phone call. This time the caller was Tim Oliphant, a staff investigator from the U.S. House Select Committee on Intelligence. The committee was organizing hearings to be held later that year for the National Wiretap Commission. They wanted to come to my shop to interview me and look at some of my invoices and customers.

"Sure," I told Oliphant. "Come on over. My records are open to you. If you have any questions about them, ask my secretary, Nancy Egan."

Several weeks later, I met with Oliphant and another investigator from the House Committee named Rich Vermiere to let them review my invoices and sales receipts.

After going through several piles of invoices Oliphant asked, "Who's U.S. Recording?"

"The FBI," I told him. "I send the gear directly to the FBI."

"Then why the invoices to U.S. Recording?"

"That's the way I've been doing it since 1965," I said, "and I've got a letter from the bureau that says this arrangement complies with the Omnibus Crime Control and Safe Streets Act of 1968."

I showed the investigators the rubber stamp that I used on my invoices; both of them seemed skeptical about it.

Oliphant asked me if I would testify at hearings to be held later that summer regarding this arrangement with the FBI. I had to think about that for a couple of moments. My clients all operated within the intelligence community and viewed publicity of any kind as more painful than a root canal without Novocain. If I agreed to testify, it could endanger my business relationship with the bureau. If I refused, it would appear that I had something to hide and the committee could subpoena me to testify anyway.

It was a no-win situation, but I decided I wasn't going to the pokey for anyone. This was still America, I thought. The truth would protect me. How naïve I was! I told the investigators I would testify, and then I dropped a bombshell.

"You know," I said, "in 1972 I was delivering some gear to the FBI and I saw something weird regarding one of my invoices. I didn't understand it at the time."

"What was that?" asked Vermiere.

"The price of my equipment was marked up by about 30 percent over the original price."

Vermiere looked at me and shook his head.

"What did you make of it?" He asked.

"As I said I thought it was a little strange, but I didn't pursue it. After all, this was the FBI."

"There's no way that's legitimate," said Oliphant. "Would you testify to that?"

I agreed, but with a sense of foreboding that events were starting to move in a direction I had not anticipated. I was trying to be a good citizen, trying to play by the rules. I hoped that everyone else would do the same. But I wasn't prepared for what happened next.

I was scheduled to testify before the House Intelligence Committee in October, several months from then. I prepared my written statement, which I gave to Oliphant. In my statement I questioned why the Omnibus Crime Bill was not being enforced uniformly among manufacturers. Under the law, it was illegal to manufacture, assemble, or offer for sale bugging equipment unless you are "under contract with a federal, state, or local agency."

That meant NO inventorying. I complained that in the early pages of its catalog, Audio Intelligence Devices (AID) of Ft. Lauderdale, Florida, claimed that it maintained an "in-depth inventory," an apparent violation of the law. Their doing just that seriously hurt my ability to run my business as a business. Often, in the eavesdropping and countermeasure business, customers will call and demand a specific device on the spot. If you have a ready supply of the equipment on hand and ready to ship, you get the sale. If you don't, the customer will often go elsewhere and you lose the sale to some other supplier. The feds had their foot on my neck by saying I could not do it, and I thought the situation was patently unfair.

Before I testified, I contacted the CIA and the FBI to see if there were any problems with my appearance before the House Committee. The CIA asked for a day's delay and then gave me the OK. There was only silence from the FBI. It was a harbinger of things to come.

Seated at the witness table with me on October 15, 1975, was Anthony Zavala, a former Houston cop who was scheduled to start a three-year federal prison term for wiretapping, and Anthony J. P. Farris, a former U.S. attorney in Houston. Zavala testified that the FBI as well as U.S. Customs and the Bureau of Narcotics and Dangerous

Drugs (later the Drug Enforcement Administration) were aware that illegal wiretaps were being carried out by Houston police. Farris confirmed that fact, recalling that he repeatedly "ran into a stone wall" in his efforts to get the FBI to conduct a serious investigation of illegal electronic surveillance supposedly used by the Houston police.

Here was another example of the FBI talking out of both sides of their mouth.

When I looked at the prepared statement sitting in front of me on the table, I was astonished. My statement had been completely rewritten. It still attacked the FBI about the use of U.S. Recording Company as a middleman in my dealings with them, and mentioned the price markups. But it made no mention whatsoever of other companies and their practice of stockpiling equipment and being allowed to market their wares without a contract, apparently in violation of the Omnibus Crime Act, and that included AID. The imposter statement made it sound as if my sole purpose in testifying was to go to war with one of my best clients.

I told Tim Oliphant that the paper in front of me wasn't my statement. I refused to read it because of the changes that had been made from my original. Oliphant didn't seem surprised or upset by my refusal. He gave me fifteen minutes to go to an anteroom to rewrite the statement. When I finally read the revised version, the committee members looked at each other, clearly confused about the discrepancies in the statement they had before them and the one I was giving. But I did testify to the 30 percent price markup I had seen on one of my invoices to the FBI.

As to who rewrote my statement and why, I can only speculate. Given the post-Watergate environment in which the National Wiretap Commission held its hearings, and the many congressional investigations into abuses by the FBI and the rest of the intelligence community, someone on the committee wanted to score points and makes headlines by attacking the bureau. Ironically, that was not the original purpose of the hearings.

An investigation by the General Accounting Office (GAO) would later reveal that for the equipment I had delivered directly to the bureau, U.S. Recording had hiked my sale prices between 30 percent and 280 percent. My gross sales to the FBI had been approximately $200,000. The markup on these sales was estimated at approximately $75,000.

I subsequently learned that U.S. Recording was what the intelligence community called a "cutout"—tradecraft terminology for a middleman in an intelligence transaction designed to hid the true source of sensitive data or hardware sold to a third party.

The FBI ultimately acknowledged that U.S. Recording Company was one of its "confidential suppliers." Federal law permitted agencies to purchase sensitive hardware from these "confidential suppliers" without competitive bidding. An internal investigation by the Justice Department and one by the GAO later determined that there was no reason to used a so-called "cutout" to purchase many of the non-sensitive items.

An FBI spokesman vehemently denied anything improper regarding using U.S. Recording as an intermediate supplier, or the price markup that I alluded to in my testimony.

My testimony caused a huge flap and an enormous embarrassment for the bureau. *Newsweek* magazine ran a story on December 15, 1975, with the headline, "Case of the Cozy Cutout." The story indicated that my testimony had prompted the Intelligence Committee to investigate an apparent conflict of interest between John Mohr, the fourth-highest official in the FBI before his retirement in 1972 (and head of purchasing for the bureau), and Joseph Tait, president of U.S. Recording. Investigators felt the relationship violated the conflict of interest statute governing federal purchases.

It later came out that Tait and Mohr were close friends and regular poker partners with other FBI agents and intel community officials, including James J. Angleton, the CIA's counterintelligence chief, at the Blue Ridge Rod and Gun Club, a hunting lodge in the

Shenandoah Valley of Virginia. It was reported that Tait always picked up the $600 tab for these weekend poker games.

The lodge mysteriously burned to the ground on November 23, 1975, the night before investigators from the House Intelligence Committee were due to inspect the club's books. The club's books were not the only documents destroyed in the fire. A former staff member of the committee suspected that some of Hoover's secret files had been stored there following his death in 1972. Those files were reported to contain potentially damaging information regarding the personal lives of current and former presidents, members of Congress, and celebrities. What happened to these files remains a mystery to this day.

Following an internal FBI investigation based on my testimony, the relationship with U.S. Recording was terminated and the use of "cutouts" was permanently ended. Several ranking FBI officials were asked to take early retirement, and the bureau underwent a complete reorganization of its accounting and purchasing procedures. The bureau's investigation also revealed that various high-ranking officials, including John Mohr, Nicholas P. Callahan, Deke DeLoach, G. Speights McMichael, as well as Hoover, had repairs done to their residences using materials and on-duty FBI personnel paid for by the bureau.

The GAO's accounting of the whole mess showed that roughly $24 million was run through U.S. Recording, of which roughly $7.5 million was "misspent" by bureau personnel.

Despite Hoover's mantra over the years that agents must avoid even the appearance of impropriety, he was, by far, the greatest offender of using FBI personnel and materials for his own benefit. During his time as director, Hoover used FBI employees to build additions to his house at 4936 Thirtieth Place NW in Washington, including a front portico and rear deck, a fishpond, a redwood garden fence, a flagstone court and sidewalks, as well as interior bookshelves. Hoover reportedly had bureau employees write the book,

Masters of Deceit for him under his name, and then banked part of the proceeds. Traditionally, celebrities like Hoover would give the profits from a book to charity.

A week after the *Newsweek* article appeared about U.S. Recording and the price markups, two FBI Special Agents knocked on my shop door. I reluctantly let them in. They proceeded to virtually hold me hostage for nearly three hours in an effort to persuade me to recant my testimony. Every half-hour one of them would leave the room to go to the "bathroom." In reality, the agent went to change the tape in the recorder hidden in his jacket pocket. He didn't even have the common sense to flush the toilet to give a logical cover for his supposed need to relieve himself with such frequency.

But getting me to say something on tape was not enough. They kept pressuring me to sign a written statement they had prepared with my name at the bottom of the page. The statement essentially repudiated the sworn testimony I had given before the House Intelligence Committee. In an effort to get the agents out of my shop, I agreed to sign it, with the notation: "I have PARTIALLY prepared the above statement," which essentially rendered my signature invalid.

A week after the visit by the agents, I received a call from the local IRS office. I was being audited, and they wanted to come to my office to interview me. The timing, to put it mildly, was highly suspicious but not unexpected. I'd never been audited before despite operating my own business for ten years at that point. I had never been late in paying my estimated taxes and had never owed back taxes. I paid an accountant to make sure my books were in order at all times. I had nothing to hide. An IRS agent showed up at my shop two days later, a few days before Christmas. He wanted an explanation for a business deduction —a $500 high-gain antenna.

"I'm in the electronics business," I told him. "I use antennas for my countermeasure equipment as well as bomb detection devices. What's the problem?"

"There was a question about whether the antenna was used for business," said the agent, "or for your personal use."

"What do you mean?" I asked.

"Well, I believe you're a licensed ham radio operator."

I felt like telling the IRS agent that it was none of his business what I did in my personal life, but I decided that silence was the smartest reaction. It was clear where the IRS had obtained information about my ham radio interest. The FBI's footprints were all over that information. I remained silent for the rest of the interview, and the agent got the message. He picked up his attaché case and left. I never heard anything further from them.

In the weeks that followed there were attempts by various strangers to set me up for violations of the wiretap sections of the Omnibus Crime Act. The most blatant example involved a so-called "private detective" who called and asked if I would show him how to "three-wire" a telephone.

The process requires short-circuiting one of the primary two wires in a telephone and connecting the third wire, usually yellow in color, to the handset earpiece that serves as a microphone. The "three-wire attack" became obsolete with the advent of touch-tone dialing, when two wires became standard connectors in a phone. Obviously, there are now "two wire attacks."

The "private detective" and I met in a conference room at a local motel in Towson, Maryland. He handed me a screwdriver and I handed it right back to him and told him if he wanted to learn the process, HE would have to do the work. About that time, I noticed a pair of polished wing-tipped shoes—a staple of the FBI agent uniform—at the bottom of the curtain that ran across the room. Finally, a guy wearing a dark suit, tie, and the wing tips came out from behind the curtain like the Great Oz and tried to persuade me to make the modifications to the phone. I refused and walked out the door.

For months afterward, an unlikely parade of strangers showed up at my office door. It seemed that every criminal in the Baltimore area wanted me to help him or her debug their car or apartment, but none of them got past my front door. One guy called and asked if I could come to his house to adapt an ultrasonic burglar alarm into a room listening device. I told him I would take a look at it if he sent it to me but I wasn't setting one foot in the house or the office of a stranger.

I never heard from him again. Another yo-yo who allegedly ran a licorice manufacturing business wanted me to bug his house, then went into great detail telling me how brown sugar is used to make licorice. I was amused at how hard he was trying to bullshit me. Hey, I'm an ex-Terpil graduate! I must have received fifteen to twenty calls like that during the months after my testimony before the National Wiretap Commission. I was actually subpoenaed by an attorney for a drug dealer to talk theoretically about how phones and offices could be bugged. The FBI thought that would put another nail in my coffin.

It didn't take a genius to figure out that the FBI was passing the word that taking Kaiser down could fix their problems. They began by essentially putting out a contract on my contacts within the entire intel community. Within weeks following my testimony before the House Intelligence Committee, my phone stopped ringing with orders from all previous customers. My calls went unanswered. I was suddenly considered a pariah within the world of electronic surveillance and countermeasures. Formerly eager customers hung up when I called.

The FBI, which had taken over operation of the National Bomb Data Center, refused to accept my information about bomb detection products for distribution to federal, state, and local law enforcement agencies. Technical records concerning current trends in bombing to which I had had free access for years were no longer available to me. This lack of access made the development of new and improved anti-bomb devices next to impossible and it amounted to a restraint of trade. No government agency would even discuss equipment purchase with me. In short, I was completely blackballed by all federal agencies regarding sale of any electronic gear.

Two members of the Interagency Technical Committee (IATC) informed me that at the FBI's urging, no federal intelligence agency should make further purchases from my company. The IATC is an interagency training committee composed of representatives of the twelve primary U.S. intelligence agencies. The goal of the committee is to share technical information about surveillance and countermeasure equipment.

As I mentioned earlier, I received other warnings during this period that the FBI would use me as a "test case" under the criminal wiretap provision of the Omnibus Crime Act in retaliation for my testimony before the National Wiretap Commission. And then there was the warning from a retired intelligence officer with the Strategic Air Command, Donald Swenholt, that the bureau would try to nail me through my customers. Although I had begun to do some surveillance sweeps in the private sector to pay the rent, I stopped for a while for fear of entrapment by the bureau.

One of the most eerie experiences during that time was receiving about thirty anonymously mailed envelopes that contained the embossed metal desk nameplates featuring my company name that I used to give out as a marketing tool. The message was loud and clear: *You're radioactive.* The only organization that did not turn its back on me during that period was the International Association of Bomb Technicians and Investigators (IABTI).

Dave Nye, chief investigator for the Miami/Dade County, Florida, bomb squad and charter member and director of IABTI, told me that as far as the association was concerned I was innocent until proven guilty. They would "stand by me until the outcome was known." I continued to attend their annual conferences and meetings. It was a far cry from the treatment I got from the intelligence agencies.

Within a few months, my business income on the surveillance and countersurveillance side dropped from approximately $500,000 annually to zero. I had to lay off all of my employees. I was close to bankruptcy. I could never prove that the FBI blacklisted me, but there was no other logical explanation. In March 1976, I was given a warning from a credible intelligence agency friend that the Justice Department had me in its crosshairs. They were going to charge me with an unspecified crime under the wiretap provisions of the Omnibus Crime Act of 1968.

That prompted me to send the following letter to Attorney General Edward Levi:

MARTIN L. KAISER, INC.
Countersurveillance • *Bomb Detection* • *Surveillance Electronics*

March 23, 1976
Hon. Edward Levi
Attorney General of the United States
Department of Justice
Washington, D.C.

Dear Mr. Attorney General:

It is with great hesitation that I write to you. However, I believe that I am in serious trouble and that you are the only person who will be able to assist me.

For over ten years, Martin L. Kaiser, Inc. has been a major supplier of electronic countermeasure, surveillance, and clandestine bomb detection equipment to law enforcement agencies from the federal level down. Among my customers, and these are but a few, were the CIA, Department of Defense, FBI, State Department, army, navy and air force intelligence, coast guard, etc. In June 1975, the National Wiretap Commission, operating under a congressional mandate, received my business records under threat of subpoena. These records were subsequently brought to the attention of the House Select Committee on Intelligence by the National Wiretap Commission.

As a result, it became publicly known that the FBI purchased its electronic countermeasure and surveillance equipment through a front known as the U.S. Recording Company. This disclosure has been of extreme embarrassment to the FBI, but I assure you it is not an embarrassment of my making. I am sure you are well aware of the media's treatment of subsequent events.

Since this fact became known, my business has fallen to virtually zero. No federal or, for that matter, local agency will even discuss purchases of equipment with me. I can only assume, but cannot conclusively prove, that the FBI has "passed the word." It is not, however, this event and the subsequent economic loss that are of primary concern, for I engage in other business activities that will carry me through this trying time. Recently, a person of known reliability has pointedly warned me that I am to be made a test case under the criminal wiretap provisions of the 1968 Omnibus Crime Act. Being thoroughly familiar with the complicated and often conflicting provisions of that act, I am fully aware of the danger existing for anyone who has committed themselves to the manufacture of electronic surveillance equipment.

I have never knowingly violated, and have always strictly insisted on compliance with, the provisions of the Omnibus Act. I am firmly convinced that I am not presently violating the Act, either. However, because of its complexity, my vulnerability, the FBI's pique, the news media's pressure, and the warning relayed to me, quite frankly, I am indeed worried. Although I know full well, based on previous attempts to receive clarification of the Act, it is not the normal business of the Justice Department to give a "clean bill of health" to a citizen, I indeed wonder if there would be some way for you to advise me whether, by the wildest stretch of imagination, I am contravening any provision of the Omnibus Act. Although I am reconciled to being driven out of this business, I desperately hope that I will not have to go through a trial in the process.

As mentioned previously, I also manufacture clandestine bomb detection equipment, again, having done this for federal and local agencies. Through a rather lengthy chain of events, the FBI now heads the National Bomb Program. Attempts to contact the FBI immediately after the LaGuardia Airport explosion (which occurred well after my congressional testimony) resulted in the most callous response I have ever received to one of my offers of assistance. The implications are hideous and further support my desire to resolve the issues as promptly as possible.

As a citizen who has consistently demonstrated his support of the law enforcement community and, therefore, his country, I need your help. Any assistance will be sincerely appreciated.

Respectfully,

Martin L. Kaiser
President

The essence of Levi's response was: *You do what you think is correct, and if you're wrong, we'll arrest you.*

Not a very comforting answer. A week later, I telephoned Clarence Kelley, who had succeeded Hoover as FBI director, and requested an appointment. Kelley agreed to meet with me two days later, March 30, 1976. Two high-ranking bureau officials were in the room. One seemed to want to help resolve the problem. The other's demeanor indicated he was not the least bit pleased with what I had done.

I reminded Kelley of my seven years of loyal service and supply to the bureau in the countermeasure, electronic surveillance, and bomb detection equipment area. I apologized for the problems that I had inadvertently caused the bureau by my testimony, but I explained that I had testified factually and truthfully.

"I did not create the issue of price markups of my equipment by the U.S. Recording Company," I told him. "I simply told the truth as I knew it. And since then I've essentially been punished for telling the truth."

I told Kelley I had asked for the meeting because the FBI's treatment of me as a pariah was resulting in a huge economic loss for my company. It was also resulting in a loss of valuable technology development by me in the bomb detection area. I emphasized my significant contribution to law enforcement and national security in the products that I made and had sold to the bureau in the past.

Kelley listened in silence without any reaction or facial expression. When I finished speaking, he leaned forward and spoke in a soft voice.

"Mr. Kaiser, do you have the names of individuals within the FBI," he asked, "who are supposedly behind this campaign to discredit you and tell other intelligence agencies not to do business with you?"

"No," I said. "but I've been warned by various sources within the intelligence community that the FBI will retaliate by charging me with some violation of Title III of the wiretapping statute of the Omnibus Crime Act."

Kelley looked at the other two agents and then back at me.

"I have no knowledge of any actions related to these allegations," said Kelley. "I'm sorry, but without names of individuals within this organization or details of their actions in pursuing this alleged retaliation, I'm afraid I can't help you."

With that statement, the meeting was over. Kelley stood and

came over to shake my hand, and his secretary escorted me out of the office. As I walked out of the FBI headquarters, I reran the memory of his plausible denial in my head—*I have no knowledge of any actions* . . . It must be a phrase they teach all new FBI recruits at the academy. Without knowledge that an action or a crime has been committed, you cannot be held liable or culpable for those actions.

Did he actually think I would give him the names of the assassins while the assassins were still walking around?

In fact, there was some proof that the FBI had taken action to stop purchasing equipment from me shortly after my National Wiretap Commission testimony. I only discovered this three years later through a Freedom of Information Act (FOIA) request during the discovery phase of my subsequent trial in North Carolina.

In an FBI memo dated 4-6-76, Bill Harward, the agent I had dealt with regularly in the Technical Lab section of the bureau, was interviewed following my testimony before the commission regarding the purchase of some of my eavesdropping equipment. The memo was dated approximately one week after my meeting with Clarence Kelley. Harward was later promoted to Section Chief of the Radio Engineering Section at the FBI labs.

The third paragraph of the memo read:

He [Harward] noted that there was a purchase in progress from Kaiser during October 1975 approximately around the time Kaiser appeared before the House Select Committee on Intelligence matters. This requisition involved the proposed purchase of a monitoring device which would have been approximately a $700 to $800 item. After Kaiser testified before the aforementioned Committee, Harward received a telephone call from G. Speights McMichael (Chief Procurement Officer) who indicated he felt it would not be wise to make this purchase from Kaiser in view of his appearance before the Committee. McMichael asked Harward for his *opinion and Harward agreed that it would not be wise for such a purchase to be made while the Committee hearings were going on and as a result of Kaiser's allegations concerning the FBI.*

I should remind the reader that it was on Bill Harward's desk back in 1972 that I had first seen evidence of price markups of my equipment by U.S. Recording Company. Harward had basically stopped talking to me several months before my testimony except for a time when I called him to ask if I could come over and show him a new surveillance product. He told me it wasn't "worth your time to come over here" and hung up. Harward later denied ever saying that, but I remember it vividly.

Harward also made it known among his colleagues at the FBI labs that he thought my equipment had "never been of the highest quality." This statement was included in the memo previously mentioned, despite the fact that the FBI had purchased nearly $200,000 of my surveillance and countermeasure equipment over the years and seemed quite pleased with its effectiveness. Clearly, Bill Harward was not one of my biggest fans.

Unfortunately, my meeting with FBI Director Kelley had had the opposite effect of what I had hoped for. The word had gone out from someone in the bureau to start raising the heat on me. That meant checking out my previous sales to other agencies and overseas customers. First on the list was my Egyptian contract.

On April 14, 1976, only two weeks following my meeting with Kelley, an "Interception of Communications (IOC)" investigation was instituted at the direction of Richard L. Thornburgh, Assistant Attorney General. The investigation was to determine whether I had violated any laws requiring licenses issued by the U.S. State Department's Office of Munitions Control to sell electronic surveillance equipment (Don't forget, it was actually countersurveillance equipment.) to foreign entities. The investigation noted that I had been turned down for a license in March 1975 to sell telephone surveillance equipment and recorders to the Sultan of Oman.

This investigation was clearly an example of harassment since I had openly discussed my trip with Special Agent Marion Wright and other agents in the Baltimore field office in November 1975 before I went to Cairo. The bureau had concluded at the time that my sales to the Sadat government were not an apparent violation of the IOC statute regarding items to foreign governments on the Munitions Control list.

I received a call in early May 1976 from a special agent in the Baltimore field office, asking if he could come over to my shop and interview me regarding the Egyptian intelligence deal.

"I don't know what else I can tell you that I haven't already told the bureau," I said, "but come on over."

They came to the office on the morning of May 17. As soon as they came in the door, I took out a cassette tape recorder and placed it on my desk. I told them I intended to tape the interview and I wanted my secretary, Nancy Egan, present. The agents did not like that. They enjoyed being in control when they conducted interviews. It gave them an edge, but not that day.

I also used my 2060 desk-mounted RF detector and 2065D desk-mounted tape recorder detector to make sure they weren't wearing body transmitters or recorders. One of the agents asked me to sign an Advice of Rights Interrogation form but I refused. Before either agent could say another word, I picked up the phone and called my CIA contact, Al Montefusco, at the Crystal City office.

"Al, this is Marty Kaiser. I've got two FBI agents in my office right now and they want to question me about the Egyptian contract. What should I tell them?"

"Tell 'em to contact the agency through normal liaison channels," said Al, and he hung up.

"Sorry, guys," I told them. "This was a classified contract with the CIA and you'll have to go through normal channels with the agency to get information on it."

"Who did you just speak to on the phone?" asked one of the agents.

"That's classified too," I said.

The interview was over and I showed them to the door.

A few days later, I received a phone call from another agent in the Baltimore field office about yet another possible IOC violation. This call had to do with a review of all invoices I had issued to U.S. Recording Company, and a cross-check to determine whether I had in fact delivered the items to the FBI. The preliminary investigation listed items on ten vouchers that could not be traced to the FBI. These items included several fountain pen microphones that were wildly popular with the field agents, as well as body mikes and miniature radio transmitters built inside a three-way AC outlet plug. I was able to account for all of the items on the vouchers and the bureau backed off on that investigation.

Despite the constant harassment from the bureau, I was no longer frightened or intimidated by their actions. My confidence was growing daily to deal with anything they threw at me. That was because I knew in my heart that I had done nothing wrong. I continued to believe that someone in authority at some point would realize what was going on and stop it, that this was still America where injustice would not be tolerated, especially by the federal government. This harassment had a negative impact on my family and especially on my relationship with my wife, Carmel. The pressure of paying the bills was constant. My daughter, Carol, was in college by then and my son, Marty, was in his "in your face" mode. We were definitely not the Partridge Family.

Carmel and I were at a low point of our marriage. We spoke very little about my problems. When we did talk, we argued. I always had the feeling that she felt I had brought the problems on myself. It was around that time that I first started seeing a therapist. That period in my life brought back bitter memories of my youth, of surviving my father's constant abuse. I was trying to hold it all together like the little

Dutch boy with his finger in the dike, always worried about how long I could hold back the dam of my emotions from breaking wide open.

I believe the reason the bureau retaliated so vigorously against me was because my testimony regarding the U.S. Recording Company had unwittingly led to the exposure of a deeper corruption that existed within the bureau. An organization that prided itself on its squeaky-clean image.

On November 3, 1975, following my testimony before the National Wiretap Commission, Attorney General Levi requested FBI Director Kelley to investigate the allegations. Kelley appointed an Ad Hoc Committee to oversee an inquiry by the FBI's Inspection Division, the bureau unit ordinarily responsible for internal investigations.

Levi subsequently found the report of the Inspection Division and the Ad Hoc Committee to be incomplete and unsatisfactory. On January 2, 1976, he directed the Office of Professional Responsibility (OPR) and the Criminal Division to review the Inspection Division report and conduct a second and more independent investigation. That investigation was completed on November 11, 1976. The findings went beyond the original allegations into other areas of misconduct uncovered by the investigation.

They included:

- The use of government material and personnel services by FBI officials for their personal benefit;
- The administrative mishandling and misapplication of appropriated funds;
- The misuse of funds of the FBI Recreation Association— a private association of FBI employees;
- Improprieties in the FBI's dealing with contractors other than U.S. Recording Company.

Aside from the issues of mishandling and misuse of funds and using bureau funds and employees for personal benefit, the part of the investigation report dealing with the U.S. Recording Company is instructive, and relevant to the part I played in this investigation. The report said in part:

> *FBI officials justified the exclusive relationship (with USRC) under a specific exemption for purchases that require confidentiality for security reasons. The following facts do not support this explanation, however. For instance, from 1971 to 1975, the Bureau made $500,000 of exclusive purchases from USRC which were not marked as confidential. Much of the equipment, including transmitters, receivers and microphones, clearly fell into the 'sensitive' category, but it was not clear why other "non-sensitive" equipment was purchased exclusively from USRC. . . .*
>
> *From Fiscal Year 1971 through 1975, 60 percent of USRC's total sales were made to the Bureau. Department investigators examined 1,339 USRC sales invoices, compared the cost of each item, where available, to the price USRC charged the Bureau and found an average markup of 23.8 percent from Fiscal Year 1969 through 1975. Individual markups varied widely and were as high as 40 to 270 percent.*
>
> *In addition to high markups, by using USRC as a middleman, the Bureau was not able to purchase equipment at discount prices offered by manufacturers for direct sales on large orders. For example, in 1971, the Bureau paid USRC $147,261.50 for burglar alarm equipment which could have been purchased from a New York supplier for $81,357.00.*

One FBI agent reportedly did complain about the price the bureau was paying for USRC equipment. His reward was a denial of promotion and a transfer to the Tampa field office, where the special agent in charge was told that the agent was not a good "team" player and did not get along with other employees. Obviously, his days with the bureau were numbered.

Essentially, my testimony at the National Wiretap Commission hearings prevented further looting of public funds by the FBI through this USRC relationship. In the private sector, companies reward employees who save the company money.

My reward for blowing the whistle on the fraud involving the FBI's confidential supplier, USRC, was to be treated like a snitch and a criminal—for the crime of telling the truth.

Chapter 9

Payback

THE REMAINDER OF 1976, following my unsuccessful meeting with FBI Director Kelley, was a bad time for me professionally. My government business in the countermeasure and eavesdropping area continued to drop like a stone. My only means of survival was to expand into the corporate countermeasure market—something I had little desire or motivation for except for the money—and to try to expand my bomb detection and disposal business.

It was also a highly charged political year in Washington, which provided some distractions from my own problems. The Church-Pike Senate hearings on the misdeeds of the FBI and CIA during the 1950s, 1960s, and the Nixon years filled the headlines, as did the presidential election between President Gerald Ford and the liberal politics of the Democratic challenger, Jimmy Carter.

In July, the Israelis launched a commando raid, rescuing 103 passengers aboard a hijacked Air France jet at Uganda's Entebbe Airport. I remembered that incident because I knew that Uganda's Idi Amin was one of Frank Terpil's biggest clients. I wondered how Frank was doing.

Another story that captured headlines for several days in Washington in September was also connected to Terpil and his partner in crime, Ed Wilson, involving their deals in guns, explosives, and bomb detonators to the highest bidders.

On September 21, Orlando Letelier, the former Chilean ambassador to the United States in the Allende government, and his assistant, Ronnie Moffit, were assassinated in a car bombing as they drove to work in downtown Washington, D.C. Letelier had been jailed by the Pinochet government for a year following the U.S.-supported overthrow of the Allende government in June 1973. Upon his release in December 1974, Letelier had been offered a position with the Institute for Policy Studies in Washington. Michael Townley, an American expatriate who was a Chilean intelligence agent, would later confess and be convicted of planting the bomb under Letelier's car.

According to one report, Terpil met Townley in New York the week before Letelier's murder. In another report, a source close to Assistant U.S. Attorney Larry Barcella (who would eventually prosecute Edwin Wilson, Terpil's partner in selling C-4 explosives and sophisticated bomb detonators to Libya) said, "The bomb that killed Letelier and Moffit was of the same type the FBI believed Ed Wilson [and Terpil] was selling with the same timer mechanism." Wilson and Terpil were also tight with the right-wing Cuban exile community in Miami. It was from there that Virgilio Paz and Guillermo Novo, the two men who actually detonated the car bomb that killed Letelier and Moffit, had come.

The assassination was part of "Operation Condor," code name for a joint South American intelligence services data collection and assassination operation, centered in Chile, that included the governments of Argentina, Bolivia, Paraguay, Uruguay, and Brazil.

As disturbing as Letelier's assassination was and Terpil's possible connection with it, I put it out of my mind. I had my own problems to deal with—primarily, to earn enough to pay my mortgage and put food on the table for my family. That meant doing countermeasure surveillance sweeps of private industry facilities and fiddling around with bombs to see how good my detection equipment was. I considered my rates exorbitant, but no more than the industry was charging at the time—about $1,000 a day.

One of my strangest countermeasure sweeps came in the summer of 1976. I received a call from someone in the office of Frank Fitzsimmons, president of the Teamsters, who had succeeded Jimmy Hoffa. At this point, Hoffa had been missing and presumed dead for about twelve months. One of Fitzsimmons's assistants said they wanted me to come over to the union headquarters and conduct a full sweep of his office for telephone taps and possible room bugs.

When I started checking the phones, I realized I was hearing room conversation, not phone conversation. What I found was unprecedented in terms of interoffice telephone eavesdropping. Every phone line in the entire building—as many as one hundred— was connected to Fitzsimmons's office (formerly Hoffa's). Every phone's earpiece had been adapted to serve as a hot microphone when the phone was in the hang-up position. (Remember hook-switch bypass?)

If Hoffa or Fitzsimmons wanted to monitor the conversation in a particular office, they would simply punch a button on the main telephone console for the telephone in that area and listen on the handset or speakerphone. None of the earpiece bypasses exited the building. This was an inside job.

Fitzsimmons's people said they inherited the system from Hoffa and I had no reason to doubt them. Hoffa had a well-known reputation for being paranoid about FBI surveillance (with good reason) as well as the loyalty and motivations of others in his own union.

When I questioned one of Fitzsimmons's assistants about the curious phone bank setup, he just shrugged his shoulders as if to say nothing surprised him. If the FBI had any taps on the phone lines to Fitzsimmons's office, they were outside the building and difficult to detect. Most court-ordered wiretaps were conducted from the local phone exchange. I did notice a very large phone trunk cable that left the building, but there was no way of knowing where it went to or came from.

As for room bugs, I found none, but that didn't surprise me. Hoffa was pretty savvy about countermeasures. I had heard from others in the business that he had his people sweep the offices on a regular basis. While I was there, Fitzsimmons's people asked me about installing a tape recorder detector on the large table in the conference room. I gave them a proposal, but nothing ever came of it.

The riots and deaths of inmates and hostages at prisons in Attica, New York, in 1971 and McAlester, Oklahoma, in the summer of 1973 indirectly created a market for a new communication system that I built in the late 1970s. In reviewing the ultimate failures that led to the hostage deaths in those prison riots, a critical and common problem was the lack of an effective communication system between the hostage takers and police negotiators.

During the late 1970s, I taught countermeasures and electronic surveillance techniques at the Pennsylvania State Police Academy in Hershey. One day, Captain Jim Regan showed me a crude hostage negotiation system that was put together by Western Electric. It consisted of two telephones, a battery box, and a wire reel. Jim and I discussed what was needed to improve on that model to make the system really effective. The result was my Model 7080 Hostage Negotiation System.

It consisted of two rotary-dial telephones plus a "throw telephone," a handset connected to a 150-foot cable that could literally be tossed over a barrier to the hostage takers. If the negotiator could talk his way through the barricade and into the hostage area, the system could be connected with an entire telephone to be given to the hostage taker to communicate with negotiators. The "throw telephone" or the complete telephone set was wired with a hot microphone to monitor room or area conversations of the hostage takers when the handset was hung up.

The Pennsylvania State Police bought the first model, which has since been updated with current telephone technology. The system was first used in the Graterford Prison Riot in October 1981. On that day, I was teaching at the academy in Hershey. Jim came into the classroom and asked if I had any tube microphones at my plant in Cockeysville, Maryland. I told him I did. A few minutes later he returned to the classroom and told me a state police helicopter was waiting outside for me. I hopped into the chopper, gave a thumbs up, and away we went to my plant about sixty miles away.

The pilot landed in a vacant lot next to my plant. I jumped out, ran inside, grabbed a couple of tube microphones, ran outside, jumped back into the chopper, and we sped back to Hershey. Jim was waiting on the landing pad. I gave him the microphones and off he went in the chopper to Graterford Prison. He later told me that they taped one of the mikes to a wooden pole and slid it up next to a drainpipe in the prisoner area to try to hear what the inmates were saying. One of them spotted the mike and promptly yanked it up, pole and all, into the cell.

Jim Regan said they were later able to use my hostage negotiation system effectively in getting the inmates to release the hostages unharmed. The system was later used successfully during a hostage situation in Jacksonville, Florida.

My bomb detection and disposal products continued to keep me afloat financially, but there was only total silence from the intelligence community in the countermeasure and surveillance marketplace. And I continued to receive my nameplates back in the mail from anonymous persons.

Then in January 1977, I received phone call from my Northwestern Bank client. It had been nearly five years since I had first met Ed Duncan, the chairman of the bank. The man on the phone was Gwyn Bowers, the bank's executive vice president, calling on behalf of Duncan.

Bowers told me the FBI had replaced the IRS as the bank's chief antagonist.

"They're totally disrupting the functions and operations of the bank," said Bowers. "They're terrorizing employees and managers with daily interrogations. They're using the divide-and-conquer route to demoralize and frighten the staff."

"What do you need from me?" I asked, wondering if Bowers and Duncan knew about my estrangement from the bureau.

"We need three long-play recorders," he said, "and a bunch of pocket tape recorders for each manager to record the conversations they have with the FBI agents. It is legal to do that, correct?"

"That's right," I told him, "as long as there is single-party consent."

Bowers flew up to my plant in one of the bank's private jets, bought some of the recorders, and returned the same day to North Carolina. Several weeks later, Bowers called again and said there was one scenario they weren't prepared for. The FBI had commandeered an office in the bank where they were conducting interviews.

"We need to know what kinds of questions they're asking and the answers they're getting," said Bowers. "Our people are being intimidated and threatened by them."

"What are you asking me to do, Gwyn?"

"We want you to put a bug in the room where the FBI is conducting those interviews," he said.

On the surface, this request appeared to offer an opportunity for a little payback for the treatment I'd received from my former customers. However, a faint voice inside my brain kept repeating the warning I had been given after my testimony before the National Wiretap Commission.

"If the FBI can't get you directly, they will get you through one of your customers . . ."

On the other hand, I was still incredibly angry. These bastards had wantonly destroyed my reputation, and this job presented an opportunity to get even. As long as I adhered strictly to the state and federal laws regarding Intercept of Communications, I felt I was on solid ground. I knew that North Carolina was a single-party-consent state in terms of monitoring conversations. But I was still suspicious of Gwyn Bowers. I had already sold the bank plenty of positive electronic surveillance equipment in the past and had trained their tech guy, Jerry Starr, about how to use it.

"Why do you need me to do it, Gwyn?" I asked. "Jerry knows how to do it."

"We need you to do this, Marty," he told me. "You're the man."

"On one condition," I said.

"What's that?"

"That you or Ed Duncan be in the interview sessions when the taping is going on."

"No problem," said Bowers.

I quoted Bowers a price for the hardware and services and we had a deal.

Three weeks later, on Saturday, April 23, I flew down to North Carolina on the bank's private jet. The bank gave me a car to use. I checked into a nearby motel and called Bowers. He came over and took me to the bank to show me the room they wanted bugged.

The room was adjacent to an empty 40-foot-by-40-foot area in one corner of the building. Large windows covered the front and one side of the room. The inside of the office was absolutely sterile. All it contained was a desk, a chair, and a telephone sitting on the floor. The FBI was no stranger to electronic surveillance environments.

Initially, I felt the agents had most likely bugged the room. On that assumption, I opted not to do a sweep, to save time. As I looked out the window, I saw a car on cinder blocks pointed directly at me from the parking lot across the street. I made a mental note to check it out.

Bowers wanted me to run a cable from the FBI interview room to his office on the second floor. When I realized the length of cable it would take to reach his office, I knew I would need some additional equipment and a lot more cable to carry sound from the interview office to a tape recorder in Bowers's office. I decided on a different approach: to use a spare set of wires in the existing telephone cable.

Bowers invited me to come to his house for a drink and I grudgingly agreed. I had a bad feeling about him. He said he needed some advice about why the base coil of the antenna on the citizen band radio in his car kept burning up. When he popped his trunk, I saw the problem.

He had a 1,000-watt linear amplifier that was way beyond the legal limit of five watts for CB radios. I suggested that his amplifier was too powerful and that he should reduce the power to the legal wattage. When we got to his house, he offered me a mason jar of moonshine. I didn't grab it, but merely put my palm out and he placed the jar on it. I handed it back to him without drinking it. Later, following my indictment, I recalled having my palm printed by the FBI as well as my fingers. I thought it was highly irregular at the time and subsequently wondered if my print possibly had been obtained from the jar of moonshine.

Before he drove me back to the motel, Bowers showed me his ham radio setup, which was also way above the legal power limits. Outside, I had seen his stacked MoonRaker antennas. Adding the effective amplification of those antennas to the 2,000 watts he was running would have put his effective output power well beyond 250,000 watts. I was surprised he didn't toast his neighbor's bread before it was put on the table. He handed me the microphone and asked if I wanted to talk on it. The last thing I wanted to do was lose my amateur radio license.

"No, thanks," I told him.

I had dinner at a local catfish restaurant and went back to the motel, where I watched a little TV. Before I went to bed, I pulled a couple of resistors, capacitors, and a transistor out of the 1059 pre-amplifier in my countermeasure kit and soldered them to a tiny microphone the size of a carpenter ant. I hung the completed assembly over the bathtub and listened to it from the end of the bed. It worked great.

The next morning I drove over to the bank and met Bowers there. On the way I stopped by the junked car I had seen earlier. It had no tires and was still sitting on cinder blocks. It was covered with dust and debris and obviously had been sitting somewhere else for a long time—but not there. The tipoff was the absence of a rain drip line around the car. I took out my contact microphone and placed it on the car. Suddenly, I heard the unmistakable sound of a time-lapse camera. The FBI was monitoring the room after all.

"C'mon, you guys," I said aloud. "You can do better than this."

I met Bowers and we went into the FBI interview room. As we walked into the room, one of the security guards keyed in at one of the security checkpoints. Bowers told me to make myself invisible. Then he walked over to the checkpoint and told the guard everything was all right.

I installed the microphone and the preamplifier inside the telephone jack cover connected to the red-yellow and green-yellow wires in the cable bundle. Red and green are standard single-line telephone wire colors, and the background color of yellow made them stand out clearly. I then went to the nearest frame room (the closet where all telephone lines are connected together) and found the cable coming from the telephone block I had just wired. I placed my 1059 amplifier across the red-yellow and green-yellow wires, said "Mellotaste" (that's the way Tom Walsh and I would say "Hello test") and heard myself as clear as a bell.

I ran the same-color wires to a frame room near Bowers's office and then to Bowers's office itself. I drilled a hole through the credenza where the wires were connected to a tape recorder. I checked out the sound coming from it and could hear my voice from across the bank. It was "five by five"—ham radio lingo for crystal clear. A sense of pride came over me as it always did when I completed a task. I had earned my money—$3,500. It never occurred to me that I would never collect it.

Before leaving the building that Sunday morning to check out of the motel and go to the airport, I took Bowers aside one more time to remind him about the single-party-consent requirement.

TOP LEFT: Me, age 7 (right), and my brothers, Al, 10 (background), and Ron, 4 (left). We are standing on our dock at Lake Nuangola in the Pocono Mountains, where we used to spend our summers.

TOP RIGHT: A photo of Carmel and me in 1955 going to her prom following the summer we met. It was love at first sight.

BOTTOM: I'm having fun with my ham radio rig at age 13 in my family's house in Wilkes Barre, Pennsylvania. Ham radio helped me overcome my lack of confidence and served as a refuge from my father's abuse.

All photos are part of the author's collection.

TOP : When I started working at RCA Labs in New Jersey in 1957, I switched from ham radio to ham TV. Here I am with my homemade TV station and camera.

LEFT: My Over-the-Horizon Radar system that I set up and ran in Barbados in 1963.

RIGHT: The 100-feet-high by 150-feet-long aerial for my Over-the-Horizon radar system in Barbados. The Soviets were so curious about it that they flew over it and photographed it.

BOTTOM: Working hard at my workbench in Cockeysville, Maryland, where I designed and built hundreds of eavesdropping, countermeasure, and bomb detection devices over my 30+ years in the business.

TOP: An abandoned landing craft allegedly left on a Cayman beach by a CIA strike team after an aborted operation during the Bay of Pigs Invasion in 1961. It was being used as a dive boat in 1975.

LEFT: Ex-CIA fugitive from justice, Frank Terpil. Despite all of the allegations against him, Frank was one of my closest friends during the 1970s.

TOP: I'm shaking hands with FBI Director Clarence M. Kelley during happier days at a law enforcement expo in 1974 when the bureau was still one of my biggest customers. Less than a year later, following my testimony before the National Wiretap Commission, my relationship with the FBI would take a darker turn. BOTTOM: A photo of me doing a sweep, circa 1974.

RIGHT: Bugs and mics I have produced next to one of my trademark cards, a spook's NO BOMBS! matchbook. The FBI's favorite fountain pen mic (left). A typical drop bug with a mile range that could be safety-pinned behind a drapery (top). A tube mic usually pushed through a hole in a light switch or wall socket box into an adjoining room (right). On the NO BOMBS! man is a typical miniature mic with hair-thin wire leading to the miniature amplifier that sent the signal through miles of wire.

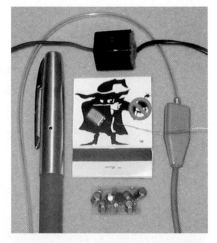

CENTER: I'm (far right) posing with other witnesses prior to my testimony before the House Select Committee on Intelligence, October 1975, which would result in one of the greatest scandals in FBI history. BOTTOM: Photos from a *Newsweek* magazine article (Dec. 15, 1975) that described the investigation of exorbitant price hikes of surveillance gear from me and other suppliers by the FBI using a "cut-out" operation.

My close friend Emil "Bill" Behre kneeling beside the remains of a car engine we blasted 30 feet into the ground with a 6-pound shape charge at a meeting of the International Association of Bomb Technicians and Investigators (IABTI).

Pennsylvania State Police Captain Jim Regan (left) and I posed with members of my State Police Academy class on eavesdropping and electronic surveillance countermeasures.

G. Gordon Liddy (right) and I at a Surveillance Expo in Washington, D.C., in the mid-1990s. Liddy spoke about his experiences during his 5-year sentence at Danbury Federal Prison following his conviction for conspiracy and burglary in the Watergate complex.

On the set of *Enemy of the State* with producer Jerry Bruckheimer (left) and Gene Hackman (right). Hackman played the role of Brill, a rogue NSA agent, and imitated some of my mannerisms. I designed many of the eavesdropping devices used in the film.

Former Congresswoman Helen Bentley (R-MD) and I remembering our past association. I did periodic sweeps of her office and home during her 10-year tenure in Congress. She tried to resolve my problems with the FBI, but was told that "the problem went too far up."

Despite the abuse my dad inflicted on me during my youth, he was a huge influence in my life. I erected a bronze plaque below the house he built at Lake Nuangola after his death at age 94. It was where I spent some of the happiest days of my life as a boy. I kneel at it often and ask him if I'm doing okay.

"Gwyn, as long as you have a consenting party in that room, you're good to go."

He nodded as if he understood, but he obviously wasn't listening. Or he had already decided he had no intention of abiding my by admonition.

"Will they find it, Marty?" he asked.

"Of course they will, Gwyn, if they look for it."

"How can you be so sure?"

"Because they use my countermeasure equipment," I told him, "and I trained most of them."

In retrospect, it took the FBI a lot longer than I expected to figure out they were bugged—nearly four months. But it took only a few minutes to find the bug in the phone jack after they had taken maximum advantage of it. I still wondered whether the entire assignment from Northwestern Bank was an FBI sting to set me up for the criminal indictment. Later, I realized that the FBI's failure to find the bug quicker was arrogance as much as anything else.

By the time of the Northwestern Bank assignment, I had moved from fear to anger and the need for revenge. These bastards were systematically destroying my business. I had tried to be reasonable and had made repeated efforts to resolve the matter amicably. I had written to everyone I knew in a position of authority asking for a fair hearing and had been dismissed. I felt it was time to go on the offensive. I heartily embraced this opportunity to engage them. I was not worried about the outcome because I had done everything by the book.

Ironically, the agents who found the bug did so with my countermeasure kit that I had sold them through U.S. Recording Company.

Part 3

Trial by Fire

Chapter 10

A Gathering Storm

THE YEAR 1977 was a great time for techies like me, offering some interesting distractions from my problems.

Two guys name Steve—Jobs and Wozniak—invented the Apple II computer, Atari introduced the first video game console, and Dennis Hayes invented the modem—that electronic magic that converts analog and digital signals and gave the world its first true global connection. For space aficionados, the Voyager spacecraft was launched on its maiden trip to other galaxies.

But those distractions wouldn't last too long

In March, two veteran FBI agents—Thomas Brereton and Zachary Lowe—had begun an investigation of Ed Duncan Jr., chairman and president of Northwestern Bank, regarding allegations of bank fraud and embezzlement. The agents were also investigating charges that Duncan had planted hidden listening devices to eavesdrop on the conversations of IRS agents who had conducted an investigation into possible tax law violations at the bank two years earlier.

I knew the IRS had investigated Duncan in the early 1970s and I suspected they were the ones who planted the bug I helped to locate a couple of years earlier. But I didn't know to what extent Duncan had also been wiring many of the offices in the bank for sound and eavesdropping on his employees to check on their loyalty. If I had known the extent of his audio surveillance, I might have had second thoughts about taking on any new assignments for him. But that was not all.

A year earlier, in 1976, the IRS had sent information to the Justice Department "relative to a possible obstruction of justice violations occurring in 1974 in connection" with the IRS investigation of Duncan. Based on an FBI document my attorney obtained through discovery, Duncan allegedly threatened an officer in one of his companies with sexual blackmail if he talked to the IRS about financial improprieties involving Northwestern Bank. In a meeting with the employee and four attorneys representing Duncan and Northwestern, including a former Assistant U.S. Attorney who later confirmed the threat, Duncan flatly warned the employee "that he was not going to talk to anyone." And if he did, Duncan said, he would send a videotape to the man's wife of him having sex with a woman in a Raleigh motel room. For unknown reasons, the FBI decided not to pursue those allegations. As it turned out, they would discover that Northwestern Bank was a target-rich environment of potentially new criminal violations.

Agents Brereton and Lowe were based in the FBI's Greensboro, North Carolina, office, and both were considered to be specialists in white-collar crimes. Both men had more than fifteen years of bureau service. I had never met either man before, but they would eventually be given extensive background information on me, my former relationship with the bureau, and my testimony before the National Wiretap Commission.

When Brereton and Lowe arrived at Northwestern Bank in Wilkesboro to start their investigation of possible BF&E (bank fraud and embezzlement), George Collins, the bank president, provided them with a room to conduct interviews with bank supervisors and staff—the surveillance target given to me by Gwyn Bowers and described in the previous chapter.

It's standard procedure for FBI agents to conduct a countermeasure sweep of any space where they are conducting investigations or holding confidential discussions with interview subjects or among themselves. Brereton said that soon after he and Lowe were assigned the work space at the bank, both Collins, the bank president, and T. V. Dunn, a lawyer for the bank, asked the agents if they did not routinely check rooms in which they worked for bugs. Brereton also testified that he had "numerous" conversations with other bank employees about whether the agents had checked for bugs.

He would later testify that his partner, Lowe, checked the phone, desk, and walls in the office where they were conducting interviews to determine whether "this apprehension expressed to us by employees had become a reality." But Lowe evidently found nothing suspicious.

The agents did not seriously suspect that they were being bugged until July 6 or July 7, when they talked with a bank employee who told them of the capabilities of certain people at the bank to carry out electronic surveillance, namely Jerry Starr, the bank's security officer, whom I had trained and to whom I had sold a variety of countermeasure equipment during the past several years.

Lowe would later testify that he found what he considered "illegal bugging equipment" in Starr's possession on July 11, the day before they found the bug I had planted. The only problem with that description was that the equipment was not illegal if the "single-consent rule" was followed—that at least one person in the room being monitored electronically knew the conversations were being recorded. It was a phrase that I had repeated to Bowers over and over when I planted the bug on April 24.

On the evening of July 12, with a court order in hand, agents Brereton and Lowe returned to the bank with Special Agent Edward J. Brennan, an FBI technician skilled in electronic countermeasures, and a technician from Southwestern Bell. Ironically, Brennan was using my countermeasure kit to find the bug, just as I had predicted to Gwyn Bowers several months before.

It took Brennan less than fifteen minutes to find the microphone hidden in the telephone jack. The agents asked the telephone company employee if the preamplifier and transmitter were standard telephone equipment and he dutifully answered in the negative. But at that point, the agents could not find the alleged tape recordings of conversations that came from the room bug. The tape recordings, which would surface later, would prove to be one of the prosecution's most dubious pieces of evidence of the alleged eavesdropping of the two agents.

In a deposition taken during the civil suit, Brereton described his initial reaction to the discovery that he and Lowe had been bugged for nearly three months without their knowledge. His anger and embarrassment over the bugging would later be directed toward me.

That night we knew what happened, there was tremendous anger. You wouldn't believe the anger that took place that night inside of me when I found out; when the agent told me there was a hot mike in that room . . .

The bank's attorney, Wesley Corle, turned to me and said, "You don't really think your conversations were private do you?" and started laughing. And it infuriated me, and I turned to him and said, "Yes, I did, and if you don't think so you're a goddamned fool."

He then walked over to me and said, "You've had your way for a long time now." He said, "But your day's coming. You're going to get it."

And I wanted to go get him and my supervisor said, "No, you stay away from him." And I said, "I want him out of this goddamned bank. I don't want to see him again because he knows what's going on. He's part of it."

And that night there was tremendous anger and frustration. Bowers sat there the whole night smirking at me when we pulled all the mikes out of the wall and traced it to

*his office. I had no authority to arrest him. I didn't have the
Department of Justice say, "Okay, arrest the guy."*

*And if you want to feel how it is to know someone's
done this to you and you can't arrest them and they're
smirking at you the whole time, it's very, very frustrating."*

But Agent Brereton's frustration would be short-lived.

Within three days of the discovery of the bug in the bank office
where the agents were conducting their interviews, Ed Duncan, the
bank president, would be charged with two counts of violations of
Intercept of Communications of IRS agents during 1971 and 1972,
and six counts of misapplication and conversion of bank funds in the
amount of $240,000 for personal use. He was arrested shortly after
the charges were filed.

Essentially, Duncan was charged with overdrafts in his personal
checking account and putting money into the account later to cover
them. Bowers and Starr would also be charged in connection with the
bugging of the IRS agents, but released on their own recognizance.
But Duncan would spend the next two days in the Guilford County
jail while attorneys argued for a reduction of bail that had been set at
$800,000.

The FBI and Brereton were sending him a message: they were
in control.

Duncan's problems with the IRS were nothing new, however.

According to a brief filed in October 1977 by the law firm representing Duncan—Smith, Moore, Smith, Schell & Hunter—he had
been a target of U.S. government prosecution since 1966, allegedly
due to a civil court case that the IRS lost to Edwin Duncan Sr.,
Duncan's father and the founder of Northwestern Bank. The brief further charged that the FBI had adopted a "studied course of conduct
designed to intimidate witnesses," including employees of Northwestern Bank.

The brief went on to allege that Special Agent Brereton "had consciously interjected himself between quarreling management factions at Northwestern Bank to successfully cause to have" Duncan fired as chairman of the board of the bank. He was forced to resign from the board of Northwestern Bank shortly after he was indicted on the initial charges of bugging the IRS agents.

The brief also alleged that Agent Brereton was to have conspired with an IRS agent in acquiring information from IRS that was in violation of Title 18, USC, Section 6103, which prohibits the disclosure of information by the IRS to other investigative agencies. The brief from Duncan's law firm further alleged that leaks within the FBI had "started a media campaign to cause embarrassment and prejudice in defense of Duncan" that led to his removal as board chairman of the bank.

As a final shot across the FBI's bow, Duncan's attorneys argued that their client had done nothing different than Bert Lance, Director of the Office of Management and Budget under President Jimmy Carter, and should therefore receive the same treatment, a not guilty verdict.

Before taking the OMB job under Carter, Lance had been president and chairman of the Calhoun First National Bank, Calhoun, Georgia. But a 1977 Justice Department investigation into irregular practices at that bank forced Lance to resign the OMB post under a cloud. He was later charged with ten counts alleging misapplications of bank funds in loans to relatives and friends and two counts alleging false financial statements. A federal jury found Lance not guilty of all charges.

The FBI denied all of the accusations charged by Duncan's attorneys and pointedly stated that the law firm representing Duncan was the same firm that represented a number of bankers in a major BF&E case in Durham, North Carolina, in 1976 who were later convicted. That statement could be interpreted to mean that Duncan's law firm specialized in representing bankers charged with fraud and embezzlement. The assumption of guilt was loud and clear.

"The case agent involved in the Durham, NC, case was SA

Thomas J. Brereton," the memo noted—the same agent leading the charge against Duncan and me.

This last statement could be interpreted two ways: that Agent Brereton had a successful track record in investigating white-collar crime cases against bankers, or that Brereton demonstrated a predisposed attitude toward Duncan—and by association, me. The FBI's attitude toward Duncan could be summed up succinctly: he was guilty!

Bowers and Starr would be charged along with Duncan of conspiracy to bug Agents Brereton and Lowe. My name would be added to theirs a few weeks later.

Unfortunately, I was totally oblivious to any of these events from the July evening when they found the bug until early December when I received word of my indictment by the grand jury. I didn't even get a courtesy call from Duncan or Bowers, but they clearly were occupied with their own legal problems.

The first indication of trouble came to me in late July. I received a letter from the U.S. District Court for the Middle District of North Carolina, in Winston-Salem, requiring my presence before a grand jury in early August. The grand jury was convened to investigate certain allegations involving the Intercept of Communications of FBI agents conducting an investigation into bank fraud and embezzlement allegations involving officers of Northwestern Bank in Wilkesboro, North Carolina.

I had not been charged with anything yet, but the message was clear. The battle was drawn. The FBI was engaged. I needed an attorney, one who had previously dealt with the FBI and was not intimidated by their tactics.

I called some friends in the countermeasure business who were still taking my calls, and asked for recommendations. One name came up frequently—Bernard "Bud" Fensterwald Jr.

Fensterwald had established a reputation as one of the preeminent JFK assassination conspiracy researchers. He founded the

Assassination Records and Research Center and the Committee to Investigate Assassinations. He also represented James Earl Ray, the convicted assassin of Martin Luther King Jr., as well as James McCord, one of the Watergate burglars, and Jack Anderson's associate, Les Whitten.

Whitten had been arrested and charged by the FBI for receiving stolen classified government documents involving a takeover at the Bureau of Indian Affairs in Washington during the Watergate investigations.

Bud Fensterwald had also represented Mitch WerBell, an arms dealer and codesigner of the MAC-10 submachine gun (and a potential customer of mine), as well as numerous people in the intelligence community in their various legal struggles with the government.

As far as I was concerned, Bud was the perfect attorney to have in a battle with the FBI. He had no illusions about government agencies and their rush to judgment against innocent, law-abiding citizens. I called him, explained my problem, and he agreed to represent me. I told him I had been subpoenaed to appear before a grand jury in Winston-Salem on August 8 and I wanted to meet with him to prepare my testimony.

"What testimony?" Bud asked.

"You know, before the grand jury," I said.

"Don't worry about it," he said. "Just read the card and don't say anything else."

"What card?"

"The one that instructs you to invoke the Fifth Amendment of the Constitution, which gives all citizens the right to refuse to answer questions that they consider self-incriminating."

Fensterwald, paralegal Marc Feldman, and I headed to Winston-Salem on August 7 for my appearance before the grand jury. Before leaving, I typed up two 3x5 cards with the Fifth Amendment statement on them. Prior to entering the grand jury room, Fensterwald told me to give them only my name and address and then "read the card."

I must have read the first card sixty to seventy times before I ceremoniously set it aside, pulled out the second card for comic relief, and started reading it. Some members of the jury laughed. One of the jurors asked whether the first card had run out of gas.

In total, I must have taken the Fifth Amendment between 150 and 175 times. Whenever I got tired, I excused myself to "converse with my attorney," but in reality to take a breather. When I reentered the jury room, Fensterwald would remind me to "read the card."

When I was finally dismissed about five hours later, Marc Feldman grabbed me by the arm and took me into an empty room.

"Marty, tell me exactly what you saw in the grand jury room," he said excitedly.

I told him that on my immediate right was the U.S. Attorney (Henry Michaux Jr.), the stenographer, the grand jurors, and finally the jury foreman's table at which sat two men. One was a gray-haired fellow and the other was Special Agent Thomas Brereton.

Feldman gasped and told me to repeat what I had just said. I did and he said, "That could be grounds for a mistrial. I have to speak to Bud."

A couple of days later I received a copy of a motion from Fensterwald to the court asking that the charges be dismissed due to improprieties by the FBI. Essentially, the motion stated that it's a violation of law for an investigating agent to be present during grand jury proceedings when a witness is questioned.

Judge Hiram H. Ward ordered a hearing on the motion. Since we expected Brereton to deny that he had been in the grand jury room, we asked the judge to provide us with a list of jurors so that we could question them under oath regarding his presence. The judge provided the list but we never got the opportunity to question the jurors.

I took the stand and under oath made my statement that I had seen Special Agent Brereton in the room during my questioning. Brereton then took the stand and swore under oath that he had not been in the room. He should have stopped talking, but his ego simply would not let him remain silent.

"Did you see me go in and out of the grand jury room," Brereton asked Fensterwald.

"No," said Fensterwald.

"I was in the library when your client was before the grand jury," Brereton added.

We then hired an ex-FBI agent, Don Wilson, to call each member of the grand jury to see if they could confirm what I had seen with my own eyes. Wilson had retired from the bureau shortly after the initial investigation at Northwestern Bank began. He also knew Brereton well. But the effort failed when every grand juror who had been called by Wilson then contacted Agent Brereton and told him of the inquiries by Wilson.

I wanted to ask the Judge to follow up Brereton's statement that he had been in the library during my testimony by asking him at precisely what time he had been in the library and in the corridor leading to the library. The door immediately behind the jury foreman's desk led into the corridor that ended at the library. Judge Ward clearly did not want to go there.

He turned to me and said, "Mr. Kaiser. You're mistaken, honest or otherwise."

He whacked the gavel and that was that. It was now pretty clear that this would be an uphill battle for the truth.

I carefully folded the list containing the names and addresses of the grand jury members and slid it into my pocket. I knew it would come in handy later.

A couple of weeks after I appeared before the grand jury, the government handed down indictments of Ed Duncan for bank fraud and embezzlement and directing others to eavesdrop on the conversations of IRS agents at the bank from 1971 to 1973.

Gwyn Bowers and Jerry Starr were also indicted for the eavesdropping of the IRS agents. On that same day the government indicted Duncan on separate charges for conspiracy to eavesdrop on agents Brereton and Lowe from April to July 1977. Bowers and Starr were also named in that indictment.

My name was mentioned as the source of the clandestine transmitters, but for the moment I was still in the clear.

Duncan went to trial on September 26, 1977, on the BF&E charges and bugging the IRS agents and he was found guilty on October 3. Sentencing was delayed pending his trial on the six-count indictment that involved the bugging of agents Brereton and Lowe. Bowers and Starr would plead guilty to the charges the following week.

On November 11, Duncan was sentenced to three years in prison on each of two counts of Intercept of Communications, two years on each of six counts of misapplication of funds with sentences to run concurrently, and $22,000 in total fines. Bowers received thirty months' suspended sentence, a $5,000 fine, and five years' probation. Starr received eighteen months' suspended sentence, a $1,000 fine, and five years' probation.

The FBI memo from the Charlotte field office informing headquarters in Washington of the developments in the prosecution of Duncan contained the following sentence:

It is interesting to note that this is the first instance in the history of the FBI that any individual has been indicted for illegally monitoring oral conversations of FBI agents.

This statement was significant for two reasons: (1) the fact that the FBI resident agency in North Carolina included it at all implied that the bureau viewed these charges with particular distaste, and (2) this acknowledgment of the rarity of these charges tacitly communicated a special motivation to its field agents to get a conviction of those responsible for these embarrassing actions.

There is an irony here that is also significant. In the majority of clandestine eavesdropping cases, the bureau is the source of the bugging, not the recipient. In other words, they are usually the bugger, not the buggee. This time the shoe was on the other foot and the bureau wanted to send a message that it would not tolerate such actions against it.

As I indicated earlier, bad news always seemed to visit me by phone. I can't say I wasn't expecting it regarding the Northwestern Bank fiasco. But I still held out hope that the bureau would realize I had done nothing wrong and wouldn't waste money on a wild goose chase. No such luck.

On December 5, 1978, the phone rang. It was Fensterwald calling to tell me we had a date for my arraignment in North Carolina a week later. At first I was angry, then in denial, and finally deeply depressed—all within a matter of moments. I should have known they would not give me a pass on bugging them. The FBI is like a junkyard dog that smells fresh meat.

Fensterwald and I flew to Winston-Salem and arrived at the courthouse early on the morning of December 12. As we stood in the hallway outside the courtroom, Henry Michaux Jr., the U.S. Attorney assigned to prosecute my case, sent word that he wanted to see us in his office.

When we entered his office, Michaux was sitting behind his desk. We chatted with him for a few minutes about our trip and the weather. Suddenly, Special Agent Brereton walked in. It was the first time I had actually met Brereton, though Fensterwald had pointed him out to me during my testimony before the grand jury months earlier. He was about an inch taller than me, with a round face, dark close-cropped hair, and the standard-issue FBI gray suit—it must have been one of Hoover's sartorial requirements. His manner reminded me of a self-righteous bureaucrat who delighted in noting the most minor infractions of those who came before him seeking counsel.

Michaux got up and took a seat next to us in front of his desk. Brereton took over Michaux's chair behind the desk and started talking to us as if he were the prosecuting attorney.

"Well, gentlemen," said Brereton, "You've had ample time to study the indictment. I believe you would agree that the only logical response for your client is to plead guilty."

I couldn't believe my ears. I wanted to scream NO FUCKING

WAY, but Bud simply looked at me—he knew my blood pressure was rising—and shook his head. He turned to look at Brereton and then at Michaux.

"Thank you, gentlemen," Bud told them, rising from his chair. "Now if you'll excuse us, we're due in court."

We left the room without another word.

As we waited in the courtroom for my name to be called and my plea to be entered, I wondered if Brereton had any idea what a guilty plea would mean to me. Not only would I lose any security clearance I now had, further affecting my ability to get work within the intelligence community, I would lose my charter membership in the International Association of Bomb Technicians and Investigators (IABTI). I would forfeit my passport and ability to travel outside the country, my right to vote, my amateur radio license that I had held for twenty-five years, and my "plank" status at the Navy Explosive Ordnance School in Indian Head, Maryland, where I taught on a regular basis.

But most of all I would lose my dignity and self-respect. For me that was tantamount to a death sentence.

Inside the courtroom, I was the last of twenty-two other cases on the docket. As each of the defendants entered a plea of guilty, the words reverberated inside my brain like the echo of a large bell. With each additional "guilty" verdict, I became more deeply depressed. It took all my will power not to get up and walk out of that courtroom.

But Fensterwald winked at me as if to indicate that this was all part of the government's intimidation process. He later told me that from his experience, the court would watch the defendant they wanted to harass and wait until he or she went to the bathroom. Then, the defendant's name and case would suddenly be called. When the defendant did not immediately respond, the judge would cite the person for contempt of court.

"If you have to go to the bathroom," he advised, "make it quick; we'll cover for you."

At the end of the afternoon, I finally had my day in court. I uttered the words "Not guilty" in a firm voice to the three charges filed against me: planting an illegal eavesdropping device in the bank boardroom, conspiring with Duncan to bug the FBI agents, and transporting an illegal eavesdropping device across state lines. The real punishment of the arraignment experience was that my "legal money meter"—at $400 an hour—had been running for the entire day. I also had to surrender my passport to the judge. The FBI convinced him that I was a flight risk.

When I returned home to Cockeysville that night, I made myself a double martini and sat down to tell my wife, Carmel, what had happened.

"What do you intend to do?" she asked.

"Obviously, I'm innocent," I told her, "and I'm going to fight the bastards with every ounce of strength and anger I have."

"What about the cost?"

"Yes, it's probably going to cost a lot of money, but I don't care about that. I'm innocent and I'm going to defend myself."

Carmel silently shook her head and I knew what was coming.

"What do you think I should do?" I asked, hoping she would be on my side in this.

"I think you should plead guilty to a lesser offense," she said, "go to jail if you have to, and put it behind us. Then the FBI will finally leave you alone."

"No way, Carm," I said. "If I plead guilty, they will have won. I will be out of business and they will have finally succeeded in destroying me. I would be a convicted felon in the eyes of everyone I've ever done business with. It would be the same as a death sentence. And, what's more, they will never leave me alone."

We didn't speak any more that evening, or for several days that followed, but I wasn't angry with her. We had been going through some rough times ever since my testimony before the National Wiretap Commission. I think she was simply in denial and couldn't believe or did not want to deal with what was happening. Without thinking of the ramifications of what she was suggesting, she was looking for the least painful solution, emotionally and financially.

I think we also had a different philosophical view about the indictment. Carmel felt you could never fight City Hall and win regardless of the truth. I, on the other hand, still believed in the old civil rights maxim, "The truth will set you free."

I believed, at least at that point in time, that there was still justice in our legal system and I would find it if I could just hang in there. I was also burning with anger and the need for retribution. I needed to fight them in order to keep my sanity.

Bud Fensterwald still had a couple of ideas up his sleeve that might help avoid the trial. One of them meant reliving the past and bringing up former embarrassments for the FBI that would offer them additional motivation to go after me. But I didn't give a damn anymore. If they were going to play hardball, we were going give as good as we got.

We decided to file a pretrial motion called a *qui tam* action—a civil suit brought by an individual plaintiff on behalf of the United States under the False Claims Act, charging fraud by government contractors or others and seeking the recovery of damages for the U.S. government.

The term *qui tam* comes from the Latin phrase "qui tam pro domino rege quam pro sic ipso in hoc parte sequitur." Roughly translated, it means "who sues on behalf of the king as well as for himself." A plaintiff, known as the relator, one who brings a *qui tam* suit, is someone who has uncovered fraud against the U.S. government and, by implication, U.S. taxpayers. As a reward for their efforts, relators receive a portion, between 15 and 30 percent, of the amount of money recovered, which is often substantial.

I wasn't looking for reward money but rather vindication, in the form of a dismissal of the charges against me.

Essentially, my *qui tam* lawsuit revisited the U.S. Recording Company (USRC) price markup scandal that accused several high-ranking FBI officials of a conspiracy to defraud the United States government.

The lawsuit described my role in bringing the USRC price markups to the attention of the House Select Committee on Intelligence. It described the resulting investigation by the General Accounting Office (GAO) that revealed the FBI had been purchasing surveillance gear through the USRC's noncompetitive bidding process that resulted in $750,000 sales annually. The lawsuit went on to call for a full and complete accounting of all electronic equipment sold by USRC to all of the U.S. intelligence agencies for the past ten years or more.

The lawsuit also mentioned that my business dealings with intelligence organizations included the CIA, the Secret Service, air force and army intelligence, and the Drug Enforcement Agency, as well as other agencies. The suit implied that a public trial could cause issues of national security to be revealed in open court.

Fensterwald met with U.S. Attorney Henry Michaux on January 6, 1978, and informed him that we would file the lawsuit in U.S. District Court in Washington, D.C., unless the charges against me were dismissed.

In an FBI memo dated 1/10/78, Michaux viewed my affidavit and possible civil action "as nothing more than blackmail" to get the charges dropped, and refused. Fensterwald then moved to Plan B: A motion describing my infamous history with the FBI and that the indictment against me was the "result of a vendetta by the FBI" and was not based on the facts.

We lost on that motion too. So much for criminal justice. An oxymoron after all.

The trial was set to start February 9, 1977, and there was a lot of preparatory work to do. My job was to contact the character witnesses my legal team had chosen and give them an approximate appearance date. My law enforcement friends would have to be subpoenaed because that was the only way I could get them out of their offices.

And then there was the question of who to call at the FBI. Who at the bureau would have the guts to appear on my behalf. My first call was to Special Agent Marion Wright of the Baltimore field office, my close friend during the four years I sold equipment to the bureau—or so I believed. I had done him some favors along the way. But he never returned my calls. Then during the document discovery phase of the trial, I found out that Marion had filed a written summary of what we talked about during our more than two dozen lunches together. When I read that I felt violated. It was as if someone I trusted had come into my house and walked off with some of my most personal possessions.

I should have known that FBI agents have no true loyalty to anyone outside the bureau. Everyone else is outside the club and a potential suspect in crimes yet to be committed.

Chapter 11

The Trial

BEFORE A TRIAL you must have a jury. Due to the intensive publicity surrounding the arrests, guilty pleas, and sentencing of Duncan, Bowers, and Starr, as well as my involvement in the case, more than 250 people would have to be interviewed by Judge Hiram Ward to find twelve jurors and an alternate who could render a fair and honest verdict.

Of the prospective jurors, the vast majority raised their hands when the judge asked if they had read or heard about the bugging of the FBI agents at Northwestern Bank last summer and fall.

"Do you have any predisposition as to the guilt or innocence of Mr. Kaiser?" Judge Ward asked them

Again, a large number responded that "based on the pretrial publicity in the case" they would vote to find me guilty.

This polling of the jury was one of the worst parts of the trial experience for me. I wondered halfway through that first day if we would ever find twelve people objective and open-minded enough to serve on the jury and able to render a verdict based solely on the facts. By the end of the day, for better or for worse, we had our jury.

After the opening statements, the prosecution's first witness was George Collins, the bank president, who testified about conversations he had with Duncan and Bowers about "wiring the entire bank building for sound."

"I told them I didn't think it was a good idea," said Collins, "but I was not in a position to order Mr. Duncan to do anything."

On the evening of July 12, when the FBI was searching for eavesdropping devices in their interview room, Collins said Bowers assured him, "Don't worry. There's nothing there."

When it came time for cross-examination, John Morrow, one of my attorneys, referring to Bowers's statement, asked Collins, "Do you trust him for his truthfulness and veracity?"

"Not a hundred percent," Collins answered.

You can say that again, I thought.

Morrow had made an important point and I hoped the jury was listening for future reference. In his opening statement, Morrow had told the jury that I had warned both Duncan and Bowers on several occasions during my time at the bank that the eavesdropping devices were legal as long as one of them was in the room when the monitoring of the FBI agents took place. The single-consent rule. When he later took the witness stand, Bowers conveniently forgot to mention that point—giving less than 100 percent of the truth.

The next witness for the prosecution was Special Agent Brereton. He testified about his suspicions that the room they were using was bugged based on random conversations with bank employees. Then he went on to relate the embarrassment he felt when another agent found the bug in the telephone wall jack. His testimony by itself was factual and straightforward.

But his behavior when he wasn't on the witness stand was something else altogether. For one thing, he had a silly giggle that could be heard throughout the courthouse. But in my view, his behavior at the prosecution table was the most troubling. He was constantly whispering into the Assistant U.S. Attorney's ear as if he— Brereton—was directing the prosecution strategy. I later learned that this was not normal procedure with most government prosecutors.

They do not want their investigators anywhere near them except when they testify. In fact, Judge Ward frequently had to tell Brereton to remain quiet. I was a little puzzled by Brereton's relentless motivation in pursuing a guilty verdict. After all, I had never met the man before. The U.S. Recording Company scandal alone surely could not generate this prosecutorial fervor on his part, I thought.

What did motivate Brereton would become patently clear a year later.

The next witness was Special Agent Edward J. Brennan, an eavesdropping expert from the Charlotte field office. Amazingly, the prosecution was able to burn up an entire day asking Brennan to describe in detail what his expertise was in technical eavesdropping and what process he used for finding the microphone and preamplifier I had planted in the phone wall jack.

In response to questions from Assistant U.S. Attorney Ben White, Brennan did his damnedest to make it sound like a sophisticated device, but he wasn't very convincing. He told the jury that the device used "crossed pairs" of telephone wires, "a technique used only by the best of eavesdroppers."

I blushed and was deeply humbled. I thought to myself, Gee, the FBI thinks I'm the best of eavesdroppers! Wow. In reality, I had simply grabbed the brightest wires of the bunch—yellow—and then looked until I found the standard single-line phone colors of red and green. That was supposed to be the so-called "crossed pairs."

After nearly six hours, the prosecution was finished with Agent Brennan. Now it was our time to cross-examine him.

Using some of the greatest courtroom theatrics since Spencer Tracy's portrayal of Clarence Darrow in the movie *Inherit the Wind,* Bud Fensterwald slowly rose and buttoned his dark brown suit jacket. He then adjusted his collar and cuffs, looked at Brennan, and paused for several moments. The jury leaned forward in their seats with anticipation.

"Special Agent Brennan," he said slowly, articulating each word, "you have been very kind in describing to the jury how you found the device. Would you be so good as to tell the jury where you got the equipment to do your job?"

Brennan sheepishly pointed at me and said, "From the defendant over there, Marty."

"No further questions, your honor," Fensterwald said and sat down.

I saw several jury members chuckle or smile and roll their eyes. The point seemed to be well taken. I hoped the jury would question the real motivation of the FBI's prosecution of one of its most trusted ex-suppliers of countermeasure equipment.

Following Brennan's testimony, the prosecution wasted another entire day with a parade of witnesses who at some point had had physical possession of the invoice for the bugging assignment. The U.S. Attorney could have simply asked us to stipulate to the fact that I had indeed billed Northwestern Bank for the equipment and installation, but they never did. I would've admitted it right away. The bank still owed me the damned money. To this day, despite a collection effort on my part, the invoice for $3,500 has never been paid.

We finally moved into the most deliberately misleading part of the prosecution's case: two cassette tapes. These tapes, the government asserted, contained the voices of the two FBI agents recorded using the eavesdropping device.

First of all, Agent Brereton testified that he had heard the tapes in question and recognized his and Agent Zack Lowe's voices discussing issues relevant to their investigation. Then the government called Gwyn Bowers to the stand to tell the jury that he had recorded the agents' discussions with a tape recorder I had provided to him. Bowers then testified that he gave the tapes to Duncan. But that's where the government's credibility began to collapse.

Ben Tennille, one of Duncan's attorneys, testified that he took the tapes back to his office in Greensboro after Duncan's daughter, Catherine Woodruff, discovered them in a box of her father's financial records. Tennille said he played the tapes on a dictating machine shortly after they were discovered and determined that they were blank, except for a "hollow, humming noise."

A week later, in late July, the court testimony revealed that Paul Weinman, an intern in the U.S. Attorney's office, was sent to Duncan's attorneys' office to listen to the tapes. Weinman testified that he had detected what he thought was a "very low-speed" recording on the tapes. Later that day, the tapes were turned over to the FBI lab in Washington. They found that most of the sound on the tapes had been recorded at one-fourth the normal cassette recording speed. That finding clashed with the evidence that the recorders I sold Northwestern Bank ran at one-third normal speed.

Something mysterious happened to the tape recorder that was supposed to be the one that recorded those eavesdropped conversations. My defense team had trouble getting the FBI to let our own technical expert, Dr. Rawdon Smith, examine it. When the court finally ordered them to let us examine it, there was evidence that someone had opened the recorder and filed the shaft down on the motor so that it now matched the one-fourth speed of the tape recordings.

Dr. Smith would not testify to these extreme measures. However, he did testify that "the low-speed portion of the conversations on the cassettes is a rerecording." That meant that the two cassettes which the government contended were originals were actually copies.

Because of the less-than-reliable physical characteristics of the tapes, as well as gaps in their chain of custody, Fensterwald tried to convince Judge Ward that the tapes were inadmissible as evidence. Ward disagreed. He said the establishment of the authenticity of the tapes outweighed the questions of custody. What authenticity? I wondered. The judge never addressed the alleged discrepancy in the speed of the tapes.

"The tapes are authentic," he ruled, "and the enhanced copies and transcripts are admissible."

It was finally my turn to take the witness stand on the sixth day of the trial and I was raring to go. Previously, Fensterwald had put Dr. Smith on the witness stand. The majority of our witnesses were friends of mine who would testify to my excellent character and my expertise as a manufacturer of high-quality electronic countermeasures devices.

During the morning session, I essentially told the story of my life and how I came to be involved in building and selling electronic surveillance equipment to the FBI, as well as to the rest of the U.S. intelligence community. I went on to tell the jury about the U.S. Recording scandal and the resulting impact on my business following my testimony.

In the afternoon session, Fensterwald told the jury that I would demonstrate why the third charge against me—that of transporting the eavesdropping device across state lines—had no basis in fact.

Then, with Judge Ward's permission, I actually built a listening device on a table in front of the entire courtroom similar to the bug I had built in the motel room in Wilkesboro last April when the bank flew me down to hook it up.

Using a battery-operated soldering iron, with tiny puffs of smoke rising from the glowing red-hot tip, I connected the subminiature Knowles BA-1501 hearing-aid microphone to the transistor, resistor, and capacitor, and presto! I had built another operable eavesdropping device. It took about five minutes, mostly due to nervousness, and because the unfamiliar weight of the soldering iron made my hands shake. The device was given to the prosecution and then to Brennan, the FBI tech expert. He hooked it up to my preamplifier and the jury heard his voice loud and clear.

At the request of Fensterwald, Judge Ward had told the jury earlier that none of the four electronic components in itself constituted an illegal bugging device. And now I had demonstrated beyond a reasonable doubt that I had made the device in my motel room.

Before I stepped down from the witness stand, I repeated what my lawyers had already stated during the opening remarks—that

Bowers never indicated he wanted to secretly monitor the FBI agents' conversations.

"Bowers told me he only wanted the conversations recorded that took place between the agents and the employees being interviewed for the sake of accuracy," I said, " because people were being intimidated and threatened."

I told the jury I must have warned him half a dozen times about making sure there was at least one person in the room who knew the agents were being monitored.

The last part of my defense consisted of my character witnesses. Most of them were police officers: a lieutenant with the Baltimore County bomb squad, a sergeant with the Baltimore County homicide section, a captain with the U.S. Capitol Police, a CIA agent, a thrice-decorated sergeant from the U.S. Army ordnance division, and a captain from the Pennsylvania State Police intelligence division. The only person I felt confident about from my intelligence community contacts was Al Montefusco, chief of the procurement division for the CIA. Before we got to him, I had to endure the U.S. Attorney's trashing of my character with every one of my witnesses and then the trashing of *their* character to the jury.

The prosecution attacked each character witness, demanding to know why they would even think of associating or doing business with a slimeball like the defendant.

Fortunately, each witness accurately related his past experience with me, ignoring the personal attacks, and described me as a "trustworthy and law-abiding citizen." I later spoke to Captain Jim Regan of the Pennsylvania State Police Intelligence Division and asked him if this witness character assassination on the part of the prosecution was common.

"It's all part of the prosecutor's game plan, Marty, "he said. "It happens to us all the time."

But from my perspective, it didn't make it right.

Just as my lawyers were about to call Al Montefusco, my CIA

contact, the doors of the courtroom crashed open and in marched three men dressed in identical gray suits and pointy-toed shoes, carrying black attaché cases. Without saying a word, they walked straight into the judge's chambers. Judge Ward whacked his gavel and barked, "Chambers, gentlemen."

With that, the lawyers from both sides, as well as Agent Brereton, went into the judge's private office. Fensterwald told me later that this action was common when it involved public testimony by a CIA officer. Each side had to prepare a list of twenty questions that would be taken to CIA headquarters by the guys in the gray suits to be approved by CIA Director Admiral Stansfield Turner. That process took an entire day, during which time the trial was in recess.

The guys with the pointy-toed shoes returned with a list of ten approved questions, and Montefusco took the stand. Fensterwald asked the questions and received the prearranged answers, including the fact that the CIA bought $60,000 worth of my equipment and that I had received "agency secret approval" clearance. Then it was U.S. Attorney White's turn to ask the questions. Instead, he began tearing up the list, demonstrating his disgust with the arrangement.

Judge Ward whacked his gavel again and insisted that all of the attorneys return to his chambers; Brereton followed. When they emerged several minutes later, White said, "No further questions, your honor."

The following morning, February 8, both sides gave closing arguments. Assistant U.S. Attorney White ended his remarks by saying that I "had once had the trust of many law enforcement organizations, but Mr. Kaiser sold that trust, ladies and gentlemen, for $3,500 (my fee from Northwestern Bank)."

In fact, I had not sold that trust from the intelligence community. The FBI had stolen it from me.

Judge Ward spent the following morning giving instructions to the jury and then they retired to deliberate. I turned to Bud Fensterwald, seeking some assurance that the verdict would go our way.

"What do you think, Bud?" I asked.

"Don't worry about it, Marty," he said. "If they come back in a couple of hours, it's a good sign. If they take longer than that, I might begin to worry."

Fensterwald called it right on the nose. The jury came back two and a half hours later and said I was not guilty of all three counts against me. When I heard the first "not guilty" verdict, I knew we were home free.

After the verdict, Fensterwald and I went into the hallway to stretch our legs. As we turned around, the jury began to file out of the courtroom. They walked in single file with a strange mixture of terror and disbelief on their faces. As they walked out, their eyes were focused straight ahead on the nape of the neck of the person in front of them.

Fensterwald nudged me and said, "Thank them." As each passed by I said, "Thank you," but not one of them turned their heads to look at me. I wondered what those guys in pointy-toed shoes had really told the judge and what he had told the jury in terms of their instructions. Probably some ridiculous story about how I was really guilty, but in the interest of national security they would have to find me not guilty.

A few minutes later, the media surrounded Fensterwald and me, asking for a statement.

"In all honesty," I said, "it's what we expected. I knew I had not done anything illegal. Needless to say, I'm satisfied."

As I was talking to the reporter, Agent Brereton walked by. The reporter turned to him and asked for a comment on the verdict.

"Mr. Kaiser is not innocent," said Brereton. "He was found not guilty only of the three charges brought against him."

Our eyes met as he spoke and I knew I had not seen nor heard the last of Special Agent Thomas Brereton.

Chapter 12

More Trials and Survival Strategies

I COULDN'T WAIT to get back to work following the trial. I needed to do something productive to shake off the lethargy that seemed to weigh on me like a hundred-pound diver's belt. At times I felt like I was drowning on dry land. I needed to focus again, reenergize my mind and body, and stop waiting for the second shoe to drop.

No one had ever told me what I could or could not do with the list I had of the grand jurors' names and addresses. I decided that now was a good time to write them a thank-you note. The letter was informative and nonthreatening and pointed out the rough costs of my trial. There is no doubt in my mind that my letters shocked the crap out of them, especially since they were told that grand jury information would be kept secret. And here was the defendant, writing to them! My God!

I had begun to see a psychologist after the indictment and had started a daily diet of antidepressants, but neither brought much relief. My relationship with Carmel was still cool, but we were at least civil to each other. The only thing that got my engine revved up was my work. For many people, "work" is nothing more than a four-letter word. For me, building things with my hands was and still is the best therapy. It was the only thing that helped me survive.

My income was still a shadow of what it had been only a few years before. In addition to the FBI passing the word to the rest of the intelligence community not to do business with me, I heard through the grapevine that they had also suggested that I was no longer to be invited to the annual and regional conferences of the National Technical Investigators Association (NATIA). And I haven't been invited since then.

NATIA is composed of over 2,000 law enforcement and intelligence officers, and support staff from various federal, state, and local agencies, as well as from the U.S. and Canadian military. Membership is restricted to full-time employees of law enforcement agencies who are actively engaged in technical surveillance, communications, and specialized support of law enforcement or intelligence activities. The value in terms of networking and sales opportunities for small electronics and communication suppliers like myself to be invited to attend NATIA conferences was incalculable. Conversely, to be intentionally shut out of these conferences was the same as being given a lifetime noncompete clause by your former employer.

Thanks to my contacts with local and state bomb squads, I was able to keep my business afloat. I was also able to pay off the legal bills of the trial, which amounted to more than $300,000 in out-of-pocket costs and millions in lost business. It was noteworthy that most of the friends who never lost faith in me and agreed to testify on my behalf were from the bomb disposal industry.

The camaraderie of the bomb guys was special. It offered the company of some of the nicest people I've ever known or worked with. It also provided the contacts that helped me reinvent myself as a bomb detection device manufacturer and kept me afloat financially at the most precarious moments of my life. Participating in their meetings was also like getting an advanced degree in bomb making and ordnance disarmament.

The International Association of Bomb Technicians and Investigators (IABTI) met annually in a different city each year. Rather than sit around drinking beer and telling war stories, we decided to add some education and fun competition to the events. At the meetings, it was mandatory that each bomb technician bring his own "inert" improvised bomb. The other technicians would then be given a timed opportunity to defuse the bomb. Obviously, no explosives were involved, but if the technician failed in his effort to disarm the device, a buzzer, flashbulb, or small firecracker would go off to inform him of his failure.

There were a LOT of failures! I absorbed all of my colleagues' ideas on disarming, and some were pretty unusual.

Defusing letter bombs was particularly dicey. That's why Ted Kaczynski, the Unabomber, was so dangerous. One of the most effective defusing strategies was to use a straightened coat hanger. Slide it through the small space left by the envelope flap, put some sort of lead paper weight on the letter and weight on one end of the hanger. Then tie a long string to the other end of the hanger, withdraw to a safe distance, and sharply pull on the string.

Other people favored the method of using a hair dryer to dry out the flap glue, which loosened the flap and permitted you to carefully examine the contents with a thin, bladed extender pole—all of course from a safe distance.

It wasn't until we took our ideas out of the classroom and into the field that I understood the power of these devices. It seemed that IABTI members had an unending supply of explosives to use as test cases and also an endless supply of old cars to blow up.

I'll never forget one of my first live-fire experiences. The meeting was held in Atlanta and the local chapter member had procured an old car from the local junkyard. We placed explosives in the trunk and around the steering column.

We blew the trunk first, did a cursory examination of the damage, and then blew the charge on the steering column. We then did a detailed examination of the alleged "crime scene." After the beer break that was a common part of our meetings, one of the techs pulled out a six-pound military shape charge.

We decided to place the charge of C-4—a terrorist's explosive of choice—directly over the engine block to see what kind of damage it would do. We retreated to what we thought was a safe distance and someone shouted the obligatory "Fire in the hole!" The explosives went off, knocking us on our collective asses. The car hood went flying about two thousand feet in the air. It was folded into the shape of a hang glider wing.

We watched as it disappeared over the horizon. We listened over a police radio and when we heard no reports of a flying saucer or a UFO taking out a low-flying aircraft, we breathed a sigh of relief. When we went back to what was left of the car, we found the engine block at the bottom of a hole six feet in diameter and thirty feet deep.

As I looked at the bomb crater, I remembered Frank Terpil's experiences in training the Libyan intelligence people in radio-concealed bombs, and what happened to his students who failed to pay attention. From that point on, I vowed never to let my mind wander in the presence of these explosives.

About six weeks after the trial, I was slowly getting back into the work groove when two events occurred within a month of each other that convinced me that the FBI had not forgotten about me or its intention for payback. Both events were precipitated, as usual, by telephone calls.

The first one came on a Saturday night. Carmel and I were home watching TV. The moment I heard the man's voice on the line, I sensed it was not a courtesy call.

"Mr. Kaiser, " said the voice. "This is the Baltimore County Police calling. We have your son, Martin, down at the station. He's been arrested for possession of marijuana. We need you to come down and take him home."

The officer went on to say that Marty had been caught with a seventeen-year-old friend of his, dividing up seven ounces of marijuana between them.

This was in an era of rampant experimentation by kids my son's age, but I was still shocked. We had a close relationship and kept no secrets from each other. Given the abuse I had received from my own father, I had made an effort to be a caring and loving dad to my own children. I was strict with them, but I never laid an angry hand on them and they never gave me any cause to do so.

When Marty was growing up, we never had a problem with him. He was just like every other kid in the neighborhood. He was in the Cub Scouts, built tree houses, and was a good craftsman. He used to fix all our neighbors' cars.

Since this was his only run-in with the law, I assumed that the judge would give him a warning that would scare him, and a slap on the wrist, as the other boy was given. I immediately hired a lawyer to defend him. The arrest had taken place two weeks after Marty's eighteenth birthday, which made him vulnerable to more serious charges as an adult. But the lawyer assured both my son and me that he had arranged for a guilty plea of simple possession. The other boy had already entered the same plea and had been given a ninety-day suspended sentence and a misdemeanor.

The trial date finally arrived and we were the only ones in the court-room. Since I had just survived a criminal trial, I was intimately aware of a courtroom setting. And this one, to put it mildly, seemed quite bizarre.

Carmel sat on my left in the second row behind the defense table. She spent the entire hearing busily balancing her checkbook, clearly not wanting to acknowledge the reality of what was happening.

The judge was on the bench, and Marty was in the witness chair explaining what happened on the night he was arrested. The lawyer was questioning him but was standing shoulder to shoulder with the prosecuting attorney. He was supposed to be defending my son, but his apparent chumminess with the prosecuting attorney did not give me much comfort. I am told that lawyers on opposing sides are often friendly, but it still bothered me.

Upon completing his testimony, Marty took a seat at the defense table. The prosecuting attorney then read the charge against him.

Instead of the simple possession charge that the lawyer had assured me he had arranged, the prosecutor charged my son with possession with intent to distribute. A felony! The lawyer then gestured to my son to accept the charge and plead guilty, which he reluctantly did.

I was absolutely livid. I wanted to jump over the rail and punch the lawyer in the face, but I was still gun-shy after my previous court experience and could not afford another legal battle.

After a few derogatory remarks, the judge gave his verdict: eighteen months' suspended sentence. For a first offense and possession of 3 ½ ounces of marijuana, my son was a convicted drug dealer. Something's wrong with this picture, I thought. This couldn't be happening.

Then, as I stood up, I looked around and noticed two men in gray suits and dark ties standing conspicuously in the back of the courtroom. I recognized them. They were FBI agents I had seen previously either in the Baltimore field office or at the Washington headquarters. I wondered why they would be wasting time in a local magistrate's court on such an innocuous case. I would see both men years later at the retirement ceremony for Master Chief Paul Shipton, who ran the Navy IEDD/EOD School at Indian Head, Maryland.

Suddenly, in my mind the harsh sentence my son was given started making sense for all the wrong reasons.

The lawyer was waiting outside the courtroom when I left. He walked over to me and said, "I didn't like Marty's lack of remorse."

I quivered with rage. I wanted to report him to the state bar for malpractice for giving my son bad advice and counsel and failing to provide effective representation. I also felt like telling him he was a lying, disreputable bastard. But I bit my tongue, and walked away from him. The last thing I wanted right then was a lawsuit with a lawyer—especially with the FBI watching.

As for my son, the experience of being convicted of a felony based on bad advice sent him into a tailspin. It took him years to finally put the past behind him, and our relationship went through some difficult times.

At one point, I demanded that he move out of our house because he refused to get a regular job. Eventually, he took responsibility for his life and got his act together. I'm proud to say that he now operates his own business, installing office cubicle partitions. Ironically, he just received a huge contract from one of the U.S. intelligence agencies with which I am quite familiar.

About a week after my son's trial ended, I received another phone call. This one was from the IRS, informing me of another audit. This would be my second audit in three years. I assumed this one was again prompted by the bureau, but I wondered what it could possibly achieve, since I had passed the audit after my National Wiretap Commission testimony with flying colors.

It would become clear to me several months later that the FBI had reasons to learn my income and whether I could afford the expense of another lawsuit—this one a civil action. I told the IRS caller to contact my accountant and deal with him. Evidently, there were no problems and I never heard from the IRS again.

There would be other, more subtle, problems related to my FBI experience. One involved my application for permanent residency in the Cayman Islands, where I had a condo.

Following my acquittal on criminal charges and my involvement in the civil suit, I applied for residency in the Caymans, requiring another $450 application fee. On the form I had to answer yes to the questions: *Have you ever been charged with a crime? Have you ever been involved in a civil action?* I noted that I had been acquitted of all charges. But that didn't count, I guess. I never heard from the residency board.

Business during this period seemed to match my mood—it sucked. I awoke most mornings wondering what would be the next crisis on my agenda. I felt like Pigpen, the character in the Peanuts comic strip who walked around with a cloud over his head. I had the feeling of impending dread and I couldn't seem to shake it. I needed a diversion, something to take my mind off my situation.

It was about that time, in May 1978, that I got call from a man named Hector Gualda. I learned later that he owned several different companies, all of them in the security field. One company was called Boxer Alarm Inc., located somewhere in New Jersey. He spoke with a Latino accent and told me he represented the government of Argentina. I asked him how he got my name and phone number. He never answered the question. I wondered if he knew Frank Terpil. Two years before, the Argentine government had been overthrown by a military junta, led by Lieutenant General Jorge Rafaél Videla. That was Frank's specialty—repressive dictatorships.

"Ah, Mister Kaiser," said Hector. "You are a famous person, no? Everyone knows you in the American intelligence community."

At first I figured this was another game the FBI was playing with me: trying to set me up to sell restricted electronic surveillance gear to a foreign government so they could bust me again.

"I'm sorry," I told Hector, "but I can't sell my products to a foreign government. It's against the law."

I always made sure to make that last statement loud and clear for anyone who was listening. I swept my office, my workshop and the phones about once a week, but I assumed someone was always listening somehow, some way.

"No, Mister Kaiser," he said. "You don't understand. My clients don't want to buy any equipment from you. They want you to evaluate the equipment they already have and give them some advice on how to use it most effectively."

"My time is extremely valuable," I told him. "My consulting fees are very high. Perhaps you should find someone else."

"Ah, Mister Kaiser," said Hector. "My clients are willing to pay you a handsome fee that I'm sure you will be happy with. After all, you've had some problems with your government recently and you would probably welcome the business. Isn't that so?"

He paused and then added, "In fact, I would like to purchase some equipment from you."

Obviously, this guy had done his homework and the money he was offering would certainly come in handy.

"What's the situation like down in Buenos Aires?" I asked him. "From what I read it seems like you've got a civil war going on down there."

"Don't believe everything you read, Mister Kaiser," said Hector. "Have you ever been to Argentina?"

"No, I haven't."

"Ah, Mister Kaiser, Argentina is like another world. It would be an unforgettable experience for you. And the women, Mister Kaiser. The women are extraordinary."

My wife would not have appreciated this sales pitch, but I needed the money and perhaps this was just the diversion I needed to lift my spirits. I told Hector I would think about it and get back to him. That gave me a few days to check him out through my own intelligence sources. I hoped he was who he claimed to be. I needed a change of scenery.

A month later, on July 9, 1978, I had a first class plane ticket on Braniff Airlines leaving JFK for Buenos Aires. When I boarded the plane, the first class section was overbooked, but the rest of the plane was totally empty, so I took a seat in coach. I didn't know if it was part of the package with Hector or whether the stewardesses were trying to make up for the lack of passengers, but they treated me like a rock star. I began to think I was going to enjoy this assignment.

First of all, I was going during one of the coolest months—June, July, and August are considered Argentina's winter. There was still a lot of humidity but the nights were pleasant and the heat was tempered by a breeze off Río de la Plata, the 170-mile-long, 25-mile-wide estuary on which Buenos Aires was built.

Hector had assured me that someone would pick me up at the airport and take care of everything. My guide's name was Arturo. He was an older man with a salt and pepper moustache. Unlike my experience in Cairo, Arturo expedited everything, including taking my luggage directly through customs without it being touched. I assumed Arturo was with the government intelligence service.

We got into a black sedan at the airport, and as we started pulling away, Arturo turned from the front seat and handed me a .45 caliber automatic pistol.

"Have you ever fired this type of gun?" he asked nonchalantly.

"Yes, but what do I need it for?" I asked.

"There are a lot of violent people here," he said. "It's for your own protection."

"No, thank you," I said, handing him back the automatic. "I'm a pacifist."

"If you will permit me to say so, Mr. Kaiser," Arturo said smiling, "you are also an optimist."

The downtown area of Buenos Aires is a gleaming swath of pink and white Greco-Roman architecture, mixed with skyscrapers that reminded me in some ways of Washington, D.C., with its broad thoroughfares, government buildings with pillars and arches, and huge marble memorials to past heroes.

On the way in from the international airport at Ezeiza, Arturo gave me a quick tour of the city and recounted its history. At the time I visited, Argentina had a population of about 20 million, and at least half of them were *porteños*, residents of Buenos Aires.

Buenos Aires was founded by the Spanish explorer Juan de Garay, on June 11, 1580, but it was only under his successor, Hernando Arias de Saavedra that the new colony became secure. The Spanish continue to rule Argentina for more than 270 years. Argentina resisted takeover attempts by the French and British. A revolution begun in 1810 led to independence in 1816, but Argentina's culture and lifestyle remain more European than any other city in the Americas. There are more Italian and German names than Spanish in the local phone directory, but more streets bore the name Juan Perón than any other.

As we drove along Avenue 9 de Julio, one of the main streets leading into the downtown area of the city, Arturo pointed out a massive stone tower rising hundreds of feet into the air.

"It is called the Obelisco," said Arturo, "in honor of the four hundredth anniversary of the city's founding."

"It reminds me of the Washington monument," I told him, "but obviously a lot older."

The other thing I noticed on the ride from the airport to my hotel was the number of heavily armed soldiers on the streets, backed up by armored cars and tanks. Every night during my stay, there was gunfire in the streets and explosions in the distance. When I asked Arturo who was doing the shooting, he would always reply, "the Communists and their sympathizers." I didn't press the subject, but it was clear that the Communists were not the only ones doing the shooting.

What I didn't realize at the time was that government of President Videla and his generals were waging a brutal counterterror campaign against the Montoneros, a left-wing Peronist faction, as well as against the People's Revolutionary Army and other left-wing groups committed to overthrowing the junta.

This period was later referred to as Argentina's "Dirty War," during which more than ten thousand people were arrested, tortured, or "disappeared," presumed to have been executed. The generals ruled until December 1983, when they were turned out of office by the democratically elected Radical Civic Union Party of Raúl Alfonsín.

To this day, I'm still not entirely clear about what the Argentine intelligence service wanted from me in the way of electronic surveillance advice. My first few days were taken up with inspecting their bugging and countermeasure equipment. It was predominately German-made. They were particularly interested in my warnings about the transmitters they were using. These were the self-excited types that could be accidentally triggered by random FM frequencies, which would compromise the surveillance operation. The rest of my ten days there was taken up by sightseeing, interspersed with lunches and dinners. I wondered whether they simply didn't know what to do with me at some point but were too embarrassed to send me home.

My fondest memories of Buenos Aires were the evenings at the tango clubs and restaurants. The tango has to be the sexiest dance ever invented. When I watched couples dancing, it was as if they were glued tight to each other from their shoulders to their calves. And then, of course, were the women of Buenos Aires. I have to admit that, in the words of Jimmy Carter, there were moments when I had lust in my heart, but that was as far as it went.

The most frightening memory of those ten days in Buenos Aires was of attending a local soccer match. The soccer field itself was surrounded by razor-topped barbed wire. A moat beyond that was filled with kerosene and two more barriers of concertina wire. There were heavily armed soldiers stationed every few feet around the soccer field itself.

I was accompanied by Arturo and some of his mates. We sat on the side of the local home team, the Bocas. The bleachers were built at a forty-five-degree angle so that fans' view of the field would not be blocked by the person sitting in front of them. When either the Bocas or the opposing team scored a goal, I felt like I was sitting at the top of a building swaying back and forth in the wake of a massive earthquake. I felt that at any minute the bleachers were going to collapse like a house of cards. Amazingly, it never happened.

Two weeks after I returned home from Buenos Aires, the second shoe, compliments of the FBI, was dropped. On July 31, 1978, Special Agents Thomas Brereton and Zachary Lowe filed a civil suit against me, as well as against Edwin Duncan Jr. and Northwestern Bank. They asked for $22 million in damages for "professional embarrassment, humiliation, and violation of their privacy." This civil suit would drag on for more than seven years, draining me financially and emotionally.

I wasn't surprised. I was reminded of the old FBI motto from the days of John Dillinger and that crowd: "The FBI always gets its man." This civil suit was confirmation to me that the bureau was not going to give up until I was behind bars or in bankruptcy court.

What I didn't realize until we began the discovery phase of the civil suit was that, in my opinion, Agents Brereton and Lowe and the FBI were guilty of conflict of interest as prohibited by the Code of Federal Regulation, Title 28, Section 45. What we found out through the discovery process was that Brereton and Lowe had sought and received permission from FBI headquarters in Washington to sue me civilly more than two months before I was even indicted in the 1977 criminal case.

On October 27, 1977, Edgar Best, special agent in charge of the Charlotte field office, had been approached by Brereton and Lowe for a legal determination regarding their status to file a civil suit against me. The Northwestern Bank incident was the first time in the history of the bureau that its agents had been the target of eavesdropping. It was also the first time that agents had sued a person for civil damages resulting from allegations in a criminal case.

Based on advice from the FBI's general counsel, John Mintz, Special Agent Best had given them the green light to proceed. Brereton and Lowe also had been allowed to continue to lead the investigation into criminal charges against me as well as Duncan and Northwestern Bank. They knew that a conviction in the criminal case would later make it far easier for them to obtain a civil judgment for damages against me and Northwestern Bank.

A potential payoff of $22 million dollars in damages was no small incentive to make sure of my conviction.

I'm not a lawyer, but it certainly seemed to me, and was argued by my attorneys, that the situation bore the appearance of conflict of interest.

Chapter 13

Searching for Bugs in Corporate America

THE YEAR 1978 ended worse than it had begun. I moved from one frying pan into another. My legal money meter continued to run, dragging me deeper into debt. The biggest story on the TV evening news was far more disturbing. It reminded me that I was still better off than a lot of other folks.

Just before Thanksgiving, more than 900 men, women, and children died in a mass suicide in Jonestown, Guyana. Most of the dead—members of a group called the People's Temple Christian Church, originally from San Francisco—had consumed Kool-Aid laced with cyanide. Jim Jones, the group's leader, reportedly died of a self-inflicted gunshot to the temple.

The eeriest part of the story was that Jones supposedly led the group in frequent rehearsals of group suicide called "White Nights," during which the faithful never knew whether this would be the night they drank the poisoned Kool-Aid or got to live for another day.

How, I wondered, could people be brainwashed to that extent and be led to their deaths like sheep to slaughter? Had they had reached the end of their personal rope? Did they view death as preferable to living?

There were moments in my life back then when I was extremely depressed, but I never got to the point of no return. I got close sometimes, I will admit, but I was always able to pull back from the abyss. Fortunately for me, my work was my saving grace, and I still had people around me who loved me and believed in me.

I was starting to expand into the bomb detection business in a big way. It began at an Explosives Ordnance Demolition (EOD) conference in Miami, where I met Master Sergeant Mike Lizak. He had stepped on a mine in Vietnam and lost one of his legs, but the experience didn't stop him from continuing as an EOD technician afterward.

We became close friends, and he told me the army was looking for a new stethoscope with a tone generator that would signal a live explosive device. I adapted my 1059 bug detector and called it the 2049M (the M is for Mike Lizak). Mike gave me an order for eighty-three of them and I turned them out in less than a month's time.

I would later sell thousands of the Model 2049M to state and local bomb squads. I eventually produced an advanced version with a contact stethoscope and ultrasonic detection capability. The bombing of the Marine barracks in Beirut in 1984 would create an increased need in the coming years for equipment that could detect gas-enhanced explosive devices.

An additional revenue generator back then was the increasing demand within the private sector for surveillance countermeasures and sweeps for eavesdropping devices or phone taps. As I have previously indicated, I had little interest in doing sweeps in the corporate sector, primarily because their expectations were so influenced by the media hype about corporate espionage.

Clearly, illegal audio surveillance is a constant and growing threat in today's private sector, primarily in the pharmaceutical, biotech, oil and gas exploration, and information technology fields. More often than not, the bugging is conducted by disgruntled employees or passed-over executives. The problem, at least back in the 1970s and 1980s, was the frequent expectation by corporate security officers or executives that the countermeasure tech would find a bug or compromised phone line in order to justify the expense of the sweep.

When I told a security person that the facilities were clean—in 95 percent of the sweeps—I often sensed a mixture of relief and disappointment.

One of the strangest reactions I ever had about finding phone compromises was from a CEO who chewed me out because I discovered the phone taps that *he* had put in place. It was also the scariest sweep I ever conducted.

The Olin Corporation in Mount Pisgah, North Carolina, produced paper for Philip Morris cigarettes. They were in the middle of a strike when I got a call from the security director. He told me it was imperative that I conduct the sweep at night after all of the employees had gone home.

When I asked him why, he said, "We have our reasons."

The security director picked me up at the airport and drove me directly to the company offices. It was already dark, but despite the late hour there was a picket line of striking employees lining the driveway as we turned in to the parking lot. The people on the picket line jeered and shouted as we drove through the front gate—we were scabs crossing the picket line. Local armed police manned the front gate.

I checked each phone line used by a department secretary in the company and to my great surprise, I found at least seventeen taps on the lines. The taps all seemed to be linked to the CEO's office, which I found a trifle bizarre.

I worked all night, and as the dawn came up, the security director and I looked out of one of the executive office windows. We saw that the strikers had poured buckets of roofing nails across the only road out of the parking lot. As the security director was calling his staff to break out the brooms to sweep up the nails, a bullet exploded through the window, hitting the wall above my head.

"That's it," I told the security director. "Unless I'm getting combat pay, I'm outta here."

"How much is combat pay?" the security director asked, laughing.

"Your company doesn't have enough money to meet it."

It took us about an hour before the security crew could clean up all of the nails from the parking lot. I was never so glad to finish a job in my life.

When I turned in the report, a couple of days later, the CEO called me and said, "Hell, Marty. Those were the taps I had put on those lines. I wanted you to find the ones the other bastards put there."

He never informed me who the "other bastards" were, though I had a pretty good idea.

One of the most critical discoveries I ever made on a sweep was at the Matthey Bishop Corporation in Malvern, Pennsylvania. The security director there had heard of me through my friends at the Pennsylvania State Police Academy. Matthey Bishop was at the time the nation's largest refiner of platinum. The company was later bought by the Johnson Corporation and is now known as the Johnson Matthey Corporation. The management felt that someone was leaking proprietary data to its competition. The job called for a complete countermeasure sweep, including all phones and executive offices.

It took me all day to check the phones, which were clean. The last office I checked for room bugs was the boardroom. The minute I entered the room, my attention was drawn to a recessed disc the size of a baseball on the ceiling, directly over the middle of the fourteen-foot mahogany boardroom table.

"What's the speaker for?" I asked pointing at it.

"The Muzak system," said the security director. "It's harmless."

Oh, how wrong he was!

"Where's the connection to it?"

"In the frame closet over there," he said, pointing to a door just off the boardroom.

I went over and located the wires to the Muzak system. Looking behind the mass of wires, I found a switch from the loudspeaker linked to a connector that would have been plugged into a tape recorder. All I found was the bare wire and no tape recorder. There was no way of telling how long this Muzak bug had been used. It was one of the crudest eavesdropping systems I had ever come across. But it was also one of the most dangerous. The Muzak speaker provided a natural microphone and its own energy source. It was centrally located and was, in fact, a dynamic microphone that sucked up every word or whisper uttered in that boardroom.

My recommendation to the security director was to remove the speaker at once. The board members would survive without listening to Perry Como and Lawrence Welk. I used the discovery of that bugged speaker in every subsequent countermeasure lecture I gave. I called it "Deep Throat," borrowing Bob Woodward and Carl Bernstein's code name for their Watergate scandal source. Bugs in Muzak speakers are the most lethal and commonly used eavesdropping device in the corporate boardroom, and a prime location for capturing sensitive corporate information.

One of the most embarrassing phone line sweeps I ever conducted was for Baltimore Gas & Electric. This was in the late 1970s and they had just introduced a new phone system with a built-in memory. It was state of the art at the time, but no one informed me about it and I'd never run across a phone with built-in memory prior to that. I was impressed.

I didn't realize that when you took the cover off the top of those telephones, it disconnected a multicontact plug at the bottom of the phone that provided the battery power to the system. This kept the memory for the entire system intact. So when I unplugged the phone, BLOOEY! The memory system instantly zeroed out.

The security director just shook his head when I told him what I'd done. BG&E had to bring a phone company tech back in to reprogram all of the phones in the building. I shudder to think what that bill must have been.

I offered to come back and conduct another sweep free of charge. But predictably, they never took me up on my offer. Despite that mistake, the sweep requests kept on coming and I kept on filling them.

During the period of the late 1970s and early 1980s, I made two trips to Canada. The first one, at the request of the Royal Canadian Mounted Police, was a training assignment rather than a counter-measure job and more oriented around bomb detection than bugs. The second trip to Canada had an amusing element to it.

I was called by the FSS Special Intelligence unit of the prime minister's office in Ottawa. They wanted a phone and office sweep of Prime Minister Pierre Trudeau's offices, as well the offices of his deputies.

The travel itinerary required me to fly to Ottawa via Montreal. When we landed in Montreal, some of the passengers got off. As we waited for the plane to taxi back onto the runway to take off, the pilot announced my name over the public address system and asked me to come forward to the cockpit. I thought that this was some sort of "red carpet" treatment for special guests of the prime minister. My reception by the pilot was decidedly the opposite.

"Mr. Kaiser," said the pilot gravely, "could you please explain the source of the beep-beep-beep coming from your checked attaché case?"

I thought for a second and realized it was the tone generator I used to turn on any voice-activated bugs when I was doing a sweep. I showed him a similar beeper on his instrument panel.

"Don't worry about it," I told the pilot, "I'll turn it off when we reach Ottawa."

"There's a problem with that," he said, ruefully, shaking his head and guiding me over to the open jet way. "You see that attaché case sitting in the middle of the tarmac? It's yours. Why don't we go out there and take a look at it."

If he thought it was a bomb, he was pretty gutsy to even risk walking over to check it out. I figured he was probably watching me to see if I exhibited any nervous, bad-guy tics. But it was all I could do to keep from cracking up laughing. The passengers had their noses plastered against the window as the pilot and I walked down the tarmac to where my attaché case was sitting.

I opened it and shut off the beeper. But the pilot was fascinated with my equipment, so I ended up giving him a short course in sur- veillance countermeasures right there on the tarmac. I'm sure the passengers must have wondered what we could be talking about for so long. About fifteen minutes later, I picked up the attaché case and gave it to the baggage handler. The pilot thanked me for my explana- tion, we boarded, and the plane took off for Ottawa.

Of course, the classified nature of my visit was clearly blown by that time, but it made the trip interesting. The actual sweep took me less than half a day. I checked all of the telephones and swept sev- eral offices for bugs. Each time I moved the spectrum analyzer to a new room, a tracking transmitter signal continued to register. The FSS had one of my 2050CAs—an FM radio frequency detector—so I told them how to test for and locate the tracking transmitter.

After I left, I was informed that they did find a tracking device on a car belonging to the secretary of one of the cabinet ministers, possibly put there by a jealous wife. In any event, that discovery never made the evening news.

I made one additional trip to Canada in the early 1980s, to con- duct a sweep of the Merck Frost Laboratories in Dorval, Quebec. I found that someone had tried to reroute telephone wire pairs in one of the frame rooms, a clear sign of a phone line compromise. But it was impossible to tell where the phone line pairs led to because the room was a rat's nest of wires. When I opened the door to the frame room, the mass of wires fell through the doorway like a dead body. I told them that the first thing they had to do was clean up the mess, and then I could get a clearer picture of what was going on. I never found any transmitters, but someone had been up to no good.

As I moved into the 1980s, the number of requests for countermea- sure sweeps began to decline. It was not because of the lack of business, but simply a matter of supply and demand. A number of self-described countermeasure "experts," most of them retired FBI and CIA officers, started entering the business. Many of these ex-spooks traded on the caché of the name recognition of their former employer rather than any expertise in the countermeasure business.

But I still had a reputation problem that followed me wherever I went to sell equipment or to lecture about it. A case in point was a seminar on bomb detection and disposal that I was asked to give in 1981 at the Redstone Arsenal in Huntsville, Alabama, the U.S. Army Explosives Ordnance Demolition (EOD) school.

I flew down the night before and took a taxi over to the base early the next morning. The security officer met me at the front gate and directed me to the classroom where I was scheduled to give the day-long lecture. As I normally did, I started off the seminar by introducing various pieces of equipment used in bomb detection, including my RF frequency detector, and explained how each worked.

The minute I turned on the RF detector, the tone generator started beeping loudly. At first, I thought it must be a glitch in the equipment. I turned it off and turned it back on, but the beeping persisted. I looked around the room and saw the confusion in the students' faces.

"What's that beeping about?" one of them asked.

"That's a good question," I told him. "It's not a bomb. What that indicates is that there is some sort of radio frequency listening device somewhere in this building. In fact, it might even be in this room."

"Why?" asked another student.

"Your guess is as good as mine," I told him.

The class was suddenly silent as the students looked at each other, trying to grasp the implication of what I had said. Several minutes later, two burly MPs entered the classroom with the security officer. Without any explanation, they took my equipment, put it back in my suitcases, physically escorted me out of the room, and threw me and my equipment out through the back gate. After waiting on a dusty road for a seemingly interminable amount of time, I was finally picked up by a passing taxi.

I went back to my motel, picked up my clothes, and flew home. The Army EOD school reimbursed me for my expenses but never gave me an explanation for why I was physically removed from the base. Obviously, the army was monitoring the training of its EOD students, and my discovery of the RF transmitter compromised that surveillance.

Was the surveillance targeting me specifically or did they monitor all training? I never learned the answer, though I wondered whether the bureau had anything to do with it. A few years later, the FBI would take over management of the National Bomb Data Program from the Army EOD, and they would make sure I was not invited to various bomb detection conferences where bureau agents were the keynote speakers.

The most blatant example of that blacklisting took place at a bomb disposal conference sponsored by the International Association of Bomb Technicians and Investigators (IABTI) in the early 1980s, after my acquittal on criminal charges.

FBI Agent Fred Smith, a bomb investigator, was the speaker. He specifically asked the IABTI to bar me from the room when he spoke. The organization acquiesced to the request, fearing that Smith would withhold potentially important data from the other members. I didn't like it, but I went along with the will of the majority.

When Smith took the stage, I left the room and went into the hotel lobby to have a cigarette. Halfway through his lecture, Smith reached the point of discussion regarding radio-controlled bombs.

According to a friend with the Bureau of Alcohol, Tobacco, and Firearms (ATF), Smith asked the audience: "Does anyone in the group know anything about radio-controlled bombs?"

My ATF friend stood and replied, "Yeah. The guy you sent out into the lobby."

There were a few chuckles at that, and Agent Smith, slightly embarrassed, continued his lecture.

Oh, yeah. I was never invited back to teach again at the Redstone Arsenal.

Chapter 14

Civil Suit and Countersuit

AS THE 1970S came to a close, my fame or infamy, depending on your point of view, was expanding globally. The day after New Year's, 1979, a story appeared in the *Daily Telegraph* of London with the headline:

BUGGED FBI MEN WITH HEMORRHOIDS SUE FOR US$22 MILLION

The first paragraph of the story summed it up:

> *A telephone tapping expert who supplied the Federal Bureau of Investigation with electronic eavesdropping devices is being sued for alleged "bugging of two FBI agents."*

The story went on to say that FBI Agents Thomas Brereton and Zachary Lowe claimed their rights as private citizens had been "grossly violated" by the eavesdropping devices that I had allegedly planted. Brereton was quoted in a court deposition as finding "five bugging devices," including special transmitters and amplifiers.

Of course, that was an exaggeration of the original criminal charge. I installed a single bug. Brereton, it seemed to me, wanted to ensure some payback for the "humiliation and embarrassment" he claims he suffered by being bugged, and for hypertension and cysts in his eyes brought on by the stress of the event.

My question was: What about me? Who was I to see about recovering my good name and reputation? What about my business, which was in shambles? What about my physical and mental health?

The answer, from the FBI, was very clear. It reminded me of the old story about the boot camp training sergeant and the recruit who can't swim. The recruit asks how he's supposed to get across the swiftly moving stream that is over his head. The sergeant replies: "Mind over matter, Private. We don't mind and you don't matter."

Initially, Bud Fensterwald assured me that there was no way these agents could win a civil judgment against me in the wake of an acquittal on all criminal charges. On the face of it, I agreed. But then, we were going up against the power of the FBI. I should have known by this time that the presence of the bureau anytime, anywhere, changed the ground rules substantially.

Each of the three criminal offenses I had been charged with— conspiracy to plant an eavesdropping device, transporting the device, and installing it—had been rendered moot by the not guilty verdict of a jury of twelve men and women. In fact, all of the charges were based on falsehoods, which we had demonstrated at trial.

In a motion filed later by my attorneys, they would argue: "The issue in the criminal trial was not whether Mr. Kaiser performed those acts (he admitted that he did), but whether the equipment's design rendered it primarily useful for surreptitious interception of communications. Mr. Kaiser contended that the equipment (which was an ordinary microphone and amplifier) was identical to the equipment that could be bought in any electronics store. The jury, by its not guilty verdicts on all three counts, agreed with Mr. Kaiser . . ."

Furthermore, after we traveled to North Carolina and started reviewing the documents requested through discovery, we found what I thought would be my single most persuasive defense in this civil case: what, in my opinion, was a conflict of interest on the part of the FBI and the two agents leading the criminal investigation against me.

I was shocked when I first saw the stack of FBI files. There, on top of the pile, were all 24 of my *original* letters that I had sent to the grand jurors. My shock then turned to anger. My seeing the originals meant that NONE of the grand jurors said to the FBI agents collecting the letters, "Hey! This guy sent me the letter and it is mine to keep." They were probably threatened with some sort of legal action if the letters were not surrendered. I later learned that the FBI tried to indict me for tampering with a grand jury, but that was ludicrous, because the grand jury had already been dismissed by the time I wrote the letters. Again, so much for grand jury secrecy.

According to the FBI Manual of Administrative Operations and Procedures, it is improper for field agents to continue any further criminal investigation of an individual if there is a potential conflict of interest involved. Section 45.735-4 [c] mandates that "no employee shall have either a direct or indirect financial interest that conflicts or *appears to conflict* with his government duties and responsibilities." [italics added]

The manual goes on to state that all agents, when receiving an assignment involving either a direct or indirect financial interest, are required to advise their superiors, and such agent or agents *shall be relieved of such assignment.* If there is a strong reason for the agent to remain involved in the case, the matter must receive direct approval from FBI headquarters in Washington.

The fact that the FBI gave its permission to these agents to sue me civilly three months before I was indicted on criminal charges and then allowed them to continue to lead the criminal investigation against me was no oversight or mistake. This was another example, in my humble opinion, of their retaliation against me.

Unfortunately, we had no knowledge of this during the criminal trial, but in our motion in response to the civil case, we called it a crystal clear example of abuse of power by the country's most powerful law enforcement agency.

"They [Brereton and Lowe] were given access and power of the federal government they should not have been given," argued Stephen Spring, a Louisiana lawyer who would later replace Fensterwald to represent me on the civil case.

Once we discovered they had been given prior permission to sue me civilly, I filed a counterclaim against Brereton and Lowe for $720,000 in damages. Several months later I added a $10.7 million suit against the FBI for "assisting and enabling [them] to gain access to information and records [about me] while on bureau time and through bureau resources of information directly bearing on the outcome of the civil action."

But as we plowed through thousands of pages of grand jury testimony, we noticed material that I didn't believe was true in statements made by Brereton. For example, Brereton presented my countermeasure equipment catalog with the comment, "Here is Mr. Kaiser's catalog of illegal equipment."

Absolutely nothing in that catalog was "illegal." The law only prohibited the sale and marketing of eavesdropping devices. My catalog contained only countermeasure and bomb disposal products, and basic electronic listening devices on sale in any electronics store. I could sell those products to whoever I wished, and I did, including to Northwestern Bank. My products were no different from a half-dozen other companies selling countermeasure equipment in the United States and advertising their equipment in similar catalogs.

More outrageous than that was the bait-and-switch game that the FBI and Brereton and Lowe played regarding the tape recorders allegedly used to tape their conversations, which were played at the criminal trial, and the tape recorder entered as evidence in the civil case.

At a hearing held before U.S. Middle District Court Judge Frank W. Bullock Jr., in February 1983, we submitted a motion and expert testimony alleging that the Panasonic tape recorder presented at my criminal trial played at a different speed—one-third—than the recorder submitted as evidence in the civil case. That recorder operated at one-fourth normal speed.

We had a nationally known tape recording expert, Dr. Rawdon Smith, testify that tests he conducted indicated the two tape recordings of Brereton and Lowe were not made on the tape recorder I had provided to Northwestern Bank in 1977. He confirmed that the two tapes were made on different recorders.

Our motion said in conclusion, "It is our belief, based upon a review of these tests, that these modifications were performed by agents and/or employees of the FBI as part of a conspiracy wherein the FBI acted in concert with plaintiffs Brereton and Lowe by attempting to convict me of a crime I did not commit and instituting the present civil suit as a retaliatory measure designed to drain me of funds necessarily spent in my defense."

During the process of discovery and requesting various documents, it also became apparent that someone had taken documents out of the FBI files regarding my case that were never returned. When we asked where they were, the bureau claimed the papers were lost. My lawyers made a motion to have the charges dismissed, but the judge didn't agree. The civil suit continued to drag on and the money meter continued to run.

The files also revealed that the FBI was still investigating me for my trip to Egypt. They had me in two other cities—Los Angeles and Chicago—at exactly the same time that I was in Cairo. I told the U.S. Attorney that I could prove I was in Egypt by 1) the date in my passport; 2) looking at a copy of the contract; 3) my plane ticket boarding passes; and 4) a letter from the CIA supporting my contention. Even with all of that supporting data, the U.S. Attorney said he would not correct their records regarding my location in these other places on the date that I was in Egypt.

This is another problem with the FBI's vaunted data collection. It's frequently incorrect, but the bureau rarely deletes anything it has entered in its files, no doubt a throwback to the Hoover era. Yet this data is often used to build cases against innocent citizens. I have the legal right to obtain my credit history in order to correct mistakes. But that legal right does not seem to apply to federal law enforcement agency files, including the FBI. Why not? I believe the only possible way to correct false information in one's FBI file is to bring a civil suit against the FBI, proving that the information is false and has resulted in damage to one's reputation or business. That seems go against every constitutional right of due process under the U.S. system of justice that holds that individuals are considered innocent until proven guilty.

Despite my acquittal on the criminal charges, Carmel still took the view that I should not go forward with the civil suit. She wanted me to settle it to save time and money. While I understood her feelings about this, I refused to give in to what I felt was a case of character assassination by the FBI. I told Bud Fensterwald to proceed.

As the civil suit was under way, I had two interesting diversions. The first one, coming in late 1979, was an on-camera interview in a British documentary titled *The Spying Game*. The documentary traced the beginning of modern electronic surveillance in 1946 to Russia's use of the passive cavity resonator hidden in the Great Seal in the U.S. Embassy in Moscow. The documentary also demonstrated how the transistor revolutionized the art of electronic espionage.

As I explained earlier, the hollowed-out center of the Great Seal, no bigger than a pencil, would be targeted with an electronic beam of light from outside the building that would collect audio from inside the room and transmit it to a remote receiver. The beauty of the device was its lack of wires or batteries, which meant it was impossible to detect.

My contribution to the documentary consisted of two of my specialty areas: the use of an existing microphone or speaker system in bugging an office, and how telephone tapping experts eliminated the proverbial "click" that was often heard in the early telephone line compromises.

I demonstrated that the easiest source of power for a room bug is to connect the transmitter to an existing microphone. It could be a telephone mouthpiece, a radio, an interoffice communication, or a Muzak system. The same principal applies: sounds goes in, electricity goes out, which is translated into live audio.

The trick to eliminating the "click" in a telephone tap is as simple as wetting your finger. Technicians discovered that by slipping the clip over a wet finger and directly onto the telephone line, you removed the static electricity that caused the click.

My other diversion came during the early 1980s, again in the form of an on-camera interview, in a BBC-produced documentary called *Confessions of a Dangerous Man*. It was about my old friend and fugitive from justice, Frank Terpil, who was interviewed in a penthouse apartment in downtown Beirut, Lebanon.

I was introduced by the interviewer as "the Michelangelo of the bugging business" and a "master craftsman who enjoys a reputation for uncompromising honesty," referring of course to my testimony before the National Wiretap Commission.

At that point in my life, I must confess that it was heartening to hear someone say some complimentary things about me.

I was interviewed about my assignment to train the Egyptian intelligence service following the Yom Kippur War, and Terpil's intimate knowledge of everything I was doing. I made the point that despite the fact that my contract and the fee were classified, Frank knew everything about my schedule and even what was in my suitcase (after it was searched by Egyptian airport police).

My remarks supported one of the primary points of the documentary: Despite Terpil's forced resignation from the CIA in 1972 and his two indictments on charges of selling explosives to Libya's Mu'mmar Gadhafi, and attempting to sell 10,000 British machine guns to undercover New York cops, he was still able to move with impunity throughout Europe and the Middle East, thanks to his connections with his former employer.

Terpil told the BBC interviewer that his flight from the United States in September 1980 was facilitated by people "in a position of authority" in the CIA.

"We were told that no one would try to stop us when we left," Terpil told the interviewer, referring to his fellow fugitive and arms dealer, Gary Korkala, "but that we would not survive a month in prison."

Terpil left the United States a day later, flying out of Washington using a phony passport. He told the interviewer that between himself and Ed Wilson, his earlier partner in crime, they were privy to an enormous amount of highly sensitive information regarding past and present CIA operations that they would divulge if brought to trial. It was their bargaining chip for a get-out-of-jail-free card.

It worked for Terpil but not for Wilson. He was lured out of Libya in 1981 to the Dominican Republic, where local officials refused entry to him and sent him on to New York. U.S. officials arrested him when his plane touched down in New York. Wilson was later convicted of selling tons of C-4 to Libya and hiring hit men to murder witnesses who would testify against him. Wilson was eventually sentenced to fifty-three years in prison without parole, but was released in September 2004, after a court overturned the conviction in connection with the sale of arms and explosives to Libya. The court found that the CIA and the Justice Department had "fabricated" evidence against him. In June 2005, Wilson's lawyers filed a motion to throw out his 1982 conviction on the basis that the CIA "not only knew of his clandestine international arms trafficking but also directed much of his activity."

One of the most alarming stories told in the documentary was about one of Terpil's couriers, who got drunk during a layover at Heathrow airport on his way to the Middle East. What made this situation particularly dicey was that the courier was reportedly packing enough binary explosives to blow up the city of London. Yet he was able to wander out of the in-transit lounge and into the concourses and bars of the airport, waiting for the connecting flight to Libya. The courier was finally taken into custody by airport authorities, but was later released and sent on his way—still carrying the explosives—thanks to a British intelligence colleague of Terpil.

Jim Hougan, a veteran reporter and author of several books about the U.S. intelligence community, was one of the only journalists to interview Terpil, and he helped the BBC arrange the interview with Terpil in Beirut.

"Frank Terpil was like a lot of people who left the CIA," said Hougan in the documentary. "He had training and skills, but not the kind he could use in the private sector. He was essentially unemployable. So he decided to offer his services to the private sector where the goal was profit, not public service."

Regardless of what the agency claims, I always thought of Frank as a member in good standing of the old boys' club of the intelligence fraternity. The fact that he was no longer on the CIA's payroll did little to diminish his privileges as a freelance spook. In many ways, he had the best of both worlds: He knew too many things about covert CIA operations to be put out of business, but he was not encumbered by the agency's rules and regulations.

I once found a reference to a book written about Terpil, titled *Beyond the CIA: The Frank Terpil Story* by Richard Lloyd and Antony Thomas. The publisher was Henry Holt & Co. and the publication date was September 1, 1984. However, in checking with more than twenty out-of-print-book Web sites, I could find no existing copies of the book.

I later found out why: The book had been mysteriously canceled prior to publication, but no reason was ever given. Did the CIA use its power to get the book pulled on grounds that it violated national security statutes regarding the release of classified information? Who knows? The CIA is not talking and Terpil has left no forwarding address.

Life for me moved at a snail's pace back then. I often felt like I was treading water, barely able to keep my mouth above the water line. But plenty of neat new technologies came along in the 1980s, especially for those, like me, obsessed with electronics and the devices the field spawned.

IBM launched its first PC in 1981, running an operating system written by Microsoft, which had been started by a Harvard dropout named Bill Gates. That same year the compact disc (CD) was introduced. Two years later the CD-ROM came on the market, and Apple revolutionized desktop publishing with the Macintosh computer. It was also the year the Internet gave us Domain Name Service, which classified Internet addresses with extensions such as .com, .net, and .org.

As the 1980s continued, the bulk of my business was in the bomb field. I was selling "bomb disrupters" (high-speed water cannons that separate bombs from their detonators), bomb suits, stethoscopes, and bomb detectors, as well as meeting the reduced demand for the old reliable Model 1059 countermeasure amplifier and RF bug detector.

But the FBI was never completely out of my mind. In July 1983, I sold four SAFECO bomb suits to the Singapore government. I had been selling countermeasure and bomb-related equipment to foreign governments and customers for more than ten years and had never had one shipment detained by U.S. Customs. That is, until then.

I received a letter from U.S. Customs that the bomb suits had been held up at Baltimore-Washington International Airport, but no reason was given. It took me four weeks and several trips to U.S. Customs at the airport to get the bomb suits cleared for shipment. The holdup was never explained. This may have been another example of the FBI flexing its muscles against me, or it could simply have been the random dysfunction of government bureaucracy. I have my opinion.

I continued to supplant my equipment sales with countermeasure sweeps. One of my favorite customers was Representative Helen Bentley, a Republican representing Baltimore County from 1985 to 1995. Representative Bentley served on the Appropriations and

Budget committees as well as Public Works and Transportation, and Maritime, Marine, and Fisheries during her five terms in Congress. Before or after hearings on some controversial piece of legislation, I would get a call from her staff director, Chris Griffin, to ask me to sweep her house.

I always looked forward to those sweeps because it gave me a chance to talk to Helen one-to-one, and to look at her husband's fantastic collection of antiques. I never found any eavesdropping devices on her property. However, I did find a carrier current "baby sitter"—one of those nursery baby monitors that became popular in the 1980s—at one of her neighbors' houses, which shared a power transformer with her. I let Helen listen to it, but I don't know if she ever told her neighbor that they had bugged themselves.

On one occasion, Griffin asked if I would check Helen's campaign headquarters. Again, I found nothing. The phones were of a newer design that contained a CPU (central processing unit) to handle the switching. I showed her staff how easy it was to bug those phones by simply pointing my 2010 Doppler Stethoscope at the CPU and listing to the conversation. Look, Ma, no hands, no wires. The staff was amazed at the ease with which their phones could be compromised.

Sometime in the late 1990s, I called to say hello to Chris and the Congresswoman. Griffin told me something that confirmed what I had known since the beginning regarding my problems with the FBI.

"You know, Marty," he said. "the boss [referring to Representative Bentley] did try to resolve your problem with the FBI, but we were told that the problem went too far up."

Translation: When you get on the wrong side of the bureau, no amount of political clout can help you.

Sales of my bomb detection and protection equipment line began to pick up after a Hezbollah truck bomb killed 241 American Marines in Beirut in the summer of 1984. I received calls from the army, navy and air force EOD teams regarding my radio-controlled bomb detection device. Unfortunately, nothing would have saved those Marines from that terrorist attack.

Try as I might, I could never completely escape the ongoing civil suit. I also had to change lawyers during the suit. I should explain that my decision was not the result of my unhappiness with Bud Fensterwald.

Bud had done a marvelous job for me and was instrumental in my acquittal in the criminal case. But there came a point in the civil proceedings when I simply ran out of funds. Bud urged me to let the lawyers for my insurance company settle with Brereton and Lowe's lawyers, but I refused. I simply could not accept defeat.

One of Bud's last letters was prophetically accurate. It read in part,

> *There are very few people that I've known in my lifetime who had the guts to try to curb the excesses of such outfits as the F.B.I. As badly as it needs doing, most people say "Let George do it."*
>
> *If and when you decide that you can't go on further, you'll get absolutely no squawk from me. You have been courageous in the extreme, and if you've had it, so be it.*
>
> *However, if you want to go on down the trail to the end, you will have to be prepared for more sacrifices. We will trim costs wherever possible, but it's going to be a long process and will end with a long trial. . . .*

About a year later, I called Steve Spring. He had been referred to me years earlier by the Louisiana State Police, for whom he was working as a paralegal on several cases. He had put himself through LSU law school doing countermeasure sweeps on oil rigs in the Gulf of Mexico, using equipment that I sold him. I explained my problem and asked if we could swap services. I would teach him the finer points of countermeasure in exchange for his pro bono representation on my civil suit. We had a deal. Steve was a blessing.

But in the end, my insurance company had lost patience. They insisted that we settle the suit regardless of my wishes. On April Fool's Day, 1986, nearly eight years after Brereton and Lowe had filed their civil suit against me, my legal battle was over.

Some people would call it a Pyrrhic victory. The only consolation for me was that the agents didn't get the payoff they were dreaming about. I am prohibited by the nondisclosure agreement from saying any more than that. I refused to sign the agreement, but the lawyers for my insurance company signed in my stead. I had no choice but to go along with it. If I had persisted, it would have ended my marriage and driven me further into an emotional and financial abyss.

Chapter 15

The Aftermath

THE YEARS FOLLOWING the civil suit settlement were mostly a blur of work and negative emotions. Or simply no emotions at all. From childhood, I had developed the ability to detach myself from my feelings. It came in handy at that point in my life. It was the only way I could get through the day. But eventually it would take its toll personally. The numbness, plus heavy doses of antidepressants—except for lithium, which made me feel like I was strapped in a leather suit—kept me going. Yet nothing seemed to relieve the feeling of hopelessness completely.

The situation at home was manageable, but not great. Carmel and I carried on polite conversations, but we avoided discussing what was really going on inside me. My son, Marty, was going through an extended period of rebellion, including a refusal to work, and I was experiencing a similar lack of motivation.

There were periods when I would wake up in the morning, eat breakfast, go to my shop, lie down on the couch in the basement, and not move all day. Sometimes I read, sometimes I watched TV (the Iran-Contra hearings), and often I did nothing but doze. Fortunately, my business didn't suffer that much. I had a very competent secretary, Janice Wheelbarger, who handled most of the equipment orders by phone. I still had enough of a reputation in the bomb disposal and detection business that my customers kept those orders coming without much sales effort on my part.

But, as Robert Capa, the legendary World War II combat photographer, wrote in the opening sentence of his memoir, *Slightly Out of Focus*, "There was absolutely no reason to get up in the mornings any more."

The Hungarian-born Capa's sense of despair was prompted by the fact that he was flat broke at the time. He had also just received a letter from the Justice Department informing him that he had been classified as a potential enemy alien, and ordering him to surrender his cameras, his only source of income.

I could empathize completely. I often felt like E.T. looking for someone to help me get home from this alien planet called Earth. There were many moments during those years when I felt like I might as well have been given the same enemy classification as Capa. The fact that I was born and raised in this country made no difference.

It was around this time I met Bill Behre through the International Association of Bomb Technicians and Investigators (IABTI). I met Bill through Dave Nye, a Miami bomb investigator, at an IABTI meeting. In my rogues' gallery of colorful characters I've run across in this business, Behre ranks near the top. Bill was a novice when it came to explosives, but he knew his way around weapons of all types and calibers. He was also one of my closest friends, who was always there for me when I started getting down on myself.

Behre said he had been involved in the Bay of Pigs invasion back in 1961, but his connection to the agency was always a mystery, as was his source of income. The one story he told about the invasion had the ring of truth if only because it seemed like a metaphor for the entire operation.

Behre's assignment in the early hours of the invasion was to attach WWII limpet mines to Cuban gunboats in Havana harbor. The only problem, Bill explained, was that when he and his UDT (Under

Water Demolition) team tried to attach the limpet mines to the wooden hulls of the Cuban boats, there was no metal to adhere to the magnet on the mines.

Bill was like a lot of people I met in the intel community, particularly in Miami in the late 1980s: independent contractors with some lethal skills for hire. For Bill, I had the impression that guns were his hobby as well as part of his occupation. And he looked the part of someone you would not want to mess with in a bar or in a dark alley. He was not tall, but he was built like an NFL linebacker, with not an ounce of fat on his broad frame.

Every time I visited Miami, I would stay with Bill and his wife, Sylvia. I was always amazed by the number and variety of weapons he had around the house, including a silenced machine pistol with a thirty-shot clip. Bill, Sylvia, and I would often go for target practice at an old CIA training area somewhere out in the Everglades and blast away at the holes inside of holes. It seemed that anything that could be shot had been shot at repeatedly.

He would give me a Glock nine-millimeter or a .45 caliber automatic to shoot, and he would blast away with what he referred to as his "pecker pistol." It was a three-shot, .22 caliber pistol slightly larger than a cigarette lighter but smaller than a derringer, and perfect, he said, for close-range targets. In other words, an assassination weapon. It was curved so that it could be hidden high up in the crotch. A hands-on body search would miss it.

I once asked him why he had a silenced machine pistol and the pecker pistol.

"To shoot people with," he said, casually. "No other reason for weapons like that." I never pursued the subject with him.

One day when we were firing weapons out in the Glades, a pickup truck drove slowly up the road toward us and stopped about a thousand yards away. The driver got out and lifted two .50 caliber machine guns from the back of the truck while a teenage girl and boy with him unloaded several ammo boxes and placed them beside the machine guns.

Without a glance in our direction—judging from the guy's nonchalance I assumed this must be a public free-fire range, or too remote to worry about getting fined—the man mounted the guns on tripods and fed the ammunition belts into the gun breaches. The two youngsters then took prone positions behind the weapons and started firing into the Glades. Within seconds, the nipa palms and shrubbery that were their targets had disintegrated.

They must have gone through thousands of rounds of ammunition before they called it a day. I always thought it was a bit strange to see a man, possibly a father, bringing his teenage kids for an afternoon of shooting recreation. The really odd thing was that these kids weren't plinking cans with .22 caliber rifles. They were learning to fire what were essentially weapons of war. I absently wondered whether there were state laws against letting kids that young fire automatic weapons, and what these kids would ultimately do with those kinds of skills. I also wondered if the local county sheriff realized that between the machine gun crew and us, we had enough firepower to have taken over a small Caribbean island.

"Do you know this guy?" I asked Bill.

He looked back in the direction of the man and the kids.

"Nope," said Bill. "Probably just another devotee of the Second Amendment, demonstrating his constitutional rights."

Weapons and explosives aside, where Bill and I really connected was our shared love for the Caribbean and scuba diving. He particularly loved the Bahamas and diving for treasure down there. He had dozens of stories about his treasure-hunting experiences, but one of them seemed unbelievable even coming from Bill.

One day he had hired a local Bahamian with a rowboat to tow him around while he snorkeled off a particular island. After several hours, Bill said he was about to give up when he spotted something shiny about fifteen to twenty feet down. He dived, and to his astonishment, he found a huge stack of silver ingots lying loose on a sandy ledge. It took him a couple of hours to haul his sunken treasure to the boat. When he had brought up the last of the silver bullion, he counted 150 five-pound ingots. In terms of silver prices at the time, he estimated the haul was worth more than $50,000.

Bill told me this story on the phone one day in the late 1980s. I didn't want to hurt his feelings, but there was no way I could buy it.

"Where could all that silver come from, Bill?" I asked, feigning belief.

"Who knows, Marty," he said. "Bank robbers, pirates, drug dealers? Who cares? Finders keepers."

"I can't wait to see all those ingots. Where you keeping them?"

"Stacked up in a corner of my living room," he said.

Yeah, right, I thought. If it's true, it's probably safer there than anywhere else. I was in Miami about a month later and called Bill.

"I want to come by and see your sunken treasure," I told him.

"Come on over, Marty."

About half an hour later, I was in Bill's living room gazing at 150 gleaming five-pound silver ingots, stacked up in several huge towers in one corner of his living room, just as he had promised. It was more precious metal than I'd ever seen in my entire life.

"Told you so, Marty," said Bill.

"You certainly did, Bill," I said, thinking that the story about planting limpet mines on the hulls of Cuban gunboats during the Bay of Pigs was probably the real deal after all.

I continued to do a substantial business in bomb detection equipment, including stethoscopes, bomb suits, and fiberglass extender poles, and I was still selling RF bug detector equipment. The CIA backed away from me in terms of countermeasure and surveillance transmitters, but in the mid-1980s, they started buying water cannons (bomb disrupters) and bomb detection equipment.

I also had a standing order from the State Department for ministethoscopes and bomb blasting machines. They were used at the U.S. government's bomb disposal school located outside New

Orleans. The feds rented property for the school at the Louisiana State Police Academy in Baton Rouge.

Even with the continuing support of the IABTI, the FBI continued its concerted effort to keep me away from its Bomb Information Program events. At one of the bureau's annual bomb conferences at the FBI academy at Quantico, Virginia, the IABTI gave me a phony registration pass during range day so that I could attend. I was "Jack Smith."

Several IABTI members came up to me during the conference, wondering how I was able to get through the front gate.

"I'm under cover," I said, laughing, showing them my name tag alias and pretending that nothing bothered me, least of all the Feebs.

But privately, I was dying inside. The FBI's vendetta toward me would never end, I realized. And this notion only deepened my paranoia and depression.

Through the 1980s, I continued to do countermeasure sweeps for corporations, most often in response to calls from ex-intelligence agency officers I had dealt with in the past who had retired and taken jobs in private-sector security.

The corporate sweeps included Ford Motor Company, Sweetheart Cup Corporation, Xerox Corporation, Eastern Airlines, McDonnell Douglas, United Aircraft, and Squibb Pharmaceutical Corporation. As usual, my sweeps tended to result in zero phone line compromises or bugs. As always, there was a mixture of relief and disappointment from the management.

One of the most amusing countermeasure jobs I ever undertook (I'm sure the client did not find it very funny) involved a Holiday Inn a few miles from my office in Cockeysville, Maryland. A gang of thieves was stealing the TV sets from the rooms on a weekly basis. They would check in, pretending to be guests, and sneak off with the TVs in the middle of the night. The manager asked me to rig up a silent alarm system that would be triggered the moment the room TV sets were moved from their original position.

It turned out he didn't need my countermeasure expertise. The same day I installed the alarm system one of the guests called the front desk to report that her TV set had just fallen off the wall. The bolts that held the TV set up on one side of the wall also held up the TV set on the other side. When the bolts were removed, down went the other set. The desk manager immediately went to the adjoining room and caught the thief with the TV in his hands, about to carry it out the door. Curiously, the thefts stopped after the man was caught.

Despite the launching of the first Iraq war in January 1991 under President George H. W. Bush, my sales in bomb equipment and detection devices remained fairly flat. Uncle Sam was throwing tons of money into the war and there was no need for the little guy. At this point, there also was no evidence of roadside bomb attacks, which might have brought business my way.

The U.S. invasion force rolled over Saddam Hussein's troops in about eight days, and the war was over. It was also around that time that I started experiencing random panic attacks at my plant. My pulse would suddenly start to rev up for no apparent reason. Then as quickly as it began, it would stop.

My insomnia grew worse, as well as my headaches. There were nights when I would toss and turn until dawn, finally falling into an exhausted stupor. I also began to receive phone calls at the office in which people would hang up after several seconds of silence.

There were days when I had trouble focusing, when hours would pass without my remembering where the time had gone. Suddenly, I would look at my watch and realize I had just wasted another afternoon.

I eventually came to the realization that I was losing the one joy in life that had always kept me going—my work, the creative juices that inspired me. It didn't seem to matter any longer. I also began to engage in behavior that would later be identified as an obsessive-compulsive disorder. Washing my hands twenty or thirty times a day, just like J. Edgar Hoover. Checking the locks on my doors at the office every few minutes. Checking the rooms and the phones for bugs more frequently. Fidgeting and unable to sit still for more than a few minutes. And the panic attacks worsened.

I also thought about ending it all for the first time. For several months in the spring of 1992, I hit bottom emotionally. I could barely force myself to get out of bed. During that period, I often thought about going to work, but I was afraid to go to the office for fear that I might use the pistol I kept there to kill myself.

Despite increased dosages of the medication I was taking— Prozac, Navane, and Paxil—nothing seemed to give me relief. I felt like I was losing altitude, psychologically and emotionally. There were times when I felt close to tears, but the tears would never come. I was crying inside but kept up a smiling front.

In the middle of June 1992, I decided to take a trip to our condo in the Cayman Islands. I thought that it might be the thing to help me snap out of my doldrums. However, just the opposite happened. When I opened the condo door, everything went black. I could hardly move and went straight to bed, where I remained for two days.

I was finally able to force myself to call my good buddy, Gwynne Ebanks, and she got me on a plane headed back to the United States. I was admitted to St. Joseph's Hospital in Baltimore and spent two weeks there, being tested and engaging in various discussions with the psychologists. Dr. Linda Meade, one of the psychologists who examined me, summed up my emotional state with these impressions:

Depression is an enduring feature of [his] personality. Comfort, satisfaction and security are missing from Mr. Kaiser's life and apparently have not been consistent companions for years. He feels lost. Early on, he established an attitude of mistrust towards the world and came to perceive people as hostile, rejecting and dangerous. Therefore, he avoids close interpersonal relationships out of a fear of emotional involvement and seems shy and withdrawn. Stemming from the mistreatment by his parents, Mr. Kaiser expects negative consequences from being dependent on people, yet as his early dependence needs were never satisfied, he cannot help latching on given the slightest opportunity. Often, he is disappointed by the responses of others and feels an absence of social support. This reinforces his paranoid leanings. . . .

I still didn't buy the paranoid label. As someone in the business once told me, just because you're paranoid doesn't mean someone's not out to get you. I was a living example of that expression.

I went home in late June 1992, still pumped up with drugs but with no interest in returning to work. It took me months to return to the office, but this time the motivation was financial survival. I had no choice. Every day was a struggle, but slowly I worked my way back to normality and financial security. I had to support my family. There was no other way but up.

Chapter 16

"Enemy of the State"

BY LATE 1995, I had worked my way back to sanity—at least on my good days. My bomb disposal equipment line was keeping me solvent and satisfied. And there was still the occasional sale of countermeasure or surveillance equipment. I was still on the meds, and they helped me get through the days. I went to work every morning, happy to have something productive to fill my days and hoping to find something that would kick up my adrenalin, a diversion to take me out of myself and my world. I needed a project in which I could totally lose myself.

The phone rang one morning in October. For a change it was something to smile about.

It was Andrew Davis, an executive producer with Walt Disney Productions/Touchstone Pictures. Years earlier I had sold Disney one of my countermeasure kits. When Davis called, I assumed it was about the kit. Instead, he told me he was calling on behalf of the movie producer Jerry Bruckheimer. He said they had a script in development that involved the National Security Agency (NSA) and had heard of my reputation and expertise in electronic surveillance. He had also read the story on my website, martykaiser.com, about my experience with the FBI.

The idea for the film was about a man whose identity is stolen and manipulated by rogue NSA agents who were trying to cover up the assassination of a public official. The man, played by Will Smith, is unwittingly passed digital photographic evidence of the murder and suddenly becomes a target of the NSA himself.

I asked Davis what the title was. He said, *Enemy of the State.*

"Sounds great," I told him. "A perfect description of me from the FBI's point of view."

The *Baltimore Sun* had just published a six-part Sunday magazine series on the NSA. Davis told me Jerry Bruckheimer had seen the articles and that they were very interested in making the film.

"They want to make it as realistic as possible, Marty," Davis told me. "Are you interested in working on the script?"

"You bet," I told him.

"Great," said Davis. "When can you come out to California to meet with Jerry Bruckheimer?"

"Yesterday," I told him. "I'm raring to go. Who're the lead actors?"

"We're hoping to get Will Smith and Gene Hackman."

"Hackman's one of my favorite actors," I told Davis. "You know I provided technical support on the movie that he starred in back in the 1970s as an eavesdropper, called *The Conversation.*"

"Really," said Davis. "Well, that's great because Bruckheimer wants this film to feature state-of-the-art eavesdropping techniques."

"No problem," I told him. "You've come to the right guy."

I wanted to tell Davis that when *The Conversation* came out in 1974 my colleagues in the surveillance business assumed that I was the inspiration for the protagonist of the story, the paranoid eavesdropper, Harry Caul, played by Hackman. But I figured Davis already knew that.

Harry Caul was your basic technological genius: detached, humorless, professionally enthusiastic, and suspicious of others' intentions to the point of paranoia. He was also haunted in his darker moments by the morality of what he did for a living. I was one step removed from the character of Harry Caul. I only made the surveillance devices to meet a specific target need. I did not conduct the eavesdropping.

I never met Francis Ford Coppola, the director and writer of *The Conversation*, but I did provide technical expertise to his assistant directors regarding how to conduct a sweep to check for bugs. I did most of it on the phone. I sent them my catalog and they were particularly interested in my telephone analyzer.

The technical aspects of the last scene of the film, which takes place in Harry Caul's apartment, were entirely my invention. Caul is being bugged by a corporation that he conducted surveillance for and which he believes is involved in the murder of the CEO. He starts to tear his place apart looking for the listening device.

I gave notes to the assistant director, who passed them on to Hackman, about how he, in the role of Harry Caul, should check his telephone for bugs. My suggestions included how Hackman should unscrew the mouthpiece and inspect it for compromises. His gestures and actions in pushing up and down on the hook switch inside the phone and looking to see if the contacts were being made were also in response to my suggestions.

But my pièce de résistance in the film was captured in the final moments as Harry Caul sits alone in the midst of the total destruction of his apartment, unable to find the device that is invading his privacy. As the camera pulls back, Harry Caul plays his saxophone, not realizing that it is the bug. Caul, the legendary eavesdropper, has been unwittingly bugged, in a figurative sense, by his own hand.

I explained to the assistant director that the saxophone serves as a natural eavesdropping device because it is made of two dissimilar metals that form the antenna for a transmitter. An RF signal is generated from a remote location to the apartment. It is detected by the instrument's two different metals and captures room audio that is bounced back out to a receiver.

It is the same concept as a nonlinear junction detector (NLJD), the device used to detect clandestine RF transmitters even when they are turned off. Most RF listening devices contain transistors or diodes (an IC, or Integrated Circuit, is made up of many, many transistors and diodes). When the signal from the transmitter in the NLJD antenna senses a transistor or diode, it acts like a mirror and reflects the signal. The signal returns with multiples of the original signal known as harmonics, and their existence indicates an RF listening device.

I thought the use of the saxophone as the ultimate bug in Harry Caul's apartment was a subtle and ironic touch in a disturbing movie, one of the first films to deal with that subject matter.

In January 1996, I flew out to California to meet with Jerry Bruckheimer and Andy Davis about working on the script of *Enemy of the State.* At the meeting, Bruckheimer gave me a fifty-page partially completed script written by David Marconi and asked me to make it real in terms of the capabilities of government electronic surveillance. While the technologies used in the film might have been a shocker to the majority of audiences, the truth is that it was probably twenty years behind what was currently possible.

When I first read Marconi's script, I knew what the Will Smith character was going through in terms of the NSA shadowing his every move and looking into every aspect of his life. In the words of Yogi Berra, it was déjà vu all over again. Only the initials of the shadow agency were different. In some ways, the film's message was a little too close to home to suit me. I was not sure that I was ready to relive the experience.

Then it dawned on me that the very thing I had been fighting for over the past twenty years—protection of individual liberties, especially privacy—was what this movie was all about. I realized that working on this film offered me the opportunity to get this point across, and at the same time start to put to rest my anger, frustration, and pain over what the FBI had put me through.

I flew back to Maryland and started working on the script. Within a couple of months I had expanded it to two hundred pages, filled with the various surveillance capabilities of the NSA.

When I first read the script I thought it was going to be a boring movie. But I saw the opportunity to show them some cutting-edge surveillance. I went through the script and made copious notes on how to make it more interesting in terms of the electronics. I helped refine every draft again and again.

Once I finished the initial suggestions, Jerry Bruckheimer flew me back to California to meet the director, Tony Scott, and add some details to the technical aspects of the script. Scott told me he was "fascinated with the idea of surveillance, especially surveillance from thousands of miles up in space." He added that he had always been a big fan of the films *Three Days of the Condor* and *The Conversation*, and he wanted to do one in that genre.

One of the first things I did was to sit down with the prop guy—he had designed a miniature NSA headquarters—and give him a list of bugs and countermeasure devices that I felt would give some edge to the film. I provided the majority of bugs used, particularly in the tracking devices used to bug Will Smith's character's suit, wristwatch, cell phone, shoe heel, and fountain pen in the hotel.

I suggested changes to the script as they rehearsed each scene. One of the toughest things about the process was making the script understandable to the average person. I wanted the guy in the audience who knows nothing about surveillance electronics to get what was happening, but not put him to sleep with jargon. Some of the technical effects they wanted were, well, clearly out of this world.

One example: Tony Scott wanted to have a scene in which the NSA techs call for diverting a KR-12 spy satellite circling hundreds of miles above the earth to target a ten-block radius in Washington. Scott also wanted the satellite sending a signal back to the techs at Fort Meade. I've never heard of a satellite sending Morse code, but in the movie script, the satellite keeps beeping the Morse letters C.Q.

over and over. Translated, it means "Will you answer me?" Clearly an oversight.

When I heard this, I thought, oh, God, you have this multibillion-dollar satellite sending a signal asking "Will you answer me?" I'm sure no one caught that humor except for the folks at NSA, the National Reconnaissance Office (the agency in charge of managing the spy satellites in orbit around the earth), and ham radio operators.

I met Gene Hackman and Will Smith when they started principal photography on location in Baltimore and Washington in the fall of 1997. Smith was always very warm and outgoing. We shook hands on the set every morning for about three months. He probably wondered who the hell I was, but he shook my hand anyway.

On the other hand, Hackman was friendly but reserved. We spoke often on the set, but he usually walked around reciting his lines and I learned not to interrupt him. When he finished his scenes, he would head straight for his trailer.

Tony Scott remarked afterward that Hackman had paid particular attention to me during our discussions about surveillance and countermeasure. He watched my mannerisms, and learned the technology lingo as well as studying my body language and gesticulations.

"That was what Gene did," said Scott. "I could see him observing Marty. He would take just a little bit here and there and it would surface a week later" with the cameras rolling.

I came up with several key sequences that Tony Scott used in the film, including the method of killing the congressman (played by Jason Robards) used by Pratt, an NSA security person in one of the film's first scenes. Pratt, played by Barry Pepper, stabs Robards in the neck with a needle that knocks him unconscious, and then pushes him and his car into the Potomac River, making it appear to be a suicide.

I suggested the duck blind camera with the compound lens that films the murder of the Robards character. I also came up with a unique way to use a potato chip bag lined with aluminum foil. The

Hackman character places the electronic tracking devices he has found on the Will Smith character inside the bag of chips. The tracking devices were hidden inside Smith's wristwatch, belt, fountain pen, hollow shoe heel, and cell phone, as well as in the lining of his pants. The purpose of the snack bag was to provide the aluminum foil that shielded the devices from transmitting their location to a remote receiver.

The other surveillance technology I suggested included the electronic scanning lock pick used by the NSA agents to open the hotel room door during the chase scene with Will Smith, and the hand-held direction finder used to find Will Smith when he's taping the conversation between Hackman and the rogue NSA official, Reynolds (played by Jon Voight). Tony Scott also used my subminiature microphones in a scene at the end of the film when they bug the hotel room of a congressman.

I was on the set for about three months when they filmed in Baltimore and Washington. I even had a walk-on, a nonspeaking part in one of the last scenes of the movie, when Hackman and Smith go to a local electronics store to pick up some surveillance equipment.

NSA did give the principal actors a sanitized tour of their facilities at Fort Meade—no interaction with employees. But the brass were initially not happy with some of the scenes in the movie. They felt too much was revealed about the classified nature of their operations and capabilities.

When given a preview screening of the rough cut, NSA officials wanted four scenes deleted. After some negotiation, the scenes remained in the movie. I wasn't privy to those discussions, but I do know that Tony Scott found a small speaking part in the film for the daughter of Deputy Director William Crowell.

All told, it was great fun to be involved in the film. More important, the experience helped me to get on with my life and put the past behind me as much as possible. I got paid a $5,000 stipend for my work as a technical adviser, as well as a screen credit. The truth is that I would have done it for nothing. It was like the old days at RCA—getting paid for having fun and doing something you loved.

Enemy was not the last of my forays into the world of film-making. In early 2003, the producers of the TV series *Threat Matrix* called me with some technical questions regarding the series pilot. The plot involved the theft of a warhead from the nose cone of a missile. They wanted to know if this kind of theft was believable and how well the government protected the nuclear missiles from this kind of theft.

I assured them that the Atomic Energy Commission (AEC) had responsibility for detecting and tracking nuclear material. The AEC had been a customer of mine for both countermeasure and surveillance equipment. I knew they had a whole department of field agents who constantly tracked nuclear, bomb-grade material, as well as the electronics associated with these missiles. They traveled around with extremely sensitive sensors for this kind of work.

By the year 2000, the majority of my business was devoted to bomb detection and disposal. It has continued to be my primary revenue source. My customers have been primarily state and local bomb squads, but also the State Department Antiterrorism Assistance Programs in Louisiana and Virginia. The State Department in conjunction with the CIA conducts training programs in bomb disposal and detection for security personnel who eventually serve in Iraq and Afghanistan. I've sold hundreds of stethoscopes and blasting machines to the ATAP that have been used to dismantle roadside bombs in Iraq.

I continue to sell some countermeasure equipment to various state and local law enforcement agencies, as well as to the security directors of corporations and to retired intelligence agency people who have gone into business. Surprisingly, I get no legitimate orders for surveillance equipment anymore. It's almost as if people have been warned to stay away.

I still get suspicious phone calls from anonymous callers who ask me to plant eavesdropping devices in someone's car, boat, or house. My answer is always the same: Sorry, but I'm no longer in that line of work. There are also the breather phone calls where someone calls, listens for a few seconds, and then hangs up.

I have tried to keep my paranoia under control in those circumstances, but my thoughts always return to the FBI. They are no longer angry thoughts, but simply a gnawing sense of loss, sadness, and resignation.

Chapter 17

Looking Back

along the brittle treacherous bright streets
of memory comes my heart, singing like
an idiot, whispering like a drunken man
who (at a certain corner, suddenly) meets
the tall policeman of my mind.

—e. e. cummings

Memory—as I interpret Cummings's words—always offers up the truth no matter how you try to spin it or pretty it up. And I know all about the "tall policeman of my mind" because he's always there to remind me of the real truth of any event that I've experienced.

My story would not be complete without recalling some of the memorable characters I've met and/or worked with (in addition to those already mentioned) during my career in surveillance and countermeasures. What follows is a fleeting glimpse at my personal rogues' gallery of those who left their impressions—good and bad—on my memory.

Jack Holcomb Jack learned the wiretapping and surveillance trade as a detective in Hollywood in the 1950s, bugging the homes of movie stars, including (he once boasted) Charlie Chaplin.

In 1969, he was deported from the Caribbean island of Anguilla after the British government representative there described him as a "gangster-type element" during an abortive coup. The following year he was kicked out of Haiti shortly before the Haitian National Guard revolted, accused by the local media of being with the CIA.

Then Holcomb met the late Leo Goodwin Jr., the ultra conservative president of GEICO Insurance Co., and heir to one of America's largest fortunes. Holcomb persuaded Goodwin to finance his establishment of Audio Intelligence Devices (AID) Inc. in 1970. Several years later Holcomb established the National Intelligence Academy (NIA) in Ft. Lauderdale, Florida.

AID and NIA trained and sold equipment to several foreign police agencies, while the academy closed its doors in late 1976 in the wake of the Church hearings on the excesses of the U.S. intelligence community. Goodwin died in January 1977.

AID and Holcomb drew some publicity during that period when it was revealed that the company sold a radio tracking device as well as other bugging equipment to Michael Townley, a Chilean secret service operative, prior to the car bomb assassination in Washington, D.C., of former Chilean diplomat Orlando Letelier and his assistant, Ronnie Moffit, in September 1976. Townley was later convicted and jailed for organizing the murders and building the bomb, which was detonated by two anti-Castro exiles.

I crossed paths with Holcomb when we both testified before the National Wiretap Commission in 1975. We had been direct competitors for years, but he was friendly and outgoing, balding and round-faced. He shook my hand and asked how my business was doing.

I nodded and said, "Well, Jack. I guess we both got what we wanted," referring to his island in the Bahamas and my place in the Cayman Islands.

I was surprised that Holcomb and AID were able to promote and sell his surveillance equipment to foreign countries without any public action from the FBI. It struck me that Holcomb may have been well connected in the government intelligence community.

G. Gordon Liddy Liddy needs no introduction for most people. But for those too young to remember the Watergate scandal, he was the warrior of the Nixon White House, the only guy who refused to rat out his fellow conspirators.

For his role in various dirty tricks, including the break-in at the Democratic National Committee offices in the Watergate complex, plus the Daniel Ellsberg conspiracy and his refusal to implicate others, Liddy was sentenced to more than twenty years in prison. He served nearly five of it, mostly in maximum security, including 106 days in solitary confinement, before being pardoned by President Jimmy Carter in the late 1970s.

I met Liddy at an annual Surveillance Expo put on by Jim Ross of Ross Engineering. He lived up to his reputation as one of the scariest people one would want to meet. Most of his speech was about how he did his time in Danbury Federal Prison and survived. I'll never forget one of the points he made. He wanted his own toilet, so he put a sign on a stall door that the toilet was to be used only by people with venereal disease.

"That assured that I had my own private palace," he said.

He also demonstrated how he held the palm of his hand over a candle flame without flinching—one of the Liddy legends from the Watergate fiasco.

"It's all in the way you hold your hand," he told the group, "as well as having a high threshold for pain."

After his speech, I went up to him and shook his hand. I told him about my business and the federal agencies I dealt with. He gave no indication that he had ever heard of me. We shook hands for the photo op, then he thanked me for coming and walked away.

As I expected, Liddy had a crushing grip. I don't recall what else he said to me. I was just happy to have him let go of my hand.

Mitchell Livingston WerBell In the world of freelance spooks, Mitch WerBell was the real deal. With his trademark handlebar moustache, his swagger stick, and swashbuckling demeanor, he looked like the perfect choice from central casting to play the role of a hit man or a spy. In fact, from what I had heard and knew of him, WerBell was no actor.

The son of a Czarist cavalry officer, WerBell had a spy lineage that could be traced back to the OSS in Southeast Asia in World War II. It ran the gamut of covert operations from the anti-Castro Bay of Pigs invasion in 1961 to "programmatic liquidation" training (Operation Phoenix) of Vietnamese military during the Vietnam War. Later on he served as a freelance adviser to attempted coups in Guatemala, the Dominican Republic, the Bahamas, and Haiti. Investigators for the House Select Committee on Assassinations considered subpoenaing WerBell for his possible involvement in the JFK assassination.

WerBell went into business in 1967 with Gordon Ingram, designer of a small submachine gun, on which WerBell's sound suppressor was mounted. The weapon was called the MAC-10, a silenced machine gun that fired 800 rounds in a quiet minute that became a favorite of drug dealers and would-be mercenaries throughout the world.

WerBell was indicted twice during the 1970s—once for trying to sell silenced MAC-10s to an undercover federal agent, and later on charges of smuggling marijuana from Colombia. In both cases, the charges were dropped. WerBell had connections in the right places.

I spoke to WerBell several times on the phone in the late 1970s when he called to inquire about my bomb detection and bomb disrupting equipment. He spoke with substantial knowledge about explosives, but of course he did not explain his interest in the equipment. I assume he intended to use the gear as part of the counterterrorist training he ran at his estate in Powder Springs, Georgia. He never did buy anything from me. The last time we spoke, he said he would be getting back in touch. I never heard from him again. About a year later, he died of cancer.

U.S. Army Captain Robert W. Doms Bob Doms was instrumental in my introduction to the intelligence community at Fort Holabird. He gave me an opportunity to demonstrate my skills and creativity in the area of countermeasures and I appreciated it immensely. But there was an unethical side to him that eventually would surface and lead to bitter feelings between us.

As Doms prepared for retirement from the army in the early 1970s, he took on an Amway distributorship. He used army personnel and vehicles to distribute the products and did it on army time. He forced vendors who supplied material to the army to become Amway distributors as the price of doing business with him.

Shortly after his retirement, he showed up at my front door and said I had an obligation to hire him. I decided to give him a chance, but within a month I learned he was selling other countermeasure manufacturer's products rather than mine, including AID products. After three months, his sales efforts were nonexistent and I fired him. Within a week I learned that Doms was working for Jack Holcomb at AID. I discovered that he had copied the schematics of every piece of surveillance and countermeasure equipment I had ever designed and had given them to Holcomb as a way of getting a job.

Doms at one point referred to my company and my products as "contributing to the criminal element." It was his way of getting free publicity, I suppose. I challenged him on that comment but he ignored me. This occurred after my testimony before the National Wiretap Commission. I was in no financial position to take him to court for slandering me. Others did, and effectively put an end to that sort of conduct from him.

Allen Bell I met Bell at Fort Holabird when I first got into the surveillance and countermeasure business. As a lieutenant colonel, he was one of the ranking officers at the army's intelligence school, and a veteran field agent. I made an effort to get to know him and thought we had a good relationship.

During the early phase of my dealings with U.S. Army Intelligence at Fort Holabird, I had developed products to detect audio and RF surveillance attacks. The next assignment was to develop something to detect telephone taps. In the late 1960s, the intel community was using a general-purpose wire analyzer to test phone lines that was essentially ineffective.

I proposed a device that would test all possible parameters of the telephone and the line. Within a week I put together a prototype that I dubbed the 1080. The guys at Fort Holabird were sold on it, and Bob Doms ordered more than two dozen of the finished product. Colonel Bell gave me a pat on the back for the quality of the 1080 and how quickly I was able to deliver it.

A few years later, a second tech meeting was called to review the telephone analyzer and suggest improvements to it. But I was not invited. Al Bell was about to retire and launch his own surveillance and countermeasure company called Dektor Counterintelligence. One of his first products was a telephone analyzer. His product, in my opinion, did essentially the same thing as mine except that it was "automatic" and housed in a prettier case.

Seeing my products knocked off by a competitor was a common problem throughout my career in the countermeasure business. I patented two of my products, but the costs were so prohibitive ($30,000 each) that I gave up trying. At least I can add "inventor" to my résumé. There are also so many loopholes under patent law that it's virtually impossible for a small company to protect a product design unless it's truly a one-of-a-kind item.

Gary Korkola I met Gary through Frank Terpil and saw him on several occasions in the late 1970s. At the time, Korkola operated his own security company, Amstech International, in Nutley, New Jersey.

He bought and resold various types of security equipment, including airport and building entrance scanners. After he met Terpil, Korkola expanded his business into more deadly items, such as briefcase bombs, letter bombs, grenades, a ballpoint pen that could fire poison darts, and other weapons.

During the time I knew him, Korkola bought some of my countermeasure and bomb disposal equipment. He was always straight and honest in his dealings with me and never tried to beat me down on price. His personality was one hundred eighty degrees from Terpil's. He was articulate, soft spoken, and not given to boasting.

The last time I saw him was at a surveillance trade show in 1978. Later, he moved some of his business operation to the Middle East at Terpil's suggestion. As previously indicated, Korkola and Terpil were busted in December 1979 trying to sell 10,000 British Sten machine guns to undercover New York detectives posing as Latin American terrorists.

For reasons known only to those high up on the U.S. intelligence totem pole, Terpil and Korkola were permitted to go free on $15,000 bail each, despite the fact that they were facing as much as fifty years in jail. Within another month, both men had fled to Damascus, Syria, where they were jailed by Syrian intelligence and held incommunicado for six months.

After his release from a Syrian prison, Korkola tried to reestablish his security business and flew to Madrid to attend an international trade show for security equipment dealers. He was arrested by U.S. DEA agents at the request of the U.S. Attorney's office in New York and taken back to stand trial.

His lawyer successfully appealed his in absentia conviction and fifty-three-year jail sentence and won Korkola a new trial. He subsequently ended up serving less than two years in jail. Upon his release, he went back to his New Jersey company, now called Security Defense Systems Corp., and took up where he had left off.

I spoke to Gary on the phone a couple of years ago when he

called to ask me about some countermeasure products. I asked him about those times with Terpil in the 1970s. His only comment: "That's ancient history, Marty."

"Have you ever heard from Frank," I asked .

"Nope," he said. End of story.

Sergio Borquez Serge was an ex-DEA wireman and one of the best countermeasure pros in the business. He was also one of the most honest people doing countermeasure work and one of my closest friends in the business. He was based in Southern California. When he retired from the agency in the early 1980s, he cornered the market on countermeasure sweeps for the Hollywood celebrity set. Sammy Davis Jr. and Frank Sinatra were two of his regular clients. Serge also did a lot of surveillance and countermeasure jobs for the Mexican government, as well as for U.S. intelligence on the Mexican border.

He used to travel to Europe on business often and would always stop at my shop either going or returning. He always brought me a gift of a new Mexican guayabera. Serge died several years ago and I really miss him. He was a sweet guy in a business that for the most part seems to mass-produce egomaniacs and the ethically challenged.

Winston Arrington Winston is a true original at developing and manufacturing quality surveillance equipment, as well exotic devices such as the "bikini bug." Winston is one of the most articulate designers of countermeasure devices. He knows what it takes to manufacture good surveillance and countersurveillance equipment.

He was one of the most successful manufacturers in this field until he sold one of his transmitters to an Illinois State Police undercover officer. Winston was arrested, convicted under the Title III statute, and put on probation. He became so disgusted with the double standard and the lack of clarity in the laws prohibiting the manufacture and sales of eavesdropping devices that he went into semiretirement.

But his depth of knowledge and wisdom about the business is still available to interested amateurs and professional TSCM practitioners alike. Winston wrote one of the most astute books ever on the various types of bugging equipment, including fully drawn schematics, entitled *Now Hear This*. It is available only from Winston Arrington at Sheffield Electronics Company, Chicago, Illinois, www.covertbug.com. He still makes a limited line of countersurveillance equipment.

Last but not least, a few words about my dad. He remained an unrepentant authoritarian to the end of his life. From the time I went away to college and got married until his last months in a nursing home back in Wilkes-Barre, we never spoke about the years of abuse. My mother died in 1988 and he lived alone for the rest of his life, dividing his time between the house on West River Street in Wilkes-Barre and the house on Lake Nuangola about ten minutes away.

I would see him three or four times a year when my brothers and my family gathered to celebrate the various holidays. I was dying to take him aside and talk about those years of my youth. The opportunity never presented itself, or perhaps I never had the will to do it. It was as if it had never happened—at least as far as he was concerned. He never stopped belittling people, including his grandchildren, or criticizing them when they failed to live up to his impossible standards.

He suffered a stroke in mid-2001 and spent the last three months of his life in a nursing home. The stroke had robbed him of his ability to speak clearly or find the words to communicate. Despite this deficit, Dad still managed to take a swing at people when he didn't like what they were doing. In this case, his nurses. By that time, he wasn't strong enough to kick them in the ass, but I'm sure he considered it.

I vividly remember the last day I saw him. It was August 31, 2001, my wife's birthday. He was ninety-four years old. I visited him at the nursing home and it was clear to me that he was at the end of his life. At this point, he spoke gibberish. I tried to figure out what he was talking about from his expression. I spoke to him about subjects I knew he liked. But at a certain point, communication was impossible.

He simply looked at me, but did not respond when I asked him how he was doing.

I finally left the nursing home and drove to the house at the lake. When I entered the house, the phone was ringing. The nurse told me he had had another stroke and had died. I felt a deep sadness, but also a large residue of unresolved resentment. The opportunity to clear the air was gone forever.

The next day I went to the funeral parlor as they were preparing Dad for burial. I saw the infamous Carnegie belt wrapped loosely around his thin frame. The memories of that belt and the abuse that it inflicted flooded back into my brain, nearly reducing me to tears. I asked the funeral director to give it to me.

"A sentimental attachment," he said. "I understand."

"Not really," I replied.

I touched the crease in the belt where he had taken it off and folded it so many times in preparation to beat me with it. I took off the belt I was wearing and slipped on the Carnegie belt with the big bronze C on the silver buckle. It felt surprisingly light. I still wear it occasionally, maybe to remind me of the old days. I really don't know why. Perhaps it's because in a very real way I earned that belt and no one will ever be able to use it against me again.

The funeral was small and attended by only a few close friends and our families. After it was over, the minister came over to me and said, "Martin, your father was very proud of you."

"How do you know that?" I asked.

"He told me he was," said the minister.

I nodded and thanked him. I wondered if he was just saying that to make me feel better. I resisted asking him why my dad had never shared that with me.

A few days later, I bought a twenty-inch by twenty-inch bronze plaque in his honor and fastened it to the rocks below the house he built at Lake Nuangola. As long as anyone can remember, the property my dad built the house on was known as "The Rocks." The plaque read:

"THE ROCKS"
M. Luther Kaiser
1907–2001

I kneel at it often and ask him if I am doing okay. I usually have a glass of champagne in my hand. Our shared drink of choice.

Part 4

The Road Ahead

Chapter 18

The Future of Privacy in America--Or What's Left of It

PRIVACY IN AMERICA these days is an illusion. Unfortunately, there are only two options left for dealing with the invasive nature of public and private sector personal data collection in the good old USA: live with it or go off the grid.

By the latter, I mean enter the underground economy and deal only on a cash basis. That would mean cutting up your credit cards, canceling all of your bank accounts, not using a telephone or cell phone, nor the local utilities to provide electricity, heat, or running water in your house. It would mean tearing up your Social Security card, refusing to pay taxes, and forfeiting the right to vote and the ability to own property. And forget about the convenience of buying anything on the Internet.

It would also mean throwing away your driver's license and car registration. That of course would make it almost impossible to earn a livable wage unless you reside in a major urban area and have access to public transportation or ride a bike. You don't need a license to ride one—yet. But regular employment would be out of the question anyway, since you would have to provide your Social Security number to your prospective employer to prove you are not an unregistered alien or part of a terrorist cell planning the next strike on the heartland.

Or you could invest in a false set of identity papers. Then you would be breaking the law, but you are already a criminal by refusing to pay your taxes.

You get the idea. There is no Plan B.

We are moving rapidly—if we are not already there—toward a total information state, a quasi-Orwellian society where the only gaps in your personal dossier held by government agencies and private data providers will be the result of temporary computer glitches and Internet viruses that cause the systems to crash. I am not implying that our civil rights will be taken away in some right-wing Saturday night coup d'état. But I do believe that what we have long taken for granted—our fundamental right to privacy—is a thing of the past.

Many privacy experts bemoan the growing intrusion of the government into the personal lives of U.S. citizens. However, I believe the greater threat to individual privacy is the burgeoning personal information market that has become one of the biggest growth sectors in the entire economy.

In a very real sense, we have enabled the demise of our own privacy by acquiescing and giving passive support to the exponential breakthroughs of information technology and the Internet. It has been an incremental and somewhat invisible process, but nevertheless a steady erosion of privacy that most Americans have ignored or have been oblivious to at their peril.

In the past four years, according to Robert O'Harrow Jr., in his compelling new book on privacy, *No Place to Hide,* what most people thought of as nobody's business has become *everybody's* business.

While the major private-sector data-mining services like Acxiom Corp, Lexis-Nexis, and Seisint have been expanding the type and amount of information collected about individual citizens since the 1990s, O'Harrow correctly points out that the last remaining privacy barrier between the government and the individual was breached in response to the terrorist attacks on 9/11. Within days afterward, the final firewall between the government intelligence agencies and the private sector information juggernaut came tumbling down.

After 9/11 our drooling politicians were busy attaching rider after rider to the PATRIOT Act, knowing they were shoo-ins. Yet each rider was one more loss for the future of privacy.

"Swept away by a patriotic fervor," O'Harrow noted, "information technology specialists slung open giant computer systems across the country to help law enforcement and intelligence agencies search for clues about the nineteen hijackers and their accomplices.

"So intent was the push for security that few people contemplated, let alone questioned," he added, "the consequences of the government's aggressive acquisition of personal information and the sudden, fearful acquiescence of American citizens."

Unfortunately, the genie will never be put back in the bottle.

As I write this, civil libertarians are anxiously debating the reauthorization of the USA PATRIOT Act that is scheduled to expire at the end of 2005. Particularly troubling is Section 213, which authorizes so-called "sneak-and-peek" entries (physical breaking and entering of an individual's home or place of business) in cases where alerting someone that a surreptitious entry took place may have an "adverse result" on a police investigation. Even though the act was created as a response to the 9/11 attacks, Section 213's powers are not limited to investigations of terrorists and spies.

Instead, sneak-and-peek searches may be used to investigate any alleged federal felony or misdemeanor, including firearms violations, marijuana possession, and copyright infringement. These kinds of searches used to be called "black bag jobs" in the intel community in the 1960s and 1970s before the Watergate scandal and the Church hearings stopped the fun and games.

According to the Justice Department, there were 108 entries and searches under Section 213 during a twenty-two-month period from October 2001 through April 2003. Eventually, the owner of the home or office is supposed to be notified of the entry, though the law says that the deadline for notification can be "extended" without limit if the law enforcement agency makes a convincing argument not to notify. In other words, they might tell you and they might not.

It sort of reminds me of the good old days of wiretapping where a warrantless ninety-day permit could be obtained with ease. After the ninety days expired, the tap was then passed along to another agency, and then to another and so on. In short, a wiretap could be in place *for years* without anyone ever obtaining a warrant.

The section of the PATRIOT Act used by the FBI that has stirred the most controversy among both political parties is Section 215. It's known by critics as the "library provision" because it allows the government to demand library records as well as other personal and business records of an individual without a showing of "probable cause," defined as the existence of specific facts to support the belief that a crime has been committed or that the items sought are evidence of a crime. Under the Foreign Intelligence Surveillance Act (FISA) and before passage of the PATRIOT Act, the FBI had the ability to request similar records but they did have to show probable cause.

Despite all the *sturm und drang*, I think the PATRIOT Act is diverting the public's attention from the real issue: the evolving technology of the private sector, bankrolled by the government intelligence community, used to delve into every nook and cranny of a person's private life with a couple of keystrokes on a computer, and without the individual's knowledge or permission.

I'm not talking about suspected terrorists as the target of this technological inquisition, but rather everyday Americans. There are computer software programs capable of browsing through billions of gigabytes of data in real time, noting the daily personal, commercial, and (once thought to be) private transactions of every person in America. Some of these software programs are available to *anyone* for under $100!

For starters, consider the Total Information Awareness (TIA) program, the brainchild of Admiral John Poindexter, who was convicted and sentenced to prison for conspiracy, obstruction of justice, and lying to Congress during the Iran-Contra scandal. Poindexter started working on the program in the days right after 9/11. He launched TIA in 2002 while working as a consultant to the Pentagon's Defense Advanced Research Projects Agency (DARPA). It's impossible to know the specific details of the TIA program or how it works due to the secrecy that surrounded it.

This much is known: According to Matthew Brzezinski, author of *Fortress America*, the TIA program "employs a network of powerful computer-generated algorithms to uncover hidden patterns in mundane life that could give early warnings of possible terrorist activity. [The program] hunts through private and public sector databases, online ticket reservations, telephone and credit card bills, medical records, or just about anywhere we leave an electronic trail, including website visits."

The TIA program smacked of such Big Brotherism that the Congress shut it down in 2003, but similar programs continue to percolate and expand in the government and private sectors under other names. One of them is called MATRIX—Multistate Antiterrorism Information Exchange.

Designed and developed by a Florida-based data company called Seisint (short for seismic intelligence), MATRIX combines commercially available information about U.S. adults with billions of criminal and government records. The program has given companies and investigators a new type of power to identify patterns and apply models that select people based on precise characteristics contained in the seemingly endless pieces of data. At this point, at least twelve states, including New York, have agreed to participate in the program, though other states have shied away due to privacy concerns.

The biggest danger of programs like this is that unscrupulous state or law enforcement officials could conduct investigations of suspected criminals who have nothing to do with terrorism. There is also the possibility that law abiding persons 1) with similar last names of terrorists or criminals, or 2) who become victims of identity theft, will be lumped in with the bad guys and suffer needlessly for it.

There are other types of information-gathering programs designed to identify potential terrorists that seem to strike a balance between privacy and security. One of them is the new Computer Assisted Passenger Pre-Screening System, called Capps 2, that is being tested by the Transportation Security Administration (TSA).

The purpose of this program is to assign all passengers at American airports a "threat index score" based on their perceived trustworthiness. Under Capps 2, each passenger's name, address, home phone number, and date of birth will be linked to two commercial databases—Lexis-Nexis and Acxiom—that collect information about consumer habits. The data may not contain medical or bank account information but may include information about passengers' magazine subscriptions and buying patterns. Based on the information, passengers will be assigned to green, yellow, or red categories (red being the highest-alert status) and will be subjected to the corresponding scrutiny.

Initially, the Bush administration proposed to share personal data from the Capps 2 software programs with national and international police to allow the prosecution of any civil or criminal violations. But critics objected that this could create widespread abuses and would permit the administration to browse the personal data of millions of people. The data would permit the political party in power to uncover relatively minor offenses and threaten its critics with vindictive prosecutions, similar to President Nixon's use of tax return audits to punish Vietnam protestors. Instead, the Congress and the Bush administration compromised. The program was allowed to move forward, but with a prohibition on sharing personal data gathered with law enforcement.

Despite the Capps 2 compromise, the fact is that the private sector continues to develop more powerful computer programs with one purpose in mind: to collect every detail possible about an individual ranging from his or her income, employment, and lifestyle to purchasing habits, desires, needs, and relationships.

An ironic footnote to the proliferation of these powerful data-mining programs created by the private sector was the FBI's January 2005 decision to shut down its custom-built Internet surveillance technology, once known as Carnivore. Created in the late 1990s, Carnivore was designed to operate in two ways: as a "content wiretap" and as a "trap and trace/pen register." It could read and copy e-mails and attached documents and other online Internet communications among suspected criminals, terrorists, and spies. The "trap and trace" technology could track all caller IDs of inbound telephone calls, while the "pen register" tracked all outbound telephone numbers dialed. It also could capture all e-mail headers, including e-mail addresses going to or from an e-mail account.

As part of the Carnivore project, the FBI also used a controversial technology they dubbed the "Magic Lantern." The program installed so-called "key logging" software on a suspect's system that was capable of capturing keystrokes typed on the computer. By tracking exactly what a suspect typed, critical encryption key information could be gathered by the FBI. The program, which acted like a Trojan Horse virus, could be sent to the suspect via e-mail—often delivered for the FBI by a trusted friend or relative.

The FBI announced that it has switched to unspecified commercial software to eavesdrop on computer traffic during their investigations and has increasingly asked Internet providers to conduct wiretaps on targeted customers on the government's behalf, reimbursing companies for their costs.

Civil liberty and privacy groups have voiced their concerns about the FBI's legally murky use of the software program to obtain e-mail and other information without a wiretap warrant. That issue was resolved by explicitly legalizing the practice in the USA PATRIOT Act in 2001.

In documents submitted to Senate and House oversight committees earlier this year, the FBI said it performed only eight Internet wiretaps in 2003 and five in 2002; none used the Carnivore software program.

Another example of a private-sector software program that government intelligence agencies are interested in using is something called "NORA." The acronym stands for Non-Obvious Relationship Awareness.

Jeff Jonas, founder and chief scientist of Systems Research & Development, a Las Vegas IT company, created the program. Some of NORA's major customers are Las Vegas casinos, which are considered the leading users of state-of-the-art surveillance equipment. The casinos have combined their facial recognition programs with NORA software to identify scam artists on an official blacklist trying to rip off the house, and their possible connection with casino employees.

NORA's analytical software examines billions of individual data points about people, their identities, and demographic characteristics, and connects the dots between them and other people. Jonas is also reportedly a consultant to the Homeland Security Administration, the Defense Department, and the National Security Agency, and was involved in discussions with John Poindexter about the Total Information Awareness (TIA) project back in 2002.

When you think of covert government electronic surveillance capability of Americans, the supersecret National Security Agency (NSA—some people say it stands for No Such Agency) is the acknowledged Big Ear on the basis of its global spy system codenamed ECHELON. With its twenty-plus acres of underground Cray X-MP supercomputers at Fort Meade, Maryland, and its land, sea, and space-based intercept facilities world wide, ECHELON captures, decrypts, and analyzes virtually every phone call, fax, e-mail and telex message sent anywhere in the world. ECHELON operates in conjunction with the governments of England, Canada, Australia, and New Zealand under a secret 1948 agreement, UKUSA, whose terms and text remain one of the most classified documents in U.S. intelligence.

NSA's intercept stations capture all satellite, microwave, cellular, and fiberoptic communications traffic on a 24/7 basis, and then process this data through its massive computer capabilities, including advanced voice recognition and optical character keyword recognition programs. It's estimated that NSA eavesdrops on as many as two million calls and e-mail messages per hour from around the world. That included Osama bin Laden, whose satellite phone number until September 11, 2001, was 00-873-68-250-5331.

NSA's voice and optical recognition systems look for target code words or phrases (known as the ECHELON "Dictionary") that carry a related national security risk factor. Intelligence analysts at each of the respective "listening posts" maintain separate keyword lists for analyzing any conversation or document flagged by the system and which is then forwarded to the respective intelligence agency headquarters that requested the intercept.

NSA is the largest employer of mathematicians and linguists in the world, including the most brilliant teams of codemakers and codebreakers ever assembled. The codebreaker's job is to crack the encryption codes of foreign and domestic electronic communications and then forward the decrypted messages to their team of skilled linguists to review and analyze the messages in over 100 languages. NSA is also responsible for creating the encryption codes that protect the U.S. government's communications.

The ECHELON network's massive listening and reception capacity is primarily provided by a classified number of satellites circling the earth twenty thousand feet overhead, which includes billion-dollar KEYHOLE-11 satellites with ultrazoom lenses that can read the headlines of a newspaper on a park bench in Pyongyang, North Korea.

There is no question that more than ever before we need this level of global, state-of-the-art electronic intelligence filter during this post-9/11 period of terrorism. And it's clear that other terrorist incidents have been averted thanks to the vigilance of ECHELON and the NSA threat analysis. That said, it's important from a constitutional and individual privacy rights perspective to be aware that NSA's surveillance capabilities have been misused in the past for partisan political purposes.

Project SHAMROCK, an NSA project that read all incoming, outgoing, and transiting telegraphs of American citizens, continued for nearly thirty years before NSA Director Lewis Allen halted the program in May 1975. The program ended after Sen. Frank Church, chairman of the Senate Intelligence Committee, described SHAMROCK as "probably the largest government interception program affecting Americans ever undertaken."

Project MINARET, a joint NSA-CIA project begun in 1967, involved the creation of "watch lists" by both agencies as well as the FBI, of those Americans accused of "subversive" domestic activities. The watch list included Martin Luther King Jr., Malcolm X, Jane Fonda, Joan Baez, and Dr. Benjamin Spock. NSA Director Allen testified before the Senate Intelligence Committee in 1975 that during Project MINARET, from 1967 to 1973, the NSA had issued 3,900 reports on watch-listed Americans. The NSA Office of Security Services maintained reports on at least 75,000 Americans between 1952 and 1974.

NSA has frequently been used by White House officials for domestic political purposes. According to Nixon aide John Ehrlichman in his memoirs, *Witness to Power: The Nixon Years*, Henry Kissinger used the NSA to intercept the messages of then-Secretary of State William P. Rogers. Kissinger reportedly used the intercepts of phone calls to convince Nixon of Rogers's incompetence.

During the Reagan administration, the NSA, under orders from the White House, eavesdropped on phone calls that Rep. Michael Barnes of Maryland placed to Nicaraguan officials, including a conversation Barnes had with the foreign minister, protesting the implementation of martial law in that country.

In 1988, Margaret Newsham, a former Lockheed software manager responsible for a dozen VAX computers that powered the ECHELON computers at Menwith Hill, England, a major NSA facility, revealed that she had heard real-time interception of phone conversations involving South Carolina's Senator Strom Thurmond. Newsham was fired from Lockheed after she filed a whistleblower lawsuit alleging that the company was engaged in flagrant waste and abuse of privacy laws.

Insight Magazine reported in 1997 that President Clinton ordered the NSA and FBI to mount a massive surveillance operation at the 1993 Asian/Pacific Economic Conference (APEC) hosted in Seattle. One intelligence source for the story said that over 300 hotel rooms had been bugged for the event. The phone intercepts were intended to pass on information regarding oil and hydroelectric deals pending in Vietnam to high-level Democratic Party contributors competing for the contract.

Personally, I don't have a problem with using the NSA's eavesdropping capacity to help American companies enjoy a level playing field on international contracts. It's a documented fact that every country in the world uses their own intelligence services to conduct economic and industrial espionage against the United States in order to provide valuable and timely information to its own corporations.

According to a report by the Office of the National Counterintelligence Executives in 2003, based on input from a cross-section of U.S. intelligence agencies, foreign businesspeople, scientists, academics, and governments from more than ninety countries continued to try to steal U.S. technologies and corporate trade secrets in 2002 and 2003.

In a 1999 survey of Fortune 1,000 companies by PricewaterhouseCoopers and the American Society for Industrial Security (ASIS), companies reported $45 billion in losses due to corporate espionage, a majority of that spying done by electronic surveillance. And that number continues to grow.

My own field of expertise continues to boom. The U.S. State Department estimated in 1997 that nearly $900 million worth of illegal bugging and eavesdropping equipment was imported and installed into unsuspecting U.S. companies annually. That figure was on top of $434 million in fees for surreptitious entry and installation of the bugs, and an additional $900 million for the cost of ongoing maintenance of the bugs and listening post operations.

Those figures could be doubled by 2006.

The majority of this equipment is illegally imported into the United States from France, Germany, Lebanon, Italy, Canada, Israel, England, Japan, Taiwan, and South Africa. If you want to do eavesdropping on the cheap and you have a soldering iron and a basic understanding of electronics, you can build and install bugs that will get you the information you want. The raw materials and schematics needed to build such devices may be easily obtained at popular national electronics stores or salvaged from consumer electronic devices such as cordless telephones, intercom systems, and televisions.

In the New York City metropolitan area alone, there are more than sixty companies or individuals that will not only sell you the eavesdropping equipment but will often break into the target's office to install the device. For an additional fee, they will provide monitoring and transcription services.

To add to the problem of privacy infringement, the major U.S. data collection agencies like Lexis-Nexis and ChoicePoint admitted that their own internal controls for selling this data are ineffective in preventing identity theft. Both companies testified before Congress in mid-April 2005 that identity thieves had stolen nearly half a million individual data files—Lexis-Nexis had 330,000 files stolen and ChoicePoint lost 145,000. Bank of America also reported a serious security breach of consumer data files during the same period. In June 2005, Citigroup reported that UPS lost a shipment of its computer tapes containing the personal information of 3.9 million Citigroup customers. And the list continues to grow almost daily.

A Federal Trade Commission study in 2003 reported that 10 million consumers were victimized by identity theft in the prior year, costing them billions of dollars. Those numbers have rapidly multiplied since then.

But the growing problem of identity theft is only a symptom of the larger problem of loss of privacy. It has much more to do with the unwitting manner in which we let these data-mining conglomerates suck us dry of every conceivable piece of information and then turn around and sell it for a fat profit. We have surrendered our privacy, particularly since 9/11, under the guise of national security, when in fact it's all about money.

Wake up, America! Someone is listening or watching or reading your personal e-mails, and it's not just those young guys in crewcuts, gray suits, and polished wingtips. Some federal agency *knows* you bought this book. The information security gurus have created technologies that have become so much a part of the everyday fabric of life that they are invisible yet ubiquitous.

Consider these advances in technology:

- The thirty million individuals who pay to have their phone numbers unlisted automatically lose that privacy when they call a toll-free number to purchase an item or make an inquiry. The telemarketing firm's caller ID device often captures the number and sells it to other data-mining firms without notifying the individual consumer.

- OnStar, a leading manufacturer of auto and personal security systems, offers voice-activated map directions based on its GPS (Global Positioning System) technology, which also acts as an antitheft tracking device. The technology also provides the convenience of opening a locked car door with a single computer keystroke. What many consumers don't realize is that the technology also gives manufacturers the ability to eavesdrop on consumers if they choose to or were ordered to by a law enforcement agency. In a landmark 2003 court case, the FBI used the system's remote capabilities to surreptitiously eavesdrop on occupants of a car under surveillance. The Court of Appeals in San Francisco left open the legality of such surveillance.

- Consumer data-mining companies are increasingly using a commercial eavesdropping service called ULTRA Customer Intelligence Analytics that enhances the ability of call centers and telemarketers to close a sale. The software, according to Verint, the company that designed it, "detects subtle, often counterintuitive patterns (of speech) and cause/effect relationships from recorded interactions to generate revenue opportunities." New customers of the technology include the IRS, Home Depot, and the Department of Homeland Security.

- RFID (radio frequency identification) tags are already embedded in almost every piece of clothing and merchandise we purchase. They are used for everything from shipment tracking to theft prevention, anti–child abduction, employee identification, and building entrance and exit security. The devices are sold as a customer convenience without mentioning their surveillance tracking capability.

- Biometric identifiers are the next generation of employee identity cards. Systems that combine face recognition systems, fingerprints, iris scanners, skin prints, and voice analyzers are all in the same security package.

I remember quite well the 1960s and 1970s when electronic surveillance was still in its relative infancy. No one, least of all the government intelligence agencies, bothered to ask for legal permission to conduct electronic surveillance of individuals or organizations. The only question back then was: Is there deniability for the operation? As long as there was no paper trail, the eavesdroppers were good to go—and hopefully didn't get caught. They seldom needed a court to give them permission to eavesdrop on someone and rummage around in their personal lives.

The Omnibus Crime Control and Safe Streets Act was passed by Congress in 1968, with a particular emphasis on the use and sale of eavesdropping devices, but it was never reviewed until the mid 1970s to see if anyone was abiding by it. It was an "anything goes" atmosphere in which agencies believed in an end-justifies-the-means strategy to nail people based more on what their politics were rather than whether they had broken the law. Government law enforcement and intelligence agencies, at the behest of President Nixon, conducted electronic and photo surveillance of various organizations and individuals protesting the Vietnam War, as well as protestors of other government policies.

The various surveillances conducted were, in my opinion, clear violations of the civil rights of these individuals, particularly in terms of privacy. These actions included an FBI counterintelligence program called COINTELPRO and a CIA operation known as CHAOS that were directed at groups and individuals "deemed to be threats to domestic security," according to the Church report.

In June 1972, there was a botched burglary at the Watergate complex. And the rest, as the saying goes, is history.

As a result of the various congressional investigations that followed, laws were passed that were designed to prevent future government abuses. The Privacy Act of 1974 was one of those laws that gave individual citizens the right to know what type of information the government was collecting about them and to expand the rights of individual privacy.

But today, thirty years later, it seems we have forgotten the lessons of that era in our anxiety to pursue the war on terrorism and prevent a replay of the tragedy of 9/11. And in the consumers' eager rush for convenience and connectedness, they are slowly giving away, moment by moment, purchase by purchase, the last vestiges of their fleeting privacy.

I think old Ben Franklin had it right when he uttered these words more than two hundred years ago:

Those who give up liberty for the sake of security, deserve neither liberty nor security.

Audio Surveillance and Countermeasures

INTRODUCTION
AUDIO SURVEILLANCE TECHNIQUES
MECHANICAL ATTACKS
MICROPHONE AND WIRE
FREE-SPACE TRANSMITTERS
CARRIER-CURRENT TRANSMITTERS
VISUAL OR OPTICAL ATTACKS
TELEPHONES
GENERAL CONSIDERATIONS FOR AUDIO SECURITY
THE AUDIO COUNTERMEASURES SURVEY

INTRODUCTION

The purpose of presenting the following material is threefold. First, it equips the layperson with a general understanding of the real threats from electronic eavesdropping. Second, it provides enough information to allow a company's general security representative to set up an effective electronic countermeasure program that would sharply limit the likelihood of a successful electronic attack. Third, it addresses and hopefully dispels many myths that have been tied to the electronic eavesdropping/countersurveillance industry.

This material is presented in a nontechnical fashion but with clarity and purpose. Individuals with an electronics background should note that this simplistic approach of holding technical language to a minimum may strain certain traditional textbook definitions. Nonetheless, any technical distortion that occurs is only the product of the omission of detail from some definitions that were not considered necessary in a general discussion. All definitions and terminology used are accurate and valid for a discussion on this basic level.

Not all eavesdropping is electronic, and the term "electronic countermeasures" is not sufficiently comprehensive to describe this branch of the security field. Audio security and audio countermeasures are the terms used to describe the specific steps taken to either detect or nullify listening devices.

A countermeasure technician is someone skilled in these techniques. In some circles, the act of eavesdropping is called technical surveillance, and the actions taken to combat such an attack are called technical surveillance countermeasures, commonly abbreviated TSCM.

The most difficult-to-detect methods of technical attack may or may not be the most expensive, and many of them represent years of experimentation by those so inclined. Often, the full resources of foreign governments support their agents. The intensity of the threat is generally in proportion to the value of the information sought. In the case of nations, it is sought-after information about national security policies and procedures. For corporations, the most sensitive information lies in its proprietary information.

With stakes high, both sides (the United States and countries spying against us) have found it worthwhile to spend great sums on the development of new surveillance techniques that, in turn, require additional sophistication in countermeasures. The presumption that most technical attacks encountered by companies in the private sector will be relatively unsophisticated and therefore more susceptible to detection or nullification is inaccurate.

To effectively plan an audio countermeasure program, one must first understand the ways a technical audio attack may be mounted. And so, the emphasis here will be on technical audio surveillance techniques, or audio attack methods.

AUDIO SURVEILLANCE TECHNIQUES

For ease of presentation, the types of technical attacks are placed in six general categories. These categories are arbitrarily established for ease of discussion. Some devices or procedures covered can fit into more than one category:

MECHANICAL ATTACKS
MICROPHONE AND WIRE
FREE-SPACE TRANSMITTERS
CARRIER-CURRENT TRANSMITTERS
VISUAL OR OPTICAL ATTACKS
TELEPHONES

MECHANICAL ATTACKS

In spite of the technological advances of the electronic age, one of the most effective "devices" used to compromise audio security is still the unaided human ear. The secretary who sits immediately outside the Board of Directors' conference room or CEO's office can often negate the large sums of money spent for sophisticated audio countermeasures equipment. So too can the security officer's failure to note that the public address system used in the boardroom amplified sound so much that anyone walking down a nearby hallway could hear it clearly.

Do not discount the effectiveness of the human ear when it is further enhanced by a plain old-fashioned water glass or the doctor's stethoscope placed against an adjoining wall. Heating/air conditioning ducts and pipes/conduits exiting the room also carry a considerable amount of room audio.

This Audio Surveillance section on countermeasures explores acoustic attenuation of walls. It also addresses variables such as thickness, nature of materials, types of construction, and acoustic impedance (the rate at which a material allows voices to pass through it). If the perimeter of a space to be protected lacks sufficient acoustic attenuation (in particular, the ability to block the transmission of voices), then without a doubt the first threat to consider and deal with is the human ear.

Tape recorders represent another type of "mechanical" attack. They can either be placed in the target area and retrieved later or carried by a person intent on intercepting details of a conference or conversation. Concealment is now quite easy, thanks to the large number of miniature, inexpensive, and very good tape recorders currently available. Some are little larger than a pack of matches. Today, it is possible to place two billion transistors on a single substrate less than one-eighth-inch square! Taking advantage of this incredible density are recent developments in "fully solid-state" electronic "tapeless" recorders that now further complicate the picture.

A recorder with a voice-activated switch (VOX) that turns on only when voices are present and which is put in place before a meeting or conference can be very damaging. There are many commercially available recorders using this technique that tape for several days. This approach is especially useful in attacking onetime events, such as conferences, where an opportunity to retrieve the device would be much greater than if the target were a corporate office or boardroom.

The recorder attack relies least upon gadgetry. Its greatest danger lies in the fact that it often hides in plain sight. A security officer oriented along lines that are more technical may completely overlook it. Cell phones have recently been added to the growing list of "mechanical" attacks. It is now possible to program a cell phone to automatically answer an incoming call while *not* ringing, and quietly eavesdrop on room conversations. The implications of this approach are enormous.

MICROPHONE AND WIRE

This is probably the oldest of the technical attacks, dating from the early days of carbon microphones and tube-type amplifiers. Today, microphone technology has advanced to the point where there are now highly sensitive units, one-quarter-inch square and one-sixteenth-inch thick, with built-in amplifiers that can transmit conversations over superthin copper wires hundreds of feet in length. There are multitudes of small, inexpensive microphones (under five dollars) commercially available that are very suitable for audio surveillance.

While microphones differ in design or specific operating principle, they all do essentially the same thing. As a group, microphones fit into that class of electrical components generally known as "transducers." A transducer is simply a device that changes mechanical energy to electrical energy, or vice versa. Thus, a radio loudspeaker is as much a transducer as the windowpane that modulates a laser beam. This interrelationship is of interest because a loudspeaker, especially an efficient one with a stiff speaker cone, makes a highly effective microphone.

It is perhaps a sign of the times that so many supposedly secure areas have speakers mounted in the walls or ceilings for the omnipresent background music or public address system. An unused speaker, i.e., one not actually broadcasting music or announcements, makes an extremely effective microphone. All that is necessary is to intercept the pair of speaker wires at any point and attach a suitable matching transformer and amplifier, recorder, or transmitter. Audio in the room causes the speaker cone to resonate in the same manner as would the diaphragm of a microphone.

Types of microphones include the dynamic (moving coil or moving magnet), ceramic, electret, carbon, crystal, and condenser. Each has its particular advantages and disadvantages. The potential attacker would carefully consider which one to use in view of the need for certain characteristics such as sensitivity, current drain, frequency response, impedance, signal output level, and detectability.

It is not necessary to go into the differences between the varieties of microphones. A veteran "wire man" will choose the appropriate microphone with the same care that a dentist chooses his instruments. Microphones may be placed in three groups: the carbon microphone, other microphones, and contact microphones.

Carbon Microphones

Once the most common, carbon microphones are fading into oblivion. There are still a large number of telephones around that use this microphone, so it deserves some discussion. Carbon microphones are characterized by their very high output signal as compared to most other types. They need an external voltage source to work. This requirement, and a progressive loss of sensitivity over time as the carbon granules settle, limits its use. Carbon microphones vary their resistance in proportion to the sound reaching them and thus are not voltage-generating microphones. It is important to remember this when searching for them.

Other Microphones

Dynamic, ceramic, crystal, or condenser microphones are usually connected to an amplifier or transmitter by a length of wire. They are self-generating transducers, similar to loudspeakers, i.e., audio taken in and equal voltage going out. Among this group is the electret microphone. This unit contains a built-in amplifier that requires an external supply voltage. The levels of current required are much lower than the carbon microphone.

A modern microphone connected to a good amplifier can pick up conversations in an average room no matter where it is placed, especially if the room is acoustically dead. These microphones are difficult to detect or locate due to their very small size. When acoustically fed through a slender plastic tube they are known as "tube microphones." The advantage of this approach is that the microphone element itself does not have to be close to the target area. This approach is incredibly effective.

Although very thin wire is sometimes used, existing electrical conductors such as power lines, telephone lines, or wire pairs that have been abandoned but remain in place inside the walls are much more effective.

Contact Microphones

The contact microphone is usually a form of dynamic, electret, ceramic, crystal, or piezo microphone designed specifically to pick up mechanical vibrations moving along a surface rather than airborne sounds. Placing it firmly against a common wall, pipe, conduit, or duct produces room audio. When mounted through a wall via a suitable fixture it becomes a "spike mike." Placed into or against the wall, it uses the entire wall as a diaphragm. Under ideal circumstances, a contact microphone is very effective. Inherent disadvantages can be overcome by use of a digital-signal-processor (DSP) filter.

"Shotgun" and Parabolic Microphones

Although "shotgun" and parabolic microphones differ in design from one another, both have the same purpose: the detection of voices at relatively great distances. Both are directional in that they focus sound waves upon the diaphragm of the microphone element somewhat the way a parabolic reflector focuses light.

These microphones can be seen at most sporting events. In that particular application, do not assume that the sound heard over the TV or radio is actually coming from a particular microphone. It is the product of the skillfully mixed output of several microphones. Parabolic microphones are also used in wildlife photography to record birdcalls or similar high-frequency sounds.

Both the shotgun and the parabolic microphone have another characteristic in common: their effectiveness is grossly exaggerated. They generally work at distances of less than 100 feet, provided the ambient noise level does not block out the targeted sound. As the distance increases, so does the "signal-to-noise" level. In other words, it is harder to distinguish target audio from background or unwanted audio. Under ideal circumstances, the best directional microphones might have a range of 300 feet, but as mentioned before, 100 feet or less is much more realistic for voice interception. Since they are difficult to conceal it is unlikely that one would select this type of microphone to further their technical efforts. These devices actually work quite well for birdcalls, for two reasons.

Bird sounds are quite loud, certainly much louder than a normal conversation. The sounds are higher in frequency. High-frequency sound is generally more directional. Additionally, the human ear tends to perceive higher-than-human-voice frequencies more easily under marginal conditions.

In summary, the microphone and wire attack is still very much with us and quite a few of the "finds" made by technical surveillance countermeasure technicians are of this type. They are attractive because of their commercial availability and low cost. Generally, the lack of technical expertise of the installer assures that most are discovered during a good physical search.

FREE-SPACE TRANSMITTERS

For purposes of clarity and convenience, free-space transmitters come in two broad categories: the radio frequency (RF) transmitter and the carrier-current transmitter. This distinction is necessary because they differ markedly in the way information is transmitted from the target area to the listening post. The countermeasure employed against each category also differs, and each will be discussed separately.

This section deals only with the free-space transmitters. In order to understand more fully the whole subject of transmitters, it would be necessary to use language that is more technical in order to explain why they are used for technical attacks and the range of countermeasures available.

As indicated earlier, a transducer is a device that changes

mechanical energy, such as human speech, into electrical energy. The proper term for this electrical energy is electromagnetic energy (EME). EME travels in waves that vibrate a given number of times per second. Various forms of electromagnetic energy vibrate at different rates, and this rate of vibration is called its "frequency." Frequency is expressed in the number of variations or cycles per second. The phrase "cycles per second" (cps) changed in recent times to "Hertz" (Hz) to honor the scientist who first described this phenomenon. One hertz equals one cycle per second.

Scientists often refer to the electromagnetic spectrum as a group of electromagnetic energy expressed in orders of frequency. At one end of the spectrum is energy that does not vibrate at all. This is direct current (DC) such as that produced by a battery. At the upper end is visible light, X-rays, and cosmic rays, which vibrate upward of 500 gigahertz. The energy used in most eavesdropping attacks is radio frequency (RF) energy. It is generally considered to be the electromagnetic energy in the spectrum from 10,000 Hz to infrared light.

It's helpful to understand these energy numbers in terms of abbreviations. Another way to say 10,000 Hz is 10 Kilohertz, or 10 KHz. The letter "K" (for kilo) is the common abbreviation for 1,000. One million Hertz or Hz is one megahertz, or 1 MHz. One thousand MHz is one gigahertz, or 1 GHz. "M" and "G" are frequently used in science for million and billion, respectively.

In reference to the transducer, energy produced in the audio range, i.e., from 20 Hz to 10 KHz, is the same range as sounds in a room. All the transducer has done is convert the mechanical energy (sound) into relatively low-frequency electromagnetic energy. Because it is low-frequency, the energy will flow along the wires attached to it and into an amplifier. Consequently, low-frequency information is retrieved from the target area along a hard-wire path.

Shifting the intercepted information to a much higher frequency, however, creates a new picture. A certain amount of the energy would still flow down the wire, but some of it radiates outward into the airways.

If the frequency were increased further, greater amounts would radiate into the airways and be intercepted by a radio receiver tuned to the same frequency.

The device that converts audio-range electromagnetic energy into radio-frequency energy is called a radio frequency (RF) transmitter. The transmitter takes the audio range information fed to it and converts it to a specific frequency in the radio frequency range. The transmitter usually includes an amplifier to magnify the converted signal. The amount of electric power used in amplifying the radio frequency signal is expressed in watts. As noted earlier, the radio frequency energy radiates from the wire leading to the listening post. Cut the wire, and the radio frequency energy continues to radiate from the section still attached to the transmitter, especially if it is of a certain length in relation to the transmitted frequency. This piece of wire becomes an "antenna," and the ideal size, its "resonant length."

Add to the above a power supply and the result is a simple broadcast station. Similar though the operating principles may be, there is a great deal of difference between a full-fledged commercial broadcast transmitter and a clandestine transmitter, or "bug." The first difference is its gross size; the "bug" must generally be very small for ease of concealment.

The requirement for electrical power needed to operate the transmitter and broadcast the signal varies widely. The need to either use small batteries or to "parasite" power from the target area's telephone line sharply limits the output power of the clandestine transmitter. This limitation does not, of course, apply when using the AC power lines. Output power is usually kept low to avoid detection. Normally, there is no need to broadcast great distances, as most listening posts are located no more than a few hundred yards of their target. While commercial broadcast stations use thousands of watts of radiated power during transmission, and typical hand-held walkie-talkies use 1 to 5 watts, the modern clandestine transmitter can effectively employ less than 1 milliwatt (a milliwatt is one one-thousandth of a watt).

Another factor affecting detection of a "bug" transmitter is the type of modulation used. A look back at the simple transmitter may be in order at this point. If the transmitter operates at a frequency of 100 MHz (as an arbitrary example), it emits a radio signal at that frequency. Somehow, the electrical information from the transducer must be impressed onto this signal to transmit the information. The way in which this intelligence superimposes itself upon the 100 MHz signal (called the "carrier wave" or "signal," or quite often, just "carrier") is modulation. The carrier wave is changed or modulated by the audio information impressed upon it during transmission.

There are several ways to modulate this carrier wave. The two most common are amplitude modulation (AM) and frequency modulation (FM). These, of course, are the two types used in commercial broadcasting. It is not necessary to understand the technical differences between them. What is important is that the countermeasure search device be able to detect the transmission that carries them.

Clandestine transmitters come in a variety of shapes and degrees of sophistication. One of the basic considerations in transmitter construction is operating time, which is determined by battery life. Generally, the larger the battery, the longer the transmitter will last. Size is not normally critical if the transmitter is to be hidden in a wall, in a location next to the target area, or if a microphone and wire run is employed.

Turning the transmitter on and off by remote control extends battery life. The advantages of this are obvious. It greatly conserves battery life during periods of inactivity, and switching the transmitter off at the first sign of an audio countermeasure survey reduces chances of its detection by means of a search receiver.

There are many small, inexpensive "throwaway" or "quick-drop" transmitters commercially available. These may have a battery life of only a few hours, but sometimes that is all that is necessary.

One type of free-space transmitter, a type that has no battery, is the so-called "resonant cavity" transmitter. The Great Seal of the

United States in the Moscow embassy concealed such a device. Many may recall the photograph of Ambassador Lodge pointing to a "bug" concealed in the back of the plaque. The embarrassment caused by the detection of this transmitter motivated the intelligence community to spring into action, and devices similar to it soon evolved.

The resonant cavity transmitter is an amazingly simple device technically known as a passive radiator, i.e., one that lacks an internal source of energy. In constructing this device, a layer of thin metalized material is stretched across a closed metal tube. The specific size of the tube determines its resonant frequency. A wire "tail," which functions as an antenna, is attached to the base of the cavity. The cavity is then flooded with a beam of radio frequency energy from an external source (usually in the microwave region, 1 GHz and up). The size of the cavity and the length of its antenna are carefully calculated so that a harmonic (multiple) of the inbound radio frequency energy that bathes the cavity is rebroadcast. The metalized diaphragm acts as a transducer, and the audio-range energy modulates the returned radio frequency signal that, in turn, is picked up by a receiver in the nearby listening post.

The Theremin microphone operates on the same principle, except that it generates two inbound signals and works with the sum or difference of those signals to recover room audio. Do not assume that these devices are the sole province of federal agencies.

The free-space transmitter remains one of the most prevalent forms of technical attacks. The most likely threat comes from one of the plentiful miniature transmitters available assembled or in kit form that use the FM broadcast band (88 to 108 MHz) or are tuned to operate just above or below it. In many instances, commercially available baby monitors make very effective listening devices. Nonetheless, regardless of sophistication, all free-space transmitters pose a threat that should receive serious consideration during an audio countermeasures survey.

CARRIER-CURRENT TRANSMITTERS

Technically, carrier-current transmitters are similar to free-space transmitters, except that they use transmitting frequencies somewhere between those in the audio frequency range and those in the radio frequency range that radiate outward from a conductor (antenna). The transmitted energy from a carrier-current device remains on the conductor. The energy is impressed upon either a power line, telephone line, cable TV line, or other single or paired conductors and is retrieved by a receiver connected to that same line somewhere outside the target area.

A common example of this is the wireless intercom. There are some obvious advantages to such a system. One is that the electrical energy needed for the transmitter comes from the power or telephone line, thus eliminating the need for a battery. Consequently, a carrier-current device can be left in place for years without the need for replacing exhausted batteries. Like the free-space transmitter, remote control signals sent over the very line powering the unit may turn it on or off.

Such carrier-current devices are easily concealed and are usually not found by a "sweep" of the radio frequency spectrum with a search receiver, because of their very low frequency. They are, however, easy to locate with either a spectrum analyzer, oscilloscope, or very-low-frequency (VLF) receiver or converter connected to the line powering them.

Carrier-current devices are commonly built into innocuous looking objects such as clocks, radios, lamps, and telephones, or sent as an expensive-looking gift to the unsuspecting target, who plugs it into the wall outlet and promptly bugs himself or herself. (Bombers sometimes use this same tactic, with devastating results.) This approach, of course, overcomes the disadvantages of having to enter the target area.

One great advantage of the carrier-current transmitter over the free-space transmitter that radiates in all directions (not only to the listening post) is that it radiates only down the wire. This can turn into a major disadvantage, however, if one cannot get to the wire. Although transmitting range (distance) can be a problem, there are many ways to overcome it. The earlier difficulties these units had with power line noise (primarily AM) have been overcome by the introduction of FM carrier-current devices.

In fact, the carrier-current transmitter is a serious threat confronting the audio countermeasures technician, particularly if installed by an adversary skilled in the concealment and use of one of these devices.

VISUAL OR OPTICAL ATTACKS (AND LIP-READING)

In some ways, this is the most interesting category, because the techniques range from the most mundane to exotic "James Bond"–type devices. Attacks in this category fit into the following areas:

Optical

Optical attacks include real-time observation via telescope or binoculars, or photography via telephoto lenses. The latter includes both motion/still pictures and video techniques. Although there is a possibility that a camera with a telephoto lens could photograph sensitive documents lying on desks, the main hazard comes from a seemingly nontechnical but in fact highly effective technique: lip-reading. Accomplished lip-readers, especially those with multilingual capability, could be of great value when armed with a good pair of binoculars and line-of-sight view of those in conversation. The conversation, of course, could be videotaped for analysis later. As obvious as this may seem, it is a technique all too often overlooked.

Television Attacks

Television is a threat in those areas where the attacker has had a chance to gain unimpeded access to the target space or occupies an adjoining room. A hole no larger than the head of an ordinary pin can produce a television picture of quite acceptable quality. With the current state of the art, light levels are no longer critical. Miniature television cameras complete with a transmitter smaller than a cigarette lighter are readily available for under $100. Cell phones with built-in TV cameras further complicate the problem.

Coupling the lens of a television camera to a high-resolution fiber-optic bundle such as those used in internal medicine is a distinct possibility. Fiber-optic systems allow for mounting the television camera some distance from the area under observation. When the target makes extensive use of briefing charts or other visual displays, it calls for a television camera attack. There are three ways to gather information intercepted by the television camera:

- videotape, retrievable at one's leisure;
- hardwire where it goes from the camera to the monitor via shielded cable (fast scan) or telephone line (slow scan);
- video transmitter that transmits the signal over the airways to a distant location.

Camera lens detectors have been the province of the three-letter agencies for several years. These units are very expensive. Fortunately there are two "poor man's" lens detectors. One can be put together for under $300 by using a simple first-generation night vision scope and a STRAIT-LINE Laser Level 30. This combination does a respectable job. A new product, the SpyFinder, was recently introduced, and it too does an effective job of locating hidden TV cameras.

Light Attacks

Now readily available and inexpensive, light-emitting diodes (LEDs) and laser diodes, primarily infrared (IR) emitters, are finding their way into surveillance equipment. These diodes have reached peak efficiencies only dreamed of a few years ago. As with any light, they need an optical path, either directly or by reflection, from the area under surveillance to the listening post. Bear in mind, though, that some materials impervious to visible light may pass IR light with little attenuation.

Both the LED and laser are used in a similar manner. A microphone attached to electrical components converts room audio into the energy needed to modulate the light beam. The type of modulation can vary but generally centers around several types of pulse modulation schemes to conserve power and thus give battery-powered units a longer life span.

It is necessary for the optical transmitter to be placed in a position so it can transmit its beam of light to the listening post (LP), where a suitable detector reverses the process, i.e., changes the light back into audible sound. Although somewhat constrained by the need for an optical path to the listening post, these devices are hard to detect.

The laser diode is perhaps the ultimate optical weapon. In some ways, the laser diode resembles the LED, except that it produces a much, much narrower or coherent beam of light at higher operating efficiency. As previously mentioned, a laser diode modulated with room conversation is an effective transmitter. There is, however, another application of the laser that is much more devious.

When a conversation takes place in a room, all objects in that room vibrate from the acoustic energy generated by that conversation. Rigid objects tend to vibrate more than soft ones. This, of course, is how a microphone works. The diaphragm, vibrated by room audio, moves back and forth, and this vibration is converted, in turn, into electrical energy. Focusing a laser on an object with a suitable beam return path returns room audio.

These systems, besides being difficult to deploy, suffer from major audio retrieval problems. Room conversation is not the only thing that vibrates the target surface. A variety of mechanical equipment noises, such as motors and fans coupled with the normal "street" noise of people walking and moving things, makes advanced filtering equipment mandatory. To make the job somewhat easier, state-of-the-art voice recognition filters called digital signal processors (DSPs) are now available.

A recently developed device sends light from an IR laser diode down a single strand of fiber-optic cable (thinner than a human hair) where it strikes a small reflective diaphragm that is modulated by room conversation and returned on another strand to the detector, where it is demodulated. This device defies all electronic detection and must be found by physical search.

TELEPHONES

Numerous embarrassing cases have served to focus public attention on the vulnerability of telephone systems to technical attack. Holding sensitive discussions in any area that contains a telephone presents a very, very serious hazard to the audio security of the entire room, no matter whether the telephone is off hook (in use) or on hook (hung up).

There are two different types of technical attacks made upon the telephone; the "tap" and the "compromise." The telephone tap is an interception of telephone communications. The interception may be of conversation or normal telephone communication, such as teletype, facsimile, or computer data. The tap results in the collection of information only when the phone is in use. A tap does not require physical access to the target area. Telephone lines are vulnerable anywhere between the target phone and a central telephone office miles away.

There are many ways to tap a telephone, ranging from direct connection with the line to inductive coupling that does not require a physical connection to the line. The latter uses a so-called induction coil/transformer to couple the energy from the line to the listening post. An induction coil works on the following principle: Electromagnetic energy flowing down a telephone wire creates a magnetic field around that wire. The information flowing down the telephone wire is, of course, electromagnetic energy modulated by the information impressed upon it. This modulation causes the magnetic field to vary at the same rate as the audio on the line itself. Placing an induction coil on or near the line so that it is within this electromagnetic field induces a similar electromagnetic energy flow in the coil. The induced signal is then fed into an amplifier and the information is recovered.

A recent development in this area replaces the induction coil with Hall-effect magnetic field sensors that detect the minute magnetic fluctuations caused by signals flowing down the wire. The induction coil, Hall effect, and similar devices are virtually impossible to detect by technical means, so a thorough visual inspection of the telephone line is mandatory.

A "compromise" is an attack upon a telephone that transforms it into a listening device capable of intercepting audio in the targeted area at all times, whether the telephone is off hook (in use) or on hook (hung up). A telephone can be compromised in many different ways, all of which require physical access to the telephone.

A transmitter, either carrier-current or free-space, concealed inside a telephone can be very difficult to find even when the phone is opened for inspection, especially if it resembles a legitimate telephone part. One of the most common of these transmitters resembles either the telephone earpiece or mouthpiece transducer. (Technically, the mouthpiece transducer is called the transmitter; the earpiece, the receiver.) This "drop-in" transmitter draws its power from the telephone. Transmitters can also be hidden within internal parts of the telephone, thus masking them from visual inspection.

Every telephone contains at least three transducers. One of these is the telephone mouthpiece (transmitter), usually either a carbon or electret microphone. As mentioned earlier, these are not "self-generating" microphones; they require external power.

The second transducer is the earpiece (receiver), which, besides being a miniature loud speaker, is a highly sensitive "self-generating" dynamic microphone that requires no external power. A spare pair of wires within the telephone connected to this device can do wonders! This is a "natural" point of attack.

The third and usually most unreliable transducer is the telephone ringer itself. The ringer assembly of many telephones is resonant at voice frequencies and thus modulated by the room audio impinging upon it. If a telephone ringer is sufficiently resonant, a high-gain amplifier with a good DSP filter can retrieve conversations emanating from nearby. Its range is quite limited, however, generally 3 to 5 feet from the instrument.

An explanation of what a telephone hook-switch does will enhance an understanding of how easily phones can be compromised. The hook-switch is the mechanical device that ostensibly disconnects the telephone from the central office (the telephone exchange) when the handset is placed upon the cradle. A telephone in this position usually has about 48 to 50 volts of DC line voltage. Lifting the handset off the cradle ("off-hook" position) connects the receiver and transmitter to a central office and the voltage drops to 7 to 9 volts DC.

In the standard, single-line instrument, all that separates the telephone handset transducers from the outside world is the hook-switch. From time to time one of these hook-switches will become accidentally bent (wink, wink), or some nonconductive deposit (fingernail polish) will build up on one of the electrical contact points (more winking). Under these circumstances the handset is never completely "hung up" and a high-gain amplifier placed across the telephone wires will retrieve room audio with astonishing fidelity.

For the same reason, there are many ways to deliberately bypass a hook-switch, thus allowing room information retrieval at the listening post. A simple rearrangement of wires takes only a few minutes and is very effective. It has the added advantage of being a deniable compromise: It may never be possible for the audio countermeasures expert to learn whether the rewiring was an actual attack or merely human error. Additionally, it is possible to insert into a telephone any number of devices such as diodes, transistors, capacitors, or resistors that compromise the hook-switch. Some of these devices have the added advantage of automatically shutting off when the handset is picked up, due to the resultant voltage drop (from 48 volts DC down to 7–12 volts DC).

Newer devices that are better able to deal with current telephone technology now replace the original "infinity transmitter" or "harmonica bug." Some of these devices require complex DTMF (Dual-Tone Multi-Frequency) tones to actuate them. These are a variation on the remotely controlled radio frequency transmitters described earlier. As with those devices, the attacker must gain access to the target area or at least arrange for a compromised telephone to be placed in the target area.

The device can also be placed anywhere along the telephone line or, worse yet, along some other person's telephone line to monitor the target area. Once on, the infinity transmitter usually stays on until the handset of the target telephone is lifted from the cradle. Most of these devices are parasitic, i.e., they draw their power from the telephone line, thus drawing the telephone line voltage down a few volts.

In summary, the telephone is susceptible to a variety of technical attacks that vary in sophistication and are extremely effective and quite difficult to detect.

- The telephone provides a hard wire path out of the target area.
- The telephone is particularly appealing to one planning a technical attack, as it provides a ready source of power.
- The telephone is large enough to simplify concealment of a variety of devices.

- The telephone does not require additional microphones because of existing microphones/transducers within the telephone instrument.

Because of its attractiveness for, and susceptibility to, technical attack, the telephone remains one of the most dangerous of surveillance devices.

GENERAL CONSIDERATIONS FOR AUDIO SECURITY

An effective audio security program should encompass two basic considerations: measures that will complicate or prevent a technical attack, and measures that will detect the presence of a technical attack. The term generally used to describe the former is "isolation and nullification." The latter would encompass the actual conduct of an audio countermeasure survey. However, before undertaking either plan, a first step is an assessment of the threat. First, determine:

- Who is the target?
- What is the potential value of the information?
- Who would be the most likely person (or persons) to mount a technical attack?

Isolation and Nullification

Generally, the areas to be protected fall into one of three basic categories:

- Permanent facilities, such as offices used by key figures on a daily basis, houses, conference rooms, etc.
- Facilities used temporarily or infrequently, such as hotel rooms, conferences in facilities such as meeting halls, or public buildings
- Automobiles

Each category presents a different challenge, relating to the amount of control the security staff has over the audio environment of the facility.

As previously noted, isolation and nullification relate to actions taken before the fact that will sharply limit the opportunity for a successful audio surveillance attack. The preventive actions one should take become more apparent if one considers the possible attacks used against the area. Despite the variety of techniques described in the six categories of technical attacks, there are only four ways to take audio from a target area:

- Carry it out. All of the techniques discussed under the heading of "Mechanical" attacks apply.
- Transmit it out. "Free-Space" techniques apply.
- Retrieve it optically. "Visual/Optical" techniques apply.
- Retrieve it via hardwire. "Carrier-Current," "Microphone and Wire," and "Telephone" techniques apply.

There is no technique that does not use one of the above methods. Therefore, these four methods must always be considered during the development of an effective isolation and nullification program. For purposes of this discussion, isolation pertains to those actions that tend to prevent the mounting of a technical attack, whereas nullification relates to those techniques that would tend to hinder the attack or prevent it from producing useful information.

The basic component of isolation is physical security. A highly effective physical security system would deny an attacker access to the target space, which would in turn sharply limit his selection of techniques. However, the security must be in effect around the clock and cannot consist solely of physical protective devices such as locks or vaults. Support all such physical security systems with either an effective alarm or television system and/or a 24-hour guard service.

Obviously, the amount of protection given a facility depends on which of the three categories it falls into, and the time and resources available.

The easiest facility to protect is, of course, the permanent facility. A security officer attempting to create an ideal audio security environment in this instance should first identify those areas in which sensitive discussions may take place. These areas are normally private offices and/or conference rooms. Every attempt should be made to confine sensitive discussions to these specific areas and concentrate security resources on just those one or two rooms rather than an entire building.

Acoustic Barriers

Consideration should be given to the type of room construction, with a view toward the acoustic attenuation characteristics of its perimeter (the ability of the walls, ceiling, and floor to act as a barrier to sound). Acoustic attenuation is greatest when there is a barrier consisting of two different types of insulating materials.

This creates what engineers call an acoustic impedance mismatch. Use of dissimilar materials, particularly when there is air space between them, is much more effective than merely thick walls. For instance, a double wall consisting of quarter-inch plywood nailed to 2-by-4-inch studs attenuate more sound than 4 inches of cinder block. And double pane, quarter-inch glass with a quarter of an inch of airspace in between is even more of a barrier.

One common insulating material that should not be used is acoustical tile. This tile was not developed to function as a sound insulator. Rather, it was designed to reduce reverberation or reflected sounds within radio broadcast studios. Its use in a room facilitates a technical attack by making the target area as acoustically "dead" as a recording studio, an ideal situation for a clandestine microphone. Additionally, the presence of thousands of dampening holes in the tile gives an opponent just that many more places to conceal a microphone, as the diameter of any one of these holes is ample for such a purpose.

It is far better to use a dense, sound-reflective material such as plywood, plasterboard, or Masonite. If the reverberations in the room become annoying to its occupants, heavy draperies can soften the sound considerably without having an adverse effect on audio security.

Room Doors

One security aspect often overlooked is the door. Although a heavy, solid-core door is often quite adequate, there is considerable sound transmission around the edges and underneath the door. This can be eliminated or reduced by the installation of an inexpensive rubber gasket around the edges of the door. A hollow-core door is an ideal place to conceal a surveillance transmitter and batteries.

Room Ductwork

Air conditioning or heating vents provide audio paths that can be exploited. There are various acoustic baffles that can be installed, but the most inexpensive approach is usually the application of nullification techniques. One example of nullification applicable in this situation is audible noise masking.

Audio Masking

Masking is the generation of sufficient noise at the perimeter of the secure area to cover or mask any conversations within the room. There are many commercially available systems designed for this exact purpose. Special transducers that create random vibrations or audible/mechanical noises are fastened to the walls, ceiling, and floor.

Transducers are also mounted in the air vents, on pipes/conduits, and in any possible avenue where sound might exit the target area. When the transducers are in operation, they virtually eliminate the chances of a successful attack using a contact microphone. The wiring of these systems should be done in such a manner that it can be visually inspected.

Failing the availability of an acoustical noise system, a radio tuned to a rock station and placed with its speaker against the unsecured wall will sometimes do. The conversations should be held as close as possible to this noise source and the tendency to talk louder than the radio should be overcome. Complete, portable, personal, secure wire communication systems are also available for use when noise sources are not available.

Room Windows

Ideally, there should be no windows in the secure room. If there are windows, they should be equipped with acoustical noise generators or, again, the radio. Cover the windows with blinds or drapes but keep in mind that IR passes through many types of material. If there are no windows, the visual/optical attack possibility is reduced to almost zero.

Room Wiring

All wiring leaving the secure area should be accounted for, with any that are not being used removed.

Room Telephones

Telephones should *not* be allowed in areas where discussions are held under any circumstances—they are an *extreme* hazard. A persuasive security officer can usually present a good argument for their removal from conference rooms, but there is no way a public figure can be talked out of having a telephone in his office. Thus, although the ideal situation is to have no phone, it will be necessary to take steps to minimize the hazard it presents.

The telephone instrument should be equipped with an easy means of disconnecting it from the telephone line. It should be unplugged when sensitive conversations take place. Do *not* use an autodisconnect device. The cheapest and simplest of these means is the plug and jack arrangement similar to that used in home telephones. With this arrangement, it is necessary to install a separate ringer to annunciate incoming calls, as the ringer in the telephone is, of course, also disconnected when the phone is not plugged in.

Ideally, the ringer should be a special, nonresonant ringer such as the Stromberg-Carlson Model 687-96A Ringer or the Kaiser RA-10 Non-Transducing Ringer. This would prevent an attacker from using the ringer as a transducer. A Kaiser RA-15 annunciator installed in the telephone ensures that it will not be left connected to the line.

Notwithstanding apocryphal stories to the contrary, there is no way that an unplugged telephone can be technically attacked. At best, it could be used to conceal a transmitter needing its own power supply. This would be detected by a basic visual search. Thus, the relatively inexpensive precaution described above nets a tremendous increase in audio security.

Telephone Disconnects and Switches

Several of these devices were commercially available years ago but they are not recommended. Since they contained extensive circuitry, the layperson was and is unable to tell if the telephone had been compromised.

Security of the Telephone Instrument

Again, physical security is paramount. The simplest countermeasures will work only if the potential adversary is denied an opportunity to gain access to the telephone instrument. Inasmuch as one attack technique consists of replacing the entire telephone with one that has been rewired, it is a good idea to discreetly mark the telephones so they can be visually inspected quickly. A control number can be engraved on the bottom of the instrument, for instance. A better method is to mark the phone in some manner with a material that fluoresces under ultraviolet light. Locking the telephone instrument in a safe is a good idea.

Telephone Taps

The adoption of all, or at least a substantial portion, of the above procedures will prevent any but the most highly sophisticated attacks. However, a word of explanation is in order. The attacks prevented are compromises designed to hear room conversation when the telephone is not in use, not taps. Short of the use of encrypted or "scrambled" telephone systems, there is no way to guarantee that a telephone is not currently tapped nor will be in the near future.

A great deal of time and considerable effort has been spent by many a technician to produce a system that can detect wiretaps. To date, *no* system has been developed that can be relied on to find even the most basic of taps all of the time.

The problem is that the line pair can be intercepted at any point between the telephone instrument and the central office. That can mean miles of unprotected wiring. Telephones are not the only devices that use the telephone lines. They are, or can be, shared with other devices such as computer modems, fax machines, and a variety of signaling and control equipment. Two telephone lines can actually carry four conversations without any one conversation interfering with the others.

A direct tap made with careful attention to impedance matching would be very, very difficult to detect. Certainly, the telephone subscriber would be unaware of it, as there would be no telltale clicks or noises on the line. Detection of a carefully installed induction coil or Hall-effect tap is simply impossible.

On the other hand, the chances of a successful tap are complicated by good physical security practices. The simplest tap is made at the nearest terminal or connecting block where the target line pair is tied to a large "house" cable or to an "outside" cable. The line pair at this point is spread out on the connecting block and is easy to both identify and attack. The terminal board or connecting block is usually found within the same building as the telephone, although it may be on an adjacent telephone pole, especially if the telephone is located in a residence. Consequently, if there is good physical security, it would possibly deny an adversary this easier point of attack.

An attacker with an understanding of how the telephone line matrix is set up can reap a bonanza simply by determining where the target company conducted its business in the past and searching for the wires outside that location. Sometimes the old wires are even left on the terminal blocks inside the old location.

Target lines can be located by means of a telephone company cable chart. Normally it would be necessary to obtain that chart from the telephone company, but it's amazing how often this information "falls off" telephone company trucks and into eager hands. Often these charts are left in the telephone frame room of the company under attack and thus are easy targets. Assume always that the attacker has access to information about the telephone lines.

Although the isolation and nullification procedures described so far are primarily applicable to permanent facilities, it should be obvious that many of them can be applied effectively to occasional-use facilities and, occasionally, to automobiles. Audio security, like any other form of security, is a percentage proposition in that every positive preventive action taken will yield a certain percentage increase in security. Therefore, it is incumbent on the security officer to carry out as many countermeasures as possible consistent with resources and common sense. A careful analysis of the isolation and nullification techniques discussed above reveal two basic points common to all the recommended countermeasures:

- Threat analysis
- Physical security

The security planner decides the most likely means of attack and plans his defenses accordingly. The material presented so far should clearly show the overwhelming importance of good physical security, which would have to be present in any event to safeguard the personal safety of any public figure or corporate executive.

If all applicable isolation and nullification techniques have been applied, then a potential technical perpetrator has been denied several means of attack. His most viable option would be planting a remote-controlled transmitter, free-space or carrier-current, and even then it would require him to breach physical security, either before or after the security perimeter was established. In short, if the security perimeter is perfect and all isolation and nullification recommendations implemented, a successful technical attack would be very difficult to carry out. However, security is never perfect or foolproof. Therefore, the security planner cannot consider his audio security program complete until he has arranged for and conducted the second major program component, the audio countermeasures survey.

THE AUDIO COUNTERMEASURES SURVEY

The audio countermeasures survey is a vital component of an effective audio security program, supplementing the application of the isolation and nullification techniques in the previous sections. It becomes necessary for two reasons.

- A technical attack may have been perpetrated before the initiation of the audio countermeasures program.
- An attack may have been successfully launched because of overlooked weakness or human error in the maintenance of adequate physical security.

As with the approach used with isolation and nullification, the survey may be conducted on a sliding scale of sophistication ranging from a simple physical examination of the area to the application of the most complex and detailed audio countermeasure equipment. As might be expected, the effectiveness of audio security tends to increase proportionately. However, the application of any audio countermeasure techniques described in this section will certainly add to the general audio security already present because of previously applied isolation and nullification techniques.

Timing of the Audio Countermeasures Survey

Perhaps the first question to be considered is exactly when and how often an audio countermeasures survey should be conducted. The answer, of course, depends upon the type of facility, permanent or occasional.

With a permanent facility, the most important criterion is the overall effectiveness of the isolation and nullification program. If the measures are all implemented, one audio countermeasures survey every year is usually sufficient. Any time there is extensive modification of the area, new construction, new electrical wiring, or any other activity that gives outsiders relatively unsupervised access to the sensitive area, a survey should be conducted upon the completion of the disrupting activity.

The survey should always be conducted during normal working hours to facilitate the discovery of remotely switchable devices. With occasional-use facilities, the survey may be conducted any time prior to its scheduled use. Upon completion of the survey, physical security procedures must be implemented. Additionally, if the activity to be protected is a conference or discussion, the security officer should arrange for some additional monitoring of the radio frequency spectrum during the initial stage of the conference. This detects any radio frequency devices missed during the survey but remotely turned on to intercept sensitive discussions. A survey will be required for the occasional facility each time there is a break in the physical security provided for it. As described later in this section, the same criterion applies to automobiles.

The equipment needed during the survey will be discussed as the steps of the audio countermeasures survey are outlined. The chances of an audio countermeasures survey detecting a clandestine device are greatly enhanced if the survey can be conducted in as nonalerting a manner as possible. There are two basic reasons for this.

If the attacker learns in advance of an audio countermeasures survey, he may have an opportunity to remove or destroy any clandestine equipment before the survey can be conducted. (A charged high-voltage capacitor placed across a microphones wires can literally vaporize the microphone element.)

If the adversary has advance notice, hears the audio countermeasures specialists in the conduct of the survey, or overhears someone in the target area mention that such a survey is in progress, he may switch off his remotely activated transmitter, preventing its detection. At the very least, he would have an opportunity to abandon his listening post, negating chances of an apprehension. Advance notice also precludes any chances of exploiting any devices found by using them to transmit false or spurious information.

This idea of strict secrecy in the conduct of audio countermeasures surveys cannot be overemphasized. Secrecy is, in fact, regarded as one of the technical surveillance countermeasures specialist's most important tools. The following is a very good rule to remember when talking about secrecy. If 1 person knows a secret then that's it. But if he or she tells another person (1) then putting those two 1s side by side looks like 11, or eleven. Adding another person (1) means it looks like 111, or one hundred and eleven, and so on. As you can see, secrets can be even harder to keep as each person is added!

Searching for Radio-Frequency Transmitters

Generally, the most important and sensitive part of the audio countermeasures survey is the search for radio frequency transmitters, both free-space and carrier-current. This is done in two ways:

- The use of electronic devices
- Physical search

The most effective pieces of electronic equipment available to assist the security officer in the detection of clandestine transmitters are specially designed detectors, a search receiver, or a spectrum analyzer (preferably capable of tuning from 10 KHz to 7 GHz). Quality detectors are available for a few hundred to a few thousand dollars. It is recognized that this cost may seem excessive to many agencies with a requirement to conduct audio countermeasures surveys, but it should be noted that relatively inexpensive "feedback" detectors could also be very effective.

The first step, then, in the conduct of an audio countermeasures survey is the search of the radio-frequency spectrum. Upon the completion of the "sweep" of the spectrum, check the power lines for the presence of a carrier-current device with equipment designed for that purpose. A similar check should be made of the telephone lines at the same time that the telephone system is checked for any compromises.

Inspection of the Telephone System

The next step in the audio countermeasures survey is inspection of the telephone system. The easiest and most efficient way to accomplish this is to check the outgoing telephone lines at their first appearance after they leave the secure area. Generally, buildings have a telephone closet where the various line pairs appear on terminal boards. This is where they are patched into the cable that eventually goes to the central office.

There are usually two wires on the terminal board for each outside line. The telephone company calls the two lines "tip and ring," a holdover from the days of operator-assisted calls. Some specialized and foreign telephones use a four-wire system. In this case, there will be a "tip and ring" for the "talk" pair (the pair connected to the transmitter/mouthpiece), and a "tip and ring" for the pair connected to the receiver/earpiece.

In telephone systems using key telephones, many wires on the board are not tip and ring. They are auxiliary conductors for such functions as the "hold" and "lamp flash" circuits. It is possible to tell a line pair by the use of a voltmeter (tip and ring will show approximately 48 volts DC between them if the line is not being used).

It is not necessary to know which wire is which for the purpose of a survey, since an adversary may have decided to use one of the auxiliary wires in the technical attack.

One of the audio countermeasures expert's most useful tools is a high-gain (amplification) audio amplifier. There are any number of commercially available units priced in the two- to four-hundred-dollar range that offer the user a choice of input and output impedances. The amplifier should include a high/low-pass filter, a tone generator for tracing wires and activating certain microphones, and a means of producing voltage to turn on external accessories such as electret and carbon microphones. Along with the amplifier there should be a set of earphones (the stethoscope type that covers both ears is best), and a two-conductor cable that terminates in alligator clips.

To check a telephone line, one wire from the amplifier is clipped to "tip," and the other to "ring." If the amplifier allows a selection of input impedances, anywhere from 10K to 500K ohms is a good choice. All that is necessary is to turn up the volume and listen. If the telephone is in use, the conversation will be heard. If the telephone is not in use and room audio is heard, the telephone hookswitch has been bypassed in some fashion, either by accident or on purpose. The sound of room audio is unmistakable.

The above procedure should be followed with all line pairs leading to the central office. If a technical attack has been initiated on a telephone in the secure area that does not utilize a radio-frequency transmitter, this procedure detects it in many, but not all, instances.

Upon completion of this audio check, the procedure should be repeated using the carrier-current detector, receiver, or spectrum analyzer. If both the radio frequency check and the audio check are negative, there is some assurance that the telephone system has not been attacked. Disassembling of the individual telephone instruments will be covered later in the survey.

There is a device available for telephone countermeasures called a telephone analyzer or telephone test set. This equipment tends to vary a great deal in cost, and the most expensive are not necessarily the best. Carefully check the capabilities of each unit to see if it matches both expectations and the existing system. Although these units are generally effective, there are drawbacks to them. First, there are devices they cannot detect for a variety of technical reasons. Second, they require a lot of understanding that translates into time. Typically, a unit can take thirty minutes to an hour to test a multiline telephone. If the space to be surveyed includes several telephones, the time can be excessive!

One of the major determinations the security officer must make is the value per audio security dollar. Sometimes money is better spent on the isolation and nullification program. In short, using the overall criterion of cost effectiveness, the telephone analyzer is not recommended for general surveys.

Total Area Inspection

Prior to initiating the audio countermeasures survey, a cursory nonalerting inspection should have been made in order to determine the possible location of listening posts and to decide the best location from which to conduct the radio frequency sweep. When the most critical portions of the survey have been completed it is not as important to remain completely nonalerting, although doing so would ensure the effective completion of the survey. Consequently, a more detailed inspection is in order starting from outside the facility.

Stand at a distance from the building. Where do the wires start from and lead to? Are there any buildings in the area not under control of the security office? Check the roof for wires and extraneous devices or antennas. Use common sense.

The inspection should continue inside the building. Are there any places in the building that might function as listening posts (a microphone and wire run could terminate in a closet, where all interceptions are recorded on tape and the tape retrieved on a daily basis)? Do unauthorized personnel securely lock the telephone closets to hinder access? Are all the keys accounted for? What conductors leave the secure perimeter? Is the closet alarmed? Every wire must be accounted for.

Room Search

Following generalized exterior and interior building examination, the potential target area itself should be considered. By this point in the audio countermeasures survey, the security officer will have a good idea of what, if any, technical attack is involved. At this juncture, the greatest obvious threat would come from a transmitter or microphone/wire feeding a nearby transmitter. The security director should have a fairly good idea of what to look for as the physical search is started.

The procedures used to search the facility are quite similar to those used to search for explosive devices, and the equipment used is basically the same. Thus, a good tool kit containing a set of screwdrivers, various pliers, wrenches, inspection mirrors and flashlights is the basic minimum needed to do the job correctly.

Priority should be given to those areas closest to where discussions normally take place, such as desks, sofas, telephones, etc. Items such as pictures and wall plaques should be removed from the wall and closely inspected for devices. The wall behind the picture or plaque should also be carefully inspected. Remember that the acoustic passage can be little bigger than a pinhole. There have been instances where transmitters have been secreted in picture frames.

An examination should be made of the underside of all furniture.

Wooden furniture should be thoroughly inspected inside and out. A beat frequency type of metal detector is useful here. Beat frequency metal detectors, unlike standard metal detectors, can tell the relative mass of both the metal and *mineral* they detect. Furniture should be picked up and moved to ensure that it does not conceal wires. The terminals of every loudspeaker should be closely examined and the wires leading to them traced to their origin.

All grates or grilles for air conditioning or heating ducts should be removed and the interiors inspected with a mirror. Be alert for any signs of recent entry such as tool marks or disturbed dust patterns. Use of an ultraviolet light is helpful in detecting recent alterations. Wear eye protection.

Examine baseboards carefully for signs of recent modification. These are popular places to hide microphones and/or wire runs. Roll back any carpeting to make sure that it does not hide wiring. Again, an ultraviolet light is useful, and don't forget the eye protection.

If the room has a false ceiling, the space between it and the true ceiling must be thoroughly inspected. Be particularly alert to the wires that often abound in these spaces. Remember that all conductors must be accounted for.

Pay particular attention to the backs of file cabinets or bookcases, as these too are good hiding places. It would be worthwhile to examine all hardbound books, as these have been successfully used in the past to hide transmitters.

The walls should be carefully inspected for any signs of microphones. Ultraviolet light is useful, as it tends to highlight paint or plaster differences better than standard light.

Light switches and electrical outlets are among the favorite places to plant carrier-current devices. These must be carefully examined. BE CAREFUL WITH HOT AC LINES! The protective covers must be removed and the inside of the box as well as the switch and socket must be carefully inspected. Quite a few off-the-shelf carrier-current devices are commercially available that are or can be packaged within wall plugs, electrical outlets, and light switches.

AGAIN, BE CAREFUL WITH HOT LINES! Use well-insulated tools. Even experienced countermeasures experts can ruefully attest to the shocking power of 117 volts AC (in some cases, 220 volts AC!) and most seasoned countermeasures tool kits contain at least one partially welded and badly scarred screwdriver.

Physical Inspection of Telephones

A physical inspection of the telephone system takes some preparation. If one is to gain anything useful from disassembling a telephone instrument, they must first know what a normal telephone looks like. Therefore, the security officer should examine a sample of the telephones in the system prior to conducting an audio countermeasures survey in order to have a general understanding of what to expect. This will greatly assist in recognizing an attack on the instrument. Attacks that are more sophisticated cannot be detected in this manner, as the devices may be hidden in telephone components or modifications made to any printed circuit boards.

The handset is examined by either unscrewing the holders for the mouthpiece and earpiece or removing the screws holding the handset together. The earpiece usually has only two wires attached to it that run through the center of the handset. Seesaw these wires back and forth to make sure nothing is in the middle. There is a small device, called a varistor, attached between the two terminals on the earpiece. On handsets designed for the hard of hearing, a coil surrounds the earpiece. There should be nothing else. The presence of any other components may represent a surveillance device. Examine the mouthpiece and the area surrounding it carefully for any abnormal signs. A common attack is the substitution for the microphone element with a drop-in surveillance device.

The wire leading from the telephone should be followed to the junction box. The cover of this box or wall jack should be removed and examined for foreign devices. Be careful to look at the insides of the covers themselves. There should be nothing there either. Some telephone systems use a plug called an Amphenol plug. The metal or plastic covers should be taken off and the inside inspected. Inspect the wires from the telephone to the wall jack.

Audio Countermeasures—Automobiles

Automobiles present an interesting and different set of problems. The basic difficulty with automobiles is that they are not afforded sufficient physical security to warrant the investment of concerted audio countermeasure efforts upon them. Consequently, a physical search is probably the most cost-effective countermeasure, and much of it could be done at the same time as any search for explosive devices. This search may require the assistance of a local auto service garage for checking under the vehicle.

There are three viable attacks against an automobile: a voice or video transmitter, a tracking transmitter (including GPS devices), and a tape recorder. A well-conducted physical search should uncover tape recorders. Keep in mind that commercially available excellent-quality voice-activated recorders are not much larger than a book of matches.

Transmitters can also be hidden easily and will be powered by either their own battery or the vehicle battery. It is important, therefore, to measure the amount of current being drawn from the vehicle battery. All current paths should be accounted for. Remember that an attacker's choice of microphone placement must always be influenced by an inherent characteristic of the automobile noise.

For this reason it follows that the microphones must be placed as close to the potential discussion area as possible. Thus, one would presume that in a chauffeur-driven car, the target area would be the backseat area rather than the front. Consequently, physical search efforts should be concentrated in that area. In short, experience and common sense will eventually formulate the audio countermeasures search procedures most effective for any given situation.

The importance of the physical search cannot be overemphasized, particularly if the audio countermeasures survey was conducted without the benefit of a radio frequency survey. For the same reason, effectiveness of a physical search should not be underrated. It is a fact that more electronic eavesdropping devices have been found by physical search and examination than by any other means. Even if a good search receiver is utilized during the audio countermeasures survey, at least 80 percent of the total person-hours expended should be devoted to the physical search.

The audio countermeasures survey is only part of an effective audio security program. True audio security will be gained by the adoption of isolation and nullification techniques. Although ideally, all of the recommendations should be incorporated into an overall audio security program, implementation of even a few will significantly decrease vulnerability to a technical attack.

Glossary of Terms

THE FOLLOWING TERMS include definitions of intelligence tradecraft, specific types of eavesdropping devices, and surveillance attacks and countermeasures.

Single-party consent: The federal wiretap law passed in 1968 permits surreptitious recording of conversations when one party consents, "unless such communication is intercepted for the purpose of committing any criminal or torturous act in violation of the Constitution or laws of the United States or of any State." Amendments to the law expand the prohibitions to unauthorized interception of most forms of electronic communications, including satellite transmission, cellular phone conversations, computer data transmissions, and cordless phone conversations. The majority of states have adopted the federal law regarding eavesdropping. Twelve states forbid the recording of private conversations without the consent of *all* parties.

Spookware: Any type of equipment that is used in the clandestine interception of electronic or spoken communications or to defeat an attempted eavesdropping.

Bug: A "bug" is a clandestine eavesdropping device that is placed in a room or vehicle, or on a person, that intercepts communications and transmits them to a listening post in another room, hundreds of feet or miles away, depending on the type of device used.

Ultrasonic bug: A technique used to convert captured audio signals to a frequency above the normal range of human hearing. The ultrasonic signal is then intercepted nearby and converted back to audio. Audio pressure waves are used instead of creating a radio signal.

RF (radio frequency) bug: This is the most common type of room eavesdropping device used in the FM band. Generally cheap and extremely easy to detect, it is highly effective and difficult to trace back to the eavesdropper who planted it.

Optical bug: A transmitter that converts sound or data into a beam of light. Expensive, but easy to detect. Example: an active or passive laser listening device.

Electronic countermeasures: Actions taken to deny interception of audio communications.

Cutout: An intermediary or front person or organization used in an intelligence transaction to disguise the true source of the information or hardware being sold or transferred.

Hook-switch bypass: A simple modification to a telephone that will convert it into an active listening device, picking up all conversations in a room when the handset is on the hook.

Harmonica bug: A small device planted inside or outside a telephone that is activated by sending a harmonica tone over the telephone line and which permits monitoring of room conversations. In older telephone systems, the tone is sounded before the person lifts the handset from the cradle. In newer phone systems, the target telephone is called and answered. An excuse is given: "Sorry, wrong number." When the target hangs up the phone, the tone is then sounded. Newer harmonic bugs use the telephone keypad to activate the bug.

Wiretapping: A preferred method of obtaining intelligence by tapping into a wire or other communications conductor. This includes telephone lines, PBX cables, local area networks, CCTV video systems, alarm systems, or any other communications medium. The goal of a wiretap is to secretly recover high-quality information and to do it without the possibility of being detected (radiated signals are easy to detect). There are four primary categories of wiretaps:

1. Hard-wired wiretap: Physically accessing a section of wire to recover the signal on those wires. A second set of wires is attached and the signal transmitted back to the monitoring location. When discovered, this type of wiretap is fairly easy to trace back to the listening post.

2. Soft wiretap: Modification to the software used to run the phone system. This can be achieved at the telephone company central office or in the case of a business, the PBX. A soft wiretap is a preferred method to tap a phone but relatively easy to catch on a PBX, although not the telephone itself. This type of tap is very popular with large law enforcement agencies, intelligence agencies, larger corporations, and hackers, who find it quite simple to gain access via maintenance software.

3. Record wiretap: A tape recorder wired to a phone line. Similar to hard-wired wiretap, but tapes must be changed on a regular basis. This is the wiretap of

choice for amateur spies and private investigators, but it carries a high risk of detection.

4. Transmit wiretap: An RF transmitter or bug connected to a wire pair. Sometimes they contain a subminiature microphone to retrieve room conversation. This is a popular eavesdropping device, but the RF energy it produces definitely increases the chances of detection by a competent TSCM practitioner.

Nonresonant ringer: To defeat placement of a listening device in a telephone ringer, you remove the ringer and replace it with a device that beeps when phone rings. National Security Agency (NSA) procedures require that all phones in overseas locations utilize a nonresonant ringer device.

Nonlinear junction detector: A microwave device that can detect a semiconductor (two different types of joined metals) inside an active or deactivated (passive) listening device that may be located inside a room or the walls of a room.

Resonant cavity transmitter: Type of bug found hidden in the Great Seal of the U.S. embassy in Moscow in the 1950s. It has no battery, making it difficult to detect. It functions by flooding its cavity with an external beam of RF energy from 300–500 meters away. The energy gathers all audio sounds in the room and rebroadcasts them back to a receiver in a nearby listening post.

The Silver Box: A telephone wiretap technology used for decades by AT&T and other competing phone companies. When it is installed in the switching equipment of a local telephone exchange, phone companies can monitor any hard-wired phone conversation in the country by punching in a special code. Phone companies use this technology to monitor customer service calls.

Foreign Intelligence Surveillance Court (FISC): Established by Congress in 1978, FISC is a special court that authorizes federal warrants sought by the Justice Department to conduct electronic eavesdropping and physical searches of individuals suspected of federal crimes. The number of so-called FISC warrants has doubled since 2001, when 934 applications were approved.

Contact microphone: Listening device designed to pick up mechanical vibrations moving along a surface, as opposed to recording airborne sounds. Placed firmly against a common wall, pipe, or air conditioning duct, it produces room audio. When mounted through a wall via a pointed probe, it becomes a "spike mike." I developed a device called a "pipe banger" to create interfering sound to defeat the contact microphone attack. The device, placed on water pipes, creates a steady vibration that drowns out audio conversations and prevents eavesdropping.

TEMPEST: U.S. government code word for a once-classified set of standards for defeating clandestine eavesdropping of electronic or electromagnetic emanations from equipment such as computers, electronic typewriters, monitors, or printers, to prevent electronic espionage.

The Black Box: Long used by bookies, two telephones are placed side by side and hooked together with a black box. When the first phone number is dialed, the second telephone dials out to the final location. When the police trace the number for the first telephone location and get a warrant to break down the door, all they find are two phones sitting side by side on the floor. The original call recipient is long gone! The same thing can be done with cellular phones. Terrorists are already wise to this trick. In reality, any number of telephones can be hooked up together, virtually circling the globe and back.

FM (frequency modulation): A type of modulation that causes the frequency of the signal to shift side to side but does not cause the amplitude to change. Think of it in terms of a trombone. As the slide moves, the pitch (frequency) changes but the loudness does not change.

AM (amplitude modulation): A type of modulation that causes the amplitude to change but not the frequency. In broadcast stations, it normally swings from 20 percent to 80 percent of the average amplitude.

Burst transmitter: Listening device that converts sound to digital form, stores it, and then transmits it in a short, high-speed burst. This makes it more difficult to find with countermeasure equipment because it is not sending a continuous signal.

Endnotes

Chapter 1: Early Survival Lessons

p. 3   "perceiving the intentions of others": Lee C. Park, M.D., et al., "Giftedness and Psychological Abuse in Borderline Personality Disorder: Their Relevance to Genesis and Treatment." *Journal of Personality Disorders* (accepted 3/7/91), 1.

p. 6   My father, Martin L. Kaiser Jr., was the first . . . furnace into northeastern Pennsylvania: Personal knowledge of the author.

p. 10   *Stockholm*, which later rammed the *Andrea Doria*: Algot Mattsson, English translation edited by Gordon W. Paulsen and Bruce G. Paulson, *Out of the Fog: The Sinking of the Andrea Dorea* (The Titanic Historical Society, 2001–2004) (jacket copy).

Chapter 2: Getting Serious About Electronics

p. 15   I called it a flying spot scanner: RCA Technical Note 76, September 1961, Martin L. Kaiser Web site; The Beginning. www.martykaiser.com. Kaiser personal papers.

p. 28   However, with the collapse of Communism: *Microwave Journal*, March 1998, 82–92.

Chapter 3: Stumbling into the Spy Racket

p. 40   Winston Arrington. . . . called it "a bikini bug.": Winston Arrington, *Now Hear This*, Sheffield Electronic Company, Chicago, Illinois.

p. 40   It was the kind of listening device: Jim Hougan, *Secret Agenda: Watergate, Deep Throat and the CIA*, Random House, 1984, 164–65.

p. 41   The Soviet Union, thanks to the brilliance of an electrical engineer named Leon Theremin: www.spybusters.com, Kevin Murray's Eavesdropping History, 1952, The Great Seal Bug, 1–10.

p. 43   The Great Seal Incident: www.spybusters.com, The Great Seal Bug, 6.

p. 47   "acting without legal authority . . . in any domestic security case . . .": Morton H. Halperin, Jerry J. Berman, Robert L. Borosage, and Christine M. Marwick, *The Lawless State: The Crimes of the U.S. Intelligence Agencies*, Penguin Books, 1976, 123.

p. 48   Between 1967 and 1970: Halperin et al., *The Lawless State*, 155.

p. 49   "a computerized Spot Report Index": Halperin et al., *The Lawless State*, 165.

p. 49   "Army [intelligence] agents infiltrated Resurrection City": Halperin et al., *The Lawless State*, 165.

p. 51   More than a decade earlier: Richard Gid Powers, *Broken: The Troubled Past and Uncertain Future of the FBI* (Free Press, 2004), 246.

p. 51   Matter had prepared at the request of William Sullivan: Powers, *Broken*, 246.

p. 51   That audiotape contained sexual conversations: Powers, *Broken*, 246.

p. 51   The tape was accompanied by an anonymous letter: Powers, *Broken*, 245–47.

p. 51   The letter read in part: Garrow, Penguin Books, 1983, 126.

p. 51   The tape and the letter were flown: Garrow, 126.

p. 52   Deke DeLoach, one of the assistant FBI directors: Garrow, 127–28.

Chapter 4: The Michelangelo of Electronic Surveillance

p. 59   According to George O'Toole: George O'Toole, "Harmonica Bugs, Cloaks & Silver Boxes," *Harper's Magazine*, June 1975, 37.

p. 60   When the bugging of the Maryland and Delaware civil defense phones: O'Toole, "Harmonica Bugs," 37.

p. 60   No one ever found out who had engaged: O'Toole, "Harmonica Bugs," 37.

p. 60   One of the most fascinating aspects: O'Toole, "Harmonica Bugs," 37.

p. 67   At the time, U.S. Representative Dick Armey: www.spybusters.com. Link re quotations about eavesdropping.

p. 69   One example involved the CIA spying: Hougan, *Secret Agenda*, 90.

Chapter 5: An Audience with J. Edgar Hoover

p. 75   The story goes that as one new agents' class: Rosemary Dew and Pat Pape, *No Backup: My Life as a Female FBI Special Agent*, Carroll & Graf, 2004, 29.

p. 78   It was estimated that Hoover's clandestine surveillance operations: Curt Gentry, *J. Edgar Hoover: The Man and the Secrets*, W. W. Norton & Co., 1991, 458–59.

p. 82   Their relationship would cause more than a few raised eyebrows: Hougan, *Secret Agenda*, 133. *Newsweek*, Dec. 15, 1975, "Case of the Cozy Cutout." *Department of Justice Report on the Relationship Between United States Recording Company and the FBI and Certain Other Matters Pertaining to the FBI*, January 1978.

Chapter 6: A Fateful Meeting

p. 83   The Weather Underground, a splinter faction: www.diyzine
.com/weatherundergroundarticle3.html.

p. 83   In 1972, the FALN: www.infoplease.com/ipa/A00001454.html.

p. 83   A Croatian nationalist set off a bomb: www.brainyhistory.com/
events/1975/december.

p. 86   The column revealed documents: Ronald Kessler, *The Bureau:
The Secret History of the FBI*, St. Martin's Press, 2002, 186.

Chapter 7: My Anwar Sadat Cadillac

p. 91   According to Butterfield: Hougan, *Secret Agenda*, 58–59.

p. 93   Martin Kaiser on Frank Terpil. Some of the information on
these pages is attributed to the author's personal knowledge
of Terpil through conversations with him. Some of the information was gained from the following sources: Peter Maas,
*Manhunt: The Incredible Pursuit of a CIA Agent Turned Ter-
rorist*, Random House, 1986, 58–65, 129–32. *Confessions of
a Dangerous Man*, BBC TV documentary, 1981. Joseph
Goulden, *The Death Merchant*, Simon & Schuster, 1984,
95–101, 306–8.

Chapter 8: Road to Ruin

p. 111   An investigation by the General Accounting Office: "Is
Kaiser Object of FBI Vendetta?," *Winston-Salem Journal*,
February 21, 1978, 1.

p. 111   It later came out that Tait and Mohr: Hougan, *Secret Agenda*,
133.

p. 112   Following an internal FBI investigation: *The Department of
Justice Report on the Relationship between United States
Recording Company and the Federal Bureau of Investigation
and Certain Other Matters Pertaining to the F.B.I.*, January
1978, 1–40.

p. 112   During his time as Director: Kessler, *The Bureau*, 111.

p. 117   Letter to Attorney General Edward Levi from Martin Kaiser. Author's personal archives.

p. 121   "He [Harward] noted that there was a purchase": FBI Memo, dated April 6, 1976. Author's personal archives.

p. 126   The report said in part: *The Department of Justice Report*, 3.

p. 126   "From Fiscal Year 1971 through 1975": *The Department of Justice Report*, 5.

p. 126   One FBI agent reportedly did complain: *The Department of Justice Report*, 6.

Chapter 9: Payback

p. 129   On September 21, Orlando Letelier: John Dinges and Saul Landau, *Assassination on Embassy Row*, Pantheon Books, 1980, jacket copy.

p. 129   In another report: Peter Maas, *Manhunt: The Incredible Pursuit of a CIA Agent Turned Terrorist*, Random House, 1986, 3–6.

p. 129   The assassination was part of "Operation Condor": Dinges and Landau, *Assassination on Embassy Row*, 185.

Chapter 10: A Gathering Storm

p. 144   "That night we knew what happened": Deposition of Thomas Brereton, September 20, 1978, U.S. District Court, Middle District of North Carolina, Greensboro Division. Civil lawsuit Nr. C-78-343-WS, *Brereton and Lowe vs. Martin L. Kaiser, et al.*, 99–101.

p. 145   According to a brief filed: FBI memo, dated September 7, 1977. This document is part of Martin Kaiser's personal archives, obtained through discovery during his criminal trial.

p. 146   The brief also alleged: FBI memo, dated September 7, 1977. This document is part of Martin Kaiser's personal archives, obtained through discovery during his criminal trial.

p. 146 Before taking the OMB job: *The New Georgia Encyclopedia.* Biography of Bert Lance. www.georgiaencyclopedia.org.

p. 151 "It is interesting to note": FBI memo, from the Charlotte, NC, field office, dated October 21, 1977. This document is part of Martin Kaiser's personal archives, obtained through discovery during his criminal trial.

p. 155 The term *qui tam*: Definition of term obtained from www.cherrylawfirm.com (Qui Tam—FAQ).

p. 156 In an FBI memo dated 1/10/78: FBI memo, Charlotte, NC, field office. This document is part of Martin Kaiser's personal archives, obtained through discovery during his criminal trial.

Chapter 11: The Trial

p. 159 "I told them I didn't think it was a good idea": Testimony by George Collins, President, Northwestern Bank, Wilkesboro, NC, during criminal trial of Martin Kaiser: *Winston-Salem Sentinel,* February 10, 1978, p. 17.

p. 159 When it came time for cross-examination: Collins testimony, *Winston-Salem Sentinel,* p. 17.

p. 160 He told the jury that the device: Testimony by FBI Special Agent Edward Brennan in criminal trial of Martin Kaiser. Quote is from notes taken by Kaiser during the trial and from part of the court transcript, February 11, 1978.

p. 161 "Special Agent Brennan": Testimony by FBI Special Agent Brennan during Kaiser trial. Part of Kaiser personal notes and court transcript, February 11, 1978.

p. 166 "Mr. Kaiser is not innocent": Attributed to FBI Agent Thomas Brereton by Martin Kaiser at the end of the criminal trial, February 21, 1978, in Winston-Salem, NC. Kaiser's personal notes.

Chapter 12: More Trials and Survival Strategies

p. 168 NATIA is composed of over 2,000 . . . law enforcement and intelligence officers: Homepage of the National Technical Investigators Association, www.natia.org/home.htm.

p. 178 They asked for $22 million: Civil lawsuit filed by FBI Agents Thomas Brereton and Zachary Lowe against Martin Kaiser, U.S. District Court, Middle District of North Carolina, Winston-Salem, NC, C-78-343, 10/4/1978. Kaiser's personal archives.

p. 179 On October 27, 1977, Edgar Best: FBI memo, dated 11/16/77, from SAC Best, Charlotte, NC, field office, to FBI legal counsel John Mintz. Kaiser's personal archives.

Chapter 13: Searching for Bugs in Corporate America

p. 180 Just before Thanksgiving: *Jonestown Massacre + 20: Questions Linger.* CNN.com. and Don Knapp, The Associated Press, 1–3. (All of the information and details related to the countermeasures sweeps described in this chapter are based on Martin Kaiser's memory, invoices, and personal notes kept by him.)

Chapter 14: Civil Suit and Countersuit

p. 189 "Bugged FBI Men With Hemorrhoids": *Daily Telegraph*, London, England. January 2, 1979. Kaiser's personal archives.

p. 190 In a motion filed later by my attorneys . . ."on all three counts agree with Mr. Kaiser . . .": (Brief in support of motion to dismiss civil suit charges against Martin Kaiser), filed March 31, 1982, 7. Kaiser's personal archives.

p. 191 According to the FBI Manual: (Defendants; brief in opposition to Plaintiffs' motion for summary judgment as to counterclaims of Martin L. Kaiser and Martin L. Kaiser Inc.), civil suit. Nr. C-78-343-WS, 1982, 11. Kaiser's personal archives.

p. 192 "They [Brereton and Lowe] were given access and power":

Brief of Stephen Spring, Kaiser's lawyer in countersuit motion of civil law suit brought by FBI Agents Brereton and Lowe. Court transcript, Kaiser's personal archives.

p. 193 "It is our belief, based upon a review": Affidavit filed by Martin Kaiser, February 4, 1983, as part of a motion to dismiss civil charges brought by FBI Agents Brereton and Lowe, 2–3. Kaiser's personal archives.

p. 196 "We were told that no one would try to stop us": Statement made by Frank Terpil in the BBC/PBS documentary *Confessions of a Dangerous Man*, aired in the early 1980s. Kaiser's personal archives.

p. 196 Wilson was eventually sentenced to fifty-three years: *New York Times* "Freed Ex-C.I.A. Officer Tries to Clear His Name," June 13, 2005, p. A14.

p. 197 "Frank Terpil was like a lot of people": statement by Jim Hougan about Terpil in the BBC/PBS documentary *Confessionals of a Dangerous Man*, aired in the early 1980s. Kaiser's personal archives.

p. 200 "There are very few people that I've known": Excerpt from private correspondence written by Kaiser's lawyer, Bud Fensterwald, to Kaiser, dated December 13, 1979. Kaiser's personal archives.

Chapter 15: The Aftermath

p. 203 "There was absolutely no reason": Robert Capa, *Slightly Out of Focus*, Henry Holt & Co., New York, 1947, p. 3.

p. 209 "Depression is an enduring feature": Excerpt of psychological evaluation of Martin Kaiser at time of admission to St. Joseph's Hospital, Baltimore, following a nervous collapse. Dated June 26, 1992, p. 5. Kaiser's personal archives.

Chapter 16: "Enemy of the State"

p. 216 "That was what Gene did": Quote from promotion material by

Don Simpson/Jerry Bruckheimer Productions, Touchstone Pictures, about the making of *Enemy of the State*. See Kaiser Web site, www.martykaiser.com. Go to link "Enemy of the State."

Chapter 17: Looking Back

p. 220   Jack learned: Jeffrey Stein, *Spy Company Linked to Hush-Up Murders*, Pacific News Service, Washington Watch, July 16, 1978, 1, 4.

p. 221   In 1969, he was deported: James M. Ellison, "A Report from the Wiretap Subculture," *Washington Monthly*, December 1975, 28. See also Jim Hougan, *Spooks: The Haunting of America—The Private Use of Secret Agents*, William Morrow & Co., 1978, 66–69.

p. 221   AID and NIA trained: Pacific News Service, Washington Watch, July 16, 1978, 1, 4.

p. 221   AID and Holcomb drew some publicity: Pacific News Service, Washington Watch, July 16, 1978, 1, 4. See also Dinges and Landau, *Assassination on Embassy Row*, p. 328.

p. 223   The son of a Czarist cavalry officer: Hougan, *Spooks*, pp. 25–48.

p. 226   The last time I saw him was at a surveillance trade show: Joseph C. Goulden, *The Death Merchant*, Simon & Schuster, New York, 1984, pp. 304–8. *Confessions of a Dangerous Man*, BBC TV documentary, 1981.

Chapter 18: The Future of Privacy in America— Or What's Left of It

p. 234   In the past four years: Andrew O'Harrow Jr., *No Place to Hide*, Free Press, 2005, pp. 4–5.

p. 234   While the major private-sector data-mining services: O'Harrow, *No Place to Hide*, pp. 6–7.

p. 235   "Swept away by patriotic fervor": O'Harrow, *No Place to Hide*, pp. 6–7.

p. 235   Particularly troubling is Section 213: Declan McCullagh,

Patriot Act's Secret Searches Used 108 Times, CNET Networks Inc., April 5, 2005, www.new.com, 1.

p. 235 According to the Justice Department: McCullagh, *Patriot Act's Secret Searches,* 1.

p. 236 The section of the PATRIOT Act: Dahlia Lithwick and Julia Turner, *A Guide to the Patriot Act, Part I,* Jurisprudence, Slate.msn.com. See also Electronic Privacy Information Center, *USA Patriot Act Sunset,* www.epic.org/privacy/terrorism/usapatriot/sunset.html, 6–7.

p. 236 For starters, consider the Total Information Awareness (TIA) program: Matthew Brzezinski, *Fortress America: On the Front Lines of Homeland Security—An Inside Look at the Coming Surveillance State,* Bantam Books, New York, 2004, pp. 55–56.

p. 237 One of them is called MATRIX: Brzezinski, *Fortress America,* p. 71. See also Jeffrey Rosen, *How to Protect America, and Your Rights, New York Times,* Op-Ed, February 6, 2005, p. A27.

p. 238 One of them is the new Computer Assisted Passenger Pre-Screening System: Brzezinski, *Fortress America,* pp. 70–71.

p. 239 An ironic footnote to the proliferation: "FBI Cuts Carnivore Internet Probe," The Associated Press, January 19, 2005, and cshink.com/2005/fbi_cuts_carnivore.htm. See also *IASSIST Quarterly,* Fall 2003, 12, and Carnivore, allen@leigh.org, 2005.

p. 239 As part of the Carnivore project: Carnivore, allen@leigh.org, 2005, 2.

p. 240 Another example of a private-sector software program: O'Harrow, *No Place to Hide,* pp. 146–47.

p. 240 When you think of covert government electronic surveillance: Patrick S. Poole, *ECHELON: America's Secret Global Surveillance Network,* copyright 1999/2000, fly.hiwaay.net/pspoole/echelon.html, 1–18.

p. 241 That included Osama bin Laden: Brzezinski, *Fortress America,* p. 57.

p. 241 NSA's voice and optical recognition systems: Poole, *ECHELON*, 8.

p. 241 The ECHELON network's massive listening and reception capacity: Brzezinski, *Fortress America*, p. 76.

p. 242 Project SHAMROCK, an NSA project: Poole, *ECHELON*, 10.

p. 242 Project MINARET, a joint NSA-CIA project: Poole, *ECHELON*, 10–11.

p. 242 NSA has frequently been used: Poole, *ECHELON*, 12.

p. 242 During the Reagan administration: Poole, *ECHELON*, 13.

p. 243 In 1988, Margaret Newsham: Poole, *ECHELON*, 13.

p. 243 *Insight Magazine* reported in 1997: Poole, *ECHELON*, 14.

p. 243 According to a report by the Office of the National Counterintelligence Executives: *Annual Report to Congress on Foreign Economic Collection and Industrial Espionage—2003*, February 2004, 1–8.

p. 243 In a 1999 survey of Fortune 1,000 companies: Symantec Enterprise Security, *Hidden Motives: Corporate Espionage*, Issue 6, Winter 2000, www.symantec.com, 1.

p. 244 My own field of expertise continues to boom: *Figures Compiled by the U.S. Department of State: 1997*. Thomas Investigative Publications, Austin, TX, www.pimall.com/nais/n.state.html, 1.

p. 244 To add to the problem of privacy infringement: "LexisNexis Chief Advocates Data Security Rule" *Los Angeles Times*, April 13, 2005, www.latimes.com, 1–2.

p. 245 OnStar, a leading manufacturer of auto and personal security systems: Brzezinski, *Fortress America*, 62–63.

p. 246 ULTRA Customer Intelligence Analytics: O'Harrow, *No Place to Hide*, p. 296.

p. 246 RFID (radio frequency identification) tags: Brzezinski, *Fortress America*, pp. 78–81.

p. 246 Biometric identifiers: O'Harrow, *No Place to Hide*, pp. 67, 91, 158, 186.

p. 247 The various surveillances conducted: Poole, *ECHELON*, 11.

Acknowledgments

MY DEEPEST HEARTFELT thanks go to the people in the trenches who stood solidly by me while the FBI drama unfolded— Kamal Sirageldin, Gwynne Ebanks, and Mary Oliver. I also want to thank Sergio Borquez, posthumously. Serge was a retired DEA wireman who, for over thirty years, actively supported my company and me to the end. Their support was of enormous value in keeping me focused on whatever task lay ahead.

My thanks to my wife, Carmel; son, Marty IV; daughter, Carol; and her husband, Andy Hundertmark, for their guidance and encouragement throughout the writing of this book. I love you all.

The job of organizing over forty years of documentation was placed in the capable hands of my administrative vice president, Joan Florentine. Without her efforts, I do not know if I would ever have seen the light at the end of the tunnel.

I met Bob Stokes more than twenty years ago when he interviewed me for a magazine story on corporate eavesdropping and espionage. From the moment I told him about my experiences in the U.S. intelligence community, Bob believed that my story would resonate with the reading public. I am forever grateful to Bob for helping me to tell my story.

For years, Bob tried to get editors interested in my story without success. We finally found, through our agent, Bob Diforio, a believer and supporter in Philip Turner, editor in chief of Carroll & Graf Publishers. From a five-page outline, Philip helped Bob and me to flesh out and organize the story. We are indebted to Philip for his continued confidence and encouragement of this project and to Keith Wallman, associate editor, for his perceptive advice and support during the editing process.

—MLK

• • •

I WANT TO thank my agent, Bob Diforio, for his continued support and enthusiasm for this project, my previous efforts, and those to come.

I also want to thank my friends and fellow writers in the Phoenix Writers Group who listened patiently to my various chapter drafts and made several helpful suggestions during the writing and rewriting of the book.

Finally, I have been blessed with the love and support of my family throughout this project. That includes my brother, Peter, and his wife, Annie; all of my children; and, most of all, my wife Cecile. Without her love and constant reassurance, as well as a keen editing eye, this book would not have been possible.

—RSS

Index

A

Agnew, Spiro, 60
Allen, Milton, 61–62
Anderson, Jack, 69–70, 85–86
Angleton, James J., 111
antiwar movement (1960s-1970s), 49–50
Argentina, 174–78
Armco Steel, 33–35
Armey, Dick, 67
Arrington, Winston, 40, 227–28
Arturo (Argentina guide), 175–78
audio surveillance
    carrier-current transmitters, 261–62
    countermeasures survey, 277–87
    free-space transmitters, 256–60
    general considerations, 269–77
    mechanical, 251–52
    microphone and wire, 253–56
    telephones, 265–69
    visual or optical, 262–65

B

Baker, William, 50
Baltimore Gas & Electric, 184–85
Barbados, 19–20
Barcella, Larry, 129
Barnes, Michael, 242
Bast, Richard, 69–70
Bell, Allen, 224–25
Bentley, Helen, 198–99
Bernstein, Carl, 184
Best, Edgar, 179
biometric identifiers, 246
black-bag jobs, 47, 78–79, 235
Black Box, The, 292
black ops jobs, 87, 91
blacklisting, 115–17, 168, 187–88. *See also* harassment
Bodden, Jim, 88
bomb detection, 83–85, 104, 199–200, 218
Borquez, Sergio, 227
Bowers, Gwyn, 132–37, 142–45, 147, 150–51
    Northwestern Bank trial, 158–59, 161, 163–64

Bradlee, Benjamin, 52
Brennan, Edward, J., 143–44, 160–61, 163
Brereton, Thomas, 141–47, 149–53
    Northwestern Bank
    civil suit, 178–79, 190–93, 201
    trial, 159–61, 165–66
Brown, Benjamin, 61
Bruckheimer, Jerry, 211–12, 214–15
Brzezinski, Matthew, 237
bugs, 244. *See also* Russians; telephone surveillance
    types of, 38–40, 45–46, 63, 289–90, ix–x
Butterfield, Alexander, 91–92

C

Callahan, Nicholas P., 112
CAMBRIDGE, Project, 16, 20–27
car bombs, 98–99
Carnivore, 239
carrier-current transmitters, 261–62
Carter, Jimmy, 222
Cayman Islands, 87–88, 173
Chile, 129
Church, Frank, 51, 242
Church Committee, 51
civil defense bugging, 59–60
civilian surveillance. *See* Hoover, J. Edgar; Hoover's FBI; PATRIOT Act; privacy in America
Clinton, Bill, 243
Cold War, 18–19, 66–68
Collins, George, 142–43, 158–59
Computer Assisted Passenger Pre-Screening System (Capps 2), 238–39
Confessions of a Dangerous Man, 195–97
consumer data-mining, 246
Conversation, The, 212–14, x
Cooper, Norval, 58–59, 61
Coppola, Francis Ford, 213
Corle, Wesley, 144
counter-drug detection, 28
countermeasure equipment, 40, 50–51, 53–55, 63–64. *See also* Fort Holabird
    private sector, 181–86

countermeasures survey, 277–87
Crowell, William, 217
cutouts, 111–112, 289

D
Davis, Andrew, 211–12, 214
Dean, John, 91
DeLoach, Deke, 52, 112
documentaries, 194–97
dollar-bill changer, 29
Doms, Robert W., 36–39, 44, 224
Duncan, Ed, 86–89, 132–34, 141–42,
    145–47, 150–51
    Northwestern Bank trial, 158–59,
        161, 178
Dunn, T. V., 142
Dwyer, Jean, xx

E
eavesdropping devices. *See* audio surveil-
    lance; bugs
Ebanks, Clint, 87
ECHELON, 240–43
Egan, Nancy, 107, 123
Egypt, 97–104, 122–23, 193–94
Ehrlichman, John, 91, 242
Eisenhower, 43
ENAC Triton Co., 29
Enemy of the State, 212, 214–16, x
Ervin, Sam, 89

F
Farris, Anthony J. P., 109–10
FBI, investigation of, 125–27
FBI and Martin Luther King, Jr. The
    (Garrow), 51–52
feedback effect, 40–41
Feldman, Marc, 148–49
Felt, W. Mark, 48
Fensterwald, Bernard ("Bud"), 147–50,
    155–56, 192, 194, 200
    Northwestern Bank
        arraignment, 152–53, xv–xx
        trial, 160–66
Fitzsimmons, Frank, 130–31
Fort Holabird, 35–50
    2050CA RF detector, 40–41, 43, 44–46
    Modal 1059 preamplifier, 38
    teaching defense, 44–49, 105

Fortress America (Brzezinski), 237
free-space transmitters, 256–60

G
Gabriel, Carmel. *See* Kaiser, Carmel (nee.
    Gabriel)
Gandy, Helen, 75–77
Garrow, David J., 51–52
German technology, 17
Global Positioning System (GPS), 245–46
Goodwin, Leo Jr., 221
Great Seal bugging, 42–43
Griffin, Chris, 199
Gualda, Hector, 174–75

H
Hackman, Gene, 212–13, 216–17, x
Haldane, Bill, 16, 19–20
Haldeman, H.R., 91
Halperin, Morton H., 47, 49
harassment, 113–14, 122–24, 170–73,
    198. *See also* blacklisting
Harward, William, 81, 121–22
Hirschman, Michael, 107
Hoffa, Jimmy, 130–31
Holcomb, Jack, 220–22, 224
hook-switch bypass, 58–59, 289
Hoover, J. Edgar, 74–77, 85–86, 112–13
Hoover's FBI, 41, 46–47, 152
    civilian surveillance, 60, 70, 78–79,
        193–94
    Martin Luther King, Jr., 51–52,
        85–86, 242
Hostage Negotiation System (Model
    7080), 131–32
Hougan, Jim, 69, 197
House Select Committee on Intelligence,
    107, 109, 112–13, 121–22, xvi

I
identity theft, 244–45
illegal surveillance, 47–48
image conversion, 14–16
Ingram, Gordon, 223
Intercept of Communications laws, 133–34,
    136–37, 159, 163–64, 288, xii
International Association of Bomb Tech-
    nicians and Investigators (IABTI),
        116, 168–69, 188

IRS tax audits, 113–14, 173
Iselin, Jay, 52
Israel, 98, 102–3

J

Johnson, Lyndon, 27, 52, 60–61
Jonas, Jeff, 240
Jones, Bob, 63, 93
Jones, Leo, 37–39

K

Kaczynski, Ted, 83, 169
Kaiser, Carmel (nee. Gabriel), 16, 124,
    154–55, 167, xviii
  Barbados, 20–23
  education of, 29–30
  meeting Martin, 12–13
  and son Marty, 170–71
Kaiser, Carol (daughter), 19, 124
Kaiser, Martin L. *See also* blacklisting;
    harassment
  abuse by father, 1–4, 124, 228–30, x
  background, ix–xiv
  early electronics interest, 1–2, 4–8, 11
  education, 4–5, 7–13
  family, 2, 6–7, 56–57
  ham radio, 5–9, 215–16
  sailing, 10–12
  teacher, 44–49
Kaiser, Marty (son), 19, 22, 25, 124, 170–73
Katzenbach, Nicholas, 52
Kelley, Clarence, 119–22, 125
key-logger, 89–90
King, Martin Luther Jr., 39, 51–52,
    85–86, 242
Kissinger, Henry, 97, 242
Kleitman, Dave, 14–15
Klensch, Richard, 17–18
Korkola, Gary, 225–27

L

Lance, Bert, 146
Lawless State: The Crimes of the U.S.
    Intelligence Agencies, The (Halperin),
    47, 49
Letelier, Orlando, 129, 221
letter bombs, 169
Levi, Edward, 117–19, 125
Lexis-Nexis, 238, 244

Libya, 195–97
Liddy, G. Gordon, 222
lie-detector systems/polygraphs, 43–44
Linville, Larry, 41, 84–85
Lizak, Mike, 181
Lodge, Henry Cabot, 43
Lowe, Zachary, 141–44, 147, 150–51, 161
  civil suit, 178–79, 189–193, 201

M

Maddox, Lester, 60
Magic Lantern, 239
Mandel, Marvin, 58–59
Marconi, David, 214
Marshall, Burke, 52
Martian Ray Detector, 66
Martin L. Kaiser, Inc., 30. *See also*
    Northwestern Bank; U.S. Recording
    Company
  Armco Steel, 33–35
  Fort Holabird, 35–50
    2050CA RF detector, 40–41, 43–46
    Modal 1059 preamplifier, 38
    teaching defense, 44–49, 105
  IRS tax audits, 113–14, 173
Matter, John M., 50–55, 73–74, 81
Matthey Bishop Corporation, 183–84
McCord, James, 40, xvi
McMichael, G. Speights, 112, 121
McPherson, Clyde, 22–23
mechanical audio surveillance, 251–52
Merck Frost Laboratories, 186–87
Michaux, Henry Jr., 149, 152–54, 156
microphone and wire, 253–56, 292
MINARET, Project, 242
Mintz, John, 179
Mitchell, John, 60
modulation (FM, AM), 293
Moffit, Ronnie, 129, 221
Mohr, John, 82, 111–12
Montanarelli, Stephen, 61
Montefusco, Al, 98, 123, 164–65
Mook, Luther, xvi–xvii
Morrow, John, 159
Morton, George, 14–16
Moyers, Bill, 52
Multistate Antiterrorism Information
    Exchange (MATRIX), 237
Muzak systems, 183–84

N

National Security Agency (NSA), 240–43
National Technical Investigators Association (NTIA), 168
National Wiretap Commission, 53, 104, 107, 110, 116, 121, 127
  retaliation for testimony, 113–17
Newsham, Margaret, 243
Nixon, Richard, 40, 91, 242, xvi. *See also* Watergate
No Place to Hide (O'Harrow), 234
Non-Obvious Relationship Awareness (NORA, 240
Northwestern Bank Wilksboro, NC, 86–89, 132–37
  FBI investigation of, 141–47
  grand jury appearance, 148–49
  trial, 156–57, 160–66
    arraignment, 152, xvi–xxi
    jury selection, 158
Novo, Guillermo, 129
Now Hear This (Arrington), 228
Nye, David, 116

O

O'Brien, Larry, 40–41
O'Harrow, Robert Jr., 234
Olin Corporation, 182–83
Oliphant, Tim, 107–10
Omar (Egypt guide), 101–2
Omnibus Crime Control and Safe Streets Act (1968), 39, 65, 107, 247
  U.S. Recording Company, 53–55, 108–12, 117, 120, xvii
On-Star, 245–46
Operation Condor, 129
Operation Mudhen, 69–70
optical or visual surveillance, 262–65
O'Toole, George, 59–60
Over-the-Horizon Radar (OTHR) system, 16, 20–27

P

Patriot Act, 235–36, 239, xiii–xiv
Paz, Virgilio, 129
Pepper, Barry, 216
Peterson, Russell, 59
Poindexter, John, 236–37, 240
polygraphs/lie-detector systems, 43–44

preamplifiers (Model 1059), 38
price markups testimony. *See* U.S. Recording Company
prison riot negotiations, 131–32
privacy in America, 233–48, xi–xiv
Project CAMBRIDGE, 16, 20–27
Project MINARET, 242
Project SHAMROCK, 242

R

radiation signals, 63–64
radio frequency detection (2050CA RF), 40–41, 43–46, 73
radio frequency identification (RFID), 246
RCA Laboratories, 13–30
  amateur TV, 16
  image conversion, 14–16
  Project CAMBRIDGE, 16, 20–27
Reagan, 48, 242
recorders, 46–47
Regan, Jim, 131–32, 164
retaliation. *See* blacklisting; harassment
Retractable Over-the-Horizon Radar (ROTHR) system, 27–28
Robards, Jason, 216
Rogers, William P., 242
Ross, Jim, 222
Rudy, John, 14
Russians, 14, 25, 41–42
  Cold War, 18–19, 66–68
  Great Seal bugging, 42–43
  radiation signals, 63–64

S

Sadat, Anwar, 97–98, 102
SCAN 23, 49–50
Scott, Tony, 215–17
Secret Agenda: Watergate, Deep Throat, and the CIA (Hougan), 69
SHAMROCK, Project, 242
Shipton, Paul, 172
single-party consent, 133–34, 136–37, 159, 163–64, 288, xii
Smith, Fred, 188
Smith, Rawdon, 162–63, 193
Smith, Will, 215–17
Sommers, Alfred, 14
Soto, Bob, 88

spookware, 288–89
Spring, Stephen, 192, 200–201
Spying Game, The, 194–95
Starr, Jerry, 88–90, 134, 143, 145, 147, 150–51
stethoscope bomb detection, 84–85, 181
strobe lights, 17
submarines, 17–18
Sullivan, William, 51
surveillance, audio
    carrier-current transmitters, 261–62
    countermeasures survey, 277–87
    free-space transmitters, 256–60
    general considerations, 269–77
    mechanical, 251–52
    microphone and wire, 253–56
    telephones, 265–69
    visual or optical, 262–65
Swenholt, 116

T

Tait, Joseph, 53–54, 82, 111–12
teaching defense, 44–49
Teamsters, 130–31
telephone surveillance, 44–45, 57–59, 265–69
Telerad Manufacturing, 28–29
Television InfraRed Observational Satellite (TIROS 1), 18–19
TEMPEST attack, 63–64, 292
Tennille, Ben, 161–62
Terpil, Frank, 93–98, 100–104, 128–29, 195–97, 225–27
terrorism, 93–97, xii–xiii
Theremin, Leon, 41–43
Threat Matrix, 218
Thurmond, Strom, 243
Timonium Racetrack, 65–66
Title III devices. *See* Omnibus Crime Control and Safe Streets Act
Total Information Awareness (TIA), 236–37, 240
Townley, Michael, 129, 221
transmitter locator and tracking system, 50–51
transmitters, 44–46, 57
    burst, 293
    carrier-current, 261–62
    free-space, 256–60

Trudeau, Pierre, 185–86
typewriters, 63–64

U

Unabomber, 83, 169
U.S. Recording Company (USRC), 52–55, xvi
    investigation of FBI, 125–27, 156
    price mark ups, 81–82, 108–12, 120, 122, 155–56

V

van Eck, Wim, 64
Vermiere, Rich, 107–8
Videla, Jorge Rafaél, 174
visual or optical surveillance, 262–65
Vogelgesang, Fred, 33–35
Voight, Jon, 217

W

Walsh, Tom, 7–9, 106, 136
Walters, Jack, 77
Ward, Hiram H., 149–50
    Northwestern Bank trial, 158, 160, 162–63, 165
Watergate, 40–41, 48, 84, 89, 222, xvi.
    See also Nixon, Richard
Weinman, Paul, 162
WerBell, Mitchell Livingston, 148, 223–24
White, Ben, 160, 165
White, Briggs, 50
Whitten, Les, 69–70, 148
Wilson, Don, 150
Wilson, Edwin, 94, 129, 196
wire and microphone, 253–56
wiretapping, 290–91
Witness to Power: The Nixon Years (Ehrlichman), 242
Woodward, Bob, 184
Wright, Marion, 78–81, 85, 123, 157
Wright, Peter, 43

Z

Zavala, Anthony, 109

MARTIN L. KAISER III is a native of Wilkes-Barre, Pennsylvania, and President of Martin L. Kaiser Inc., an electronics company located in Cockeysville, Maryland, specializing in the manufacture of electronic eavesdropping devices, bomb detection, and improvised explosive device detection equipment. A graduate of Rider University, Lawrenceville, New Jersey, Kaiser was a senior research technician at RCA Laboratories in Princeton, New Jersey, in the late 1950s and early 1960s where he was instrumental in the development of a new link in the U.S. anti-missile system. He has served as a technical adviser on films including *The Conversation*, *Enemy of the State*, and the TV show, *The Matrix*, and he was featured in the BBC Emmy Award-winning documentary, *Confessions of a Dangerous Man* in the 1980s, which was about the life of fugitive CIA agent Frank Terpil.

ROBERT S. STOKES is the author of the novel *Walking Wounded*. He covered the Vietnam War and the Chicago Seven trial for *Newsweek* and the Attica Prison riot for *Life* magazine. Mr. Stokes lives in Los Angeles, California.